CLARENDON LIBRARY OF LOGIC AND PHILOSOPHY

General Editor: L. Jonathan Cohen

METAPHYSICS AND THE MIND-BODY PROBLEM

ALSO PUBLISHED IN THIS SERIES

The Probable and the Provable by L. Jonathan Cohen
Relative Identity by Nicholas Griffin
Experiences: An Inquiry into some Ambiguities by J. M. Hinton
Knowledge by Keith Lehrer
The Cement of the Universe: A Study of Causation by J. L. Mackie
Truth, Probability and Paradox by J. L. Mackie
The Nature of Necessity by Alvin Plantinga
Divine Commands and Moral Requirements by P. L. Quinn
Simplicity by Elliott Sober
The Coherence of Theism by Richard Swinburne
The Emergence of Norms by Edna Ullmann-Margalit
Ignorance: A Case for Scepticism by Peter Unger

METAPHYSICS AND THE MIND-BODY PROBLEM

MICHAEL E. LEVIN

CLARENDON PRESS · OXFORD
1979

Oxford University Press, Walton Street, Oxford OX2 6DP

OXFORD LONDON GLASGOW
NEW YORK TORONTO MELBOURNE WELLINGTON
KUALA LUMPUR SINGAPORE JAKARTA HONG KONG TOKYO
DELHI BOMBAY CALCUTTA MADRAS KARACHI
NAIROBI DAR ES SALAAM CAPE TOWN

British Library Cataloguing in Publication Data

Levin, Mjchael E
Metaphysics and the mind-body problem. – (Clarendon library of logic and philosophy).
1. Metaphysics
I. Title
110 BD111 78–41138

ISBN 0–19–824415–0

Printed in Great Britain by
Billing & Sons Limited, Guildford, London and Worcester

Preface

THIS book defends the ancient thesis that a man is a piece of matter, that all his states are physical states, and all his properties physical properties. It would be pointless to anticipate here my reasons for accepting this thesis, but a brief overview of the topics I treat might prove helpful to the reader.

The first two chapters are preparatory. Chapter I discusses the general apparatus needed for stating the mind–body problem: identity (I.2), ontological commitment (I.3), and reduction. My treatment differs in important details from those of Quine, Nagel, Putnam, Enç and others. Its main feature—developed in I.5—is that, while not allowing properties to exist, it admits non-trivial notions of property identity and reduction by treating properties as 'virtual entities'. Mastery of chapter I through the first two paragraphs of I.6 is not essential for an understanding of what follows. Chapter II presents the three basic positions on the mind–body problem: substance dualism, property dualism, and property monism (or materialism) (II.1). Such other positions as the double-aspect theory and neutral monism are dismissed (II.2) and in II.3 behaviourism is absorbed into the basic trichotomy. In II.4 I defend, rather tentatively, characterizing matter in terms of present-day physics.

Chapter III considers and rejects substance dualism; the reader may experience a mild form of *déjà vu* as he works through my treatment of this obligatory topic. I concede in III.2 that the Cartesian can conceive the non-existence of the physical world, and in III.3 that in a suitable sense his own non-existence is inconceivable; I even concede in III.4 his use of Leibniz's Law against opacity complaints. But his argument still fails, and I propose two objections to substance dualism. (1) While defending in III.5 the idea that the mind is a thing, I argue in III.6 that the dualist cannot specify it via a mass term and a term of divided reference. (2) After discussing causation, epiphenomenal causation, and the conservation of energy, I conclude in III.7 that the old problem of interaction is fatal.

In IV and V I present and defend a version of materialism. My main innovation is the suggestion in IV.5 that the topic-neutral descriptions introduced by Smart and Lewis be taken to fix the reference of, rather than analyse, psychological expressions. This formulation blocks the main objections to topic neutralism, and almost all the most compelling objections to materialism. I digress in IV.4 to discuss phenomenalism in the light of topic neutralism, and in IV.6 I criticize the 'functional state' theory—which, as Dennett has recently noted, has almost become the new orthodoxy. In V.1 I argue that our knowledge of our internal states is not logically infallible, but is non-inferential and causally necessarily reliable. I provide a physicalistic model for introspective awareness thus construed. In V.2 I go on to reject Rorty's suggestion that psychological language be eliminated as a consequence of rejecting the general idea that languages can have built-in prejudices. Finally, I argue in V.4 that nothing in the phenomenon of intensionality, our ability to identify the objects of our intensional states, or the indeterminacy of intensional ascriptions relative to physicalistic evidence prevents their physicalistic reduction.

VI and VII consider issues that naturally arise from materialism. VI defends the possibility of computer consciousness, arguing that a computer can be as sensitive to context as a man is (VI.5), capable of basic recognition responses (VI.6), and creative (VI.7). I stress in VI.4 that Chomsky's discoveries about language add nothing to the debate. VII is a sustained defence of compatibilism, the position on free will most congenial to materialism, and one which, I think, fully satisfies our intuitions about ourselves as autonomous and morally responsible beings (VII.5). I conclude in VII.6 and VII.7 with a solution to the paradoxes of self-prediction that integrates materialism and compatibilism with some Existentialist insights, a theme already broached in VII.2.

I presuppose a smidgin of set theory throughout—about as much as is in the first forty-five pages of Halmos's *Naive Set Theory*.

Acknowledgements

RATHER than clutter the text with acknowledgements for particular points, references, and arguments, let me thank my various friends and former students here: David Thomas, Mark Alley, Carolyn White, Alan Brody, Ted Kornfeld, Robert Mayhew, Bill Lycan, Arthur Danto, Jonathan Adler, Joseph Fulda, Louis Nordstrom, and Arthur Collins; Jerry Samet prepared the index. Some remark by each has found its way into the text. The last two chapters exist because James Bayley convinced me that materialism must make its peace with all our moral intuitions. Ed Erwin and George Sher have provided criticism, discussion, and friendship over many years. A comment by Saul Kripke made many things clear to me about identity; and a few suggestions about style and organization by Jonathan Cohen had a salubrious effect on earlier drafts quite out of proportion to their brevity. Keen readers will detect the influence of several works, barely cited or not cited a tall, on my thinking: they include: Carnap's 'Meaning and Synonymy in Natural Language'; Quine's 'Mental Entities', *Word and Object*, and *Set Theory and Its Logic*; Hinckfuss's *The Existence of Space and Time*; Sayre's *Consciousness*, Dennett's *Content and Consciousness*, Broad's *Mind and Its Place in Nature*; and the many writings of Russell. I would also like to thank the editors of the *Journal of Philosophy* and of the *Australasian Journal of Philosophy* for their permission to use large portions of articles that originally appeared in those journals: 'Kripke's Argument Against the Identity Thesis', in the *Journal of Philosophy* (1975), and 'Descartes' Argument that He is not His Body', in the *Australasian Journal of Philosophy* (1973).

An author usually thanks his wife for encouragement during the trials of composition. I do so with full sincerity. I am also fortunate enough to be able to thank her for her assistance in preparing this book. Her easy familiarity with set theory and mathematical logic allowed her to check my own use of their devices and to suggest simplifications. Her sensitivity to the nuances of English has helped make the prose style of this work immeasurably more graceful than it would have been. And I have learned much from her about the topic itself.

Much of the work for this book was done under the aegis of the CUNY Research Foundation.

Contents

But leaving these vain trifles of men's souls . . .

(*Doctor Faustus* I. iii)

I

A General Setting For The Mind-Body Problem

1. Introduction

THE universe appears to contain two fundamentally different kinds of phenomena: consciousness and non-consciousness, the mental and the physical. Philosophy of mind aims at giving an account of this distinction, or apparent distinction. The universe, to be sure, exhibits countless dichotomies of no interest to philosophy. Everything is either a rock or a non-rock; this distinction does not worry philosophers because it gives no evidence of being fundamental. Rocks and non-rocks are not, in general, very different kinds of things, and the question of how there can be both kinds of things exerts no pressure. But the difference between mental and physical phenomena is so intuitively striking as to prompt the question of how there can be both kinds of things.

Spelling out just what the difference between the mental and the physical is supposed to be is itself a philosophical problem. It might even be maintained that further questions in the philosophy of mind cannot be raised until this difference is brought into further relief. Can the problem of mentality be raised in the absence of a reasonably clear statement of what material objects are? Indeed, if 'matter' is understood as the subject-matter of physics, and 'physics' in turn is taken to denote whatever science turns out to be all-competent, might not the mind–matter dichotomy eventually disappear by definitional fiat? To keep this from happening, do we not first have to circumscribe the domain of physics?

These obscurities that attend an initial characterization of the problem of mind do not undercut it. The problem of mind emerges, and can be formulated, at a level below that of characterizing mind or matter. *Whatever* rocks turn out to be, selves seem to be very different from them. If Occamist scruples dictate that any global distinction demands explanation, an explanation is needed for this.

Some philosophers, indeed, accept this as a sufficient statement of the mind–matter problem: 'material' means 'like rocks' and 'mental' means 'like us'.[1] I argue in chapter II that this is too loose, and that the mind–matter problem must be relativized to what current physics tells us matter is. But this is to refine the problem, not introduce it.

Talk of identity and difference, of what there is, and of prospects for reducing the apparent mind–matter dualism to a single underlying unity, focuses attention on the notions of identity, ontology, and reduction. Progress in the mind–matter, or mind–body, problem is impossible without first clarifying these notions, and this clarification is the subject of the present chapter.

Before turning to these matters, however, a caveat is in order. Just as the problem of mind can be raised using merely a preanalytic understanding of thoughts and rocks, so in a limited way can the thesis that the mental is reducible to the physical be understood in terms of a merely preanalytic notion of reduction. One need not possess a definition of reduction that passes muster among logicians to recognize that surface tension has been reduced to electrostatic attraction and that lightning has turned out to be nothing 'over and above' electrical discharge. The issue of whether mentality is ultimately a material phenomenon is just whether, *whatever* the relation is between lightning and electrical discharge, mind stands in that kind of relation to matter. Materialism is the claim that this is so, and various dualisms all claim that this is not so. The issue of identifying mind and matter can thus be taken up in the absence of a full analysis of what that relation is.

Using unarguable cases of scientific reduction simply as paradigms permits the issue of materialism to be taken up, but it provides little guidance as to how the issue is to be decided. Whether mind actually is to matter as lightning is to electricity is unanswerable without a clear account of the relation between lightning and electricity. None the less, a useful methodological precept can be extracted from the availability of paradigm scientific reductions: whenever an objection to materialism works equally well against identifying lightning with electrical discharge, the objection has misfired by proving too much. If there is a mind–matter dualism only in a sense in which there is a lightning–electrical discharge dualism, the materialist will gladly give

[1] Thus see J. Cornman, *Materialism and Sensations* (Yale U.P., New Haven, Conn.: 1971), chapter 1.

the dualist his dualism and rightfully claim that his own position has so far been left untouched.

With this caveat entered, we turn to the issues of identity, ontology, and reduction. The discussion that follows treats these issues in their own right, in full generality. However, some general conclusions are especially pertinent to the mind–body problem, and due notice is taken of their application.

2. *Identity*

Defining identity amounts to defending a principle which implicitly defines the expression '='. The concept of identity thus defined is usually called *strict* identity. The present section argues that strict identity is the 'right' concept—the interesting identity questions are those in which identity means strict identity.

The principle in question is the Principle of Leibniz, or PL: every instance of the schema $(x)(y)(x = y \supset (A(x) \equiv A(y)))$ is true, where 'A' is schematic for open sentences with one free variable. (For convenience I will sometimes refer to properties x has rather than open sentences x satisfies.) PL's most convenient form is its contrapositive: if there is some open sentence that x satisfies and y does not, $x \neq y$. PL must be distinguished from its converse, the claim that if all instances of the schema $A(x) \equiv A(y)$ are true, then $x = y$. This is the much more controversial identity of indiscernibles, the claim that no two things can differ only by being different. We will have no need of this latter.

The concept of identity introduced by PL is called strict because it appears, at least, to be violated by some cases that common sense takes to be identities. Thus, it might seem that the author of *Macbeth* (call him S_m) is not strictly identical to the author of *Hamlet* (call him S_h), since Shakespeare was 30 when he wrote *Macbeth* and 40 when he wrote *Hamlet*. Since S_m differs from S_h in age, $S_m \neq S_h$. Perhaps they are identical in some 'loose and popular' sense, but not in the sense of identity captured by PL. PL must be defended against the charge of counterintuitiveness or deviance from ordinary use because the mind–body problem draws its primitive sense from the ordinary notion of identity. A discussion of that problem in terms of a neologistic sense of identity risks failing to address the original issue.

To preserve ordinary judgements, some philosophers have distinguished four-dimensional entities from their momentary three-dimensional time-slices. (Taking things to be bounded regions of spacetime is not distinctively consonant with relativity theory: the idea of spacetime worms and their time-slices is available in classical physics. All relativity adds is the impossibility of global time-slices.) Time-slices of enduring things sustain strict identity only to themselves, but two different time-slices of the same entity sustain to each other the weaker equivalence relation 'is part of the same entity as' which goes proxy for identity. In the way we say two glasses contain the same wine when they contain wine from the self-same vintage, we can say of S_h, the time-slice of Shakespeare that wrote *Hamlet*, that it is part of the same entity as is S_m, the time-slice of Shakespeare that wrote *Macbeth.* Ordinary judgements about identity, and identity through time, are preserved if ordinary identity is construed as 'is part of the [self-]same entity as'.

This account still implies that, strictly speaking, what wrote *Hamlet* is not what wrote *Macbeth.* It says that they bear to each other a strong equivalence relation which, in loose speech, merges with identity. Thus, the time-slice theory still accuses ordinary speech of error. There is, however, a more natural account of identity through time compatible with both PL and ordinary speech.[2] When we talk about S_h and S_m we are talking about the enduring Shakespeare both times. Of this enduring entity we may correctly predicate two characteristics: writing *Hamlet* at age 30 in 1600 and writing *Macbeth* at age 40 in 1610. Thus, S_h is *strictly* identical to S_m, since they are both simply Shakespeare. It is true of S_h that he wrote Hamlet in 1600 and *Macbeth* in 1610. When predicates are given time references we need not worry about how self-identical entities can change through time—how one and the same thing can be both a *Hamlet*-writer and a non-*Hamlet*-writer. The two relevant properties Shakespeare has are 'writing *Hamlet* in 1600' and 'not writing *Hamlet* in 1610'.

The two foregoing accounts of identity coalesce.[3] On the account of the last paragraph Shakespeare is a four-dimensional entity, where this is now seen as the commonsensical fact that Shakespeare lasted some finite amount of time. Also, there *are* on this account such

[2] See R. Chisholm, 'Identity through Time', in *Language, Belief and Metaphysics*, ed. H. Kiefer and M. Munitz (SUNY Press, Albany, N.Y.: 1970).

[3] J. Smart dissents from this in 'Space-Time and Individuals', in *Logic and Art*, ed. I. Scheffler and R. Rudner (Bobbs-Merrill, N.Y.: 1962), on the grounds that talk of enduring entities is erroneously committed to absolute simultaneity. On p. 17 of this essay, however, he seems to withdraw this accusation.

entities as time-slices of enduring entities, if one wants to allude to them. Thus, 'the entity which came into existence on 1 January 1610, went out of existence on 31 December 1610, and occupied the region of space Shakespeare occupied during that interval' denotes a year-thick time-slice of Shakespeare. The present account just insists that there is no reason to identify the author of *Macbeth* with the time-slice of Shakespeare whose temporal bounds are the beginning and ending of the writing of *Macbeth.* That time-slice entity is not the author of *Macbeth*, merely a time-slice of the author of *Macbeth.*

The commonsense ontology of entities enduring through time dissolves other spurious puzzles about identity, such as the one about the statue and its bronze. A statue, it is said, cannot be identical to the bronze that composes it, since after the bronze statue is melted down the bronze exists but the statue does not. Now, what is shown decisively by the fact that the bronze exists when the statue does not is that the statue is not identical to the piece of bronze considered in its full temporal extension. But this is compatible with the statue being identical to a *proper part* of the piece of bronze—that is to say, a sufficiently thick time-slice of the piece of bronze. During a proper part of its history the piece of bronze had a certain arrangement; the entity which coincides with the bronze for that part of the bronze's history *is* the statue in the strict sense of identity. *That temporal part* of the bronze has ceased existing after the bronze has been melted down just as surely as the statue has ceased existing. So we can now say in a very strong sense that the statue is the bronze that composes it; not the whole of the piece of bronze, but a proper temporal part of the piece of bronze.

This point bears on the mind–body problem. S. Kripke[4] and others have argued that a person cannot be his body because his body can and normally does exist after the person himself has ceased existing. But, to follow the account of the bronze and the statue, this shows only that a person is not identical to the *whole* of his body conceived as a temporally extended thing. The fact that your body goes on existing after you have ceased existing is quite compatible with your being identical to some *proper segment* of your body, in particular that time-slice of your body during which it was in working order. Moreover, construing the relation of a person to his body as simply a special case of the part–whole relation also permits the

[4] 'Identity and Necessity', in M. Munitz, ed., *Identity and Individuation* (N.Y.U. Press, N.Y.: 1971), pp. 163–4.

difference between them to be explained in terms of the different conditions the two are in without having to reify the condition or 'form'[5] that a human body has when it is a person.

Geach has attacked strict identity in a quite different way. He argues[6] that judgements of identity are really of the form 'x is the same A as y', where A is a sortal. There are no 'pure' judgements of the form '$x = y$'. This attempt to relativize identity is implausible. Clearly, if $x = y$, x will be the same A as y for all A. In particular, if x is an A, where A is the (or a) sort of thing x is, and $x = y$, then certainly y is an A and indeed the same A as x. Suppose that every x is a thing of some sort: some instance of 'x is an A' is true. So for any x, any y that is strictly identical to x will also satisfy some instance of the schema 'y is the same A as x'. Thus, the truth of strict identities is compatible with the truth of any number of sortal identities. Moreover, strict identity can always be recovered from sortal identity. Consider a language lacking '=' but containing count nouns and the expression 'is the same A as'. We can define '$x = y$' to hold just in case all instances of the schema 'x is the same A as y' are true. One would suppose that $\langle x,y \rangle$ always satisfies one instance of this schema iff it satisfies all of them (although Geach insists that this is not so). At any rate, whenever sortal identity is definable, so is strict identity. Not only is strict identity compatible with sortal identity, any apparatus sufficient for sortal identity brings strict identity with it.[7]

[5] See P. Geach and G. Anscombe, *Three Philosophers* (Cornell U.P., Ithaca: 1961), pp. 78–84; see also p. 48.

[6] See 'Identity' in Geach's *Logic Matters* (U. of California, Berkeley: 1972). N. Griffin's main reason for rejecting PL is that it offers no decision-procedure for determining identity; see his *Relative Identity* (O.U.P., Oxford: 1977), chapter 1. This is so; someone bent on identifying a with b can always reverse the argument 'Since Fa and $-Fb$, $a \neq b$' to 'Since $a = b$ and Fa, it must be that Fb as well'. The law $a = b \supset (Fa \equiv Fb)$ is of course incompetent to decide whether we shall affirm the antecedent or deny the consequent; very few definitions provide algorithms for their definienda. If a is a man and b is a balloon, we need to know something about men and balloons to evaluate the significance of 'b burst' for $a = b$. But this does not show that the concept of identity changes when the subject does; for more on this, see Quine's review of *Identity and Individuation* (ed. M. Munitz. N.Y.U. Press, N.Y.: 1971) in *Journal of Philosophy* (Sept. 1972), pp. 488–97.

[7] One may wonder why I don't acquiesce in the relative theory and take materialism as the thesis that mental entities are the same A as (some) physical entities. However, as things stand, there is no sortal A which both mental and physical things are already known to be. The best we can do is replace A by 'entity', which the relativist will rightly reject as a mere dummy sortal. Since it might be that we will find out what sorts of things mental things are by finding

A final argument for the relativity of identity is its alleged relativity to given stocks of predicates. To see the point of this allegation, reflect that PL is a schema for first-order sentences. The natural second-order formulation of PL, $(x)(y)(x = y \supset (P)(P(x) \equiv P(y)))$, uses a quantifier that ranges over properties, and this seems a sufficient reason for rejecting it.[8] In sections 4 and 5 below properties are explicitly repudiated; but even philosophers more tolerant of properties than I am will shy away from linking PL as closely to the reification of properties as does its second-order formulation. The first-order form of PL requires only (informal) quantification over the open sentences for which '*A*' is schematic. So construed, however, PL and identity become relativized to language. Two things might be indiscriminable relative to one set of predicates but discriminable relative to another. The trouble is not simply that there could be two languages L and L' such that for any L-definable open sentence $A(...)$, $A(x) \equiv A(y)$ held, while there was an open sentence $A'(...)$ of L' such that $A'(x)$ & $-A'(y)$. (The first condition implies $x = y$ only if the identity of indiscernibles is assumed.) The problem is deeper. To see what it is, consider not only PL—the infinitely many axioms (4_A) below—but the three other axioms of standard identity theory. Any relation that satisfies these conditions satisfies all the conditions on identity expressible in first-order logic:

(1) $(x)I(x,x)$
(2) $(x)(y)(z)((I(x,y) \;\&\; I(y,z)) \supset I(x,z))$
(3) $(x)(y)(I(x,y) \supset I(y,x))$
(4_A) $(x)(y)(I(x,y) \supset (A(x) \equiv A(y)))$.

Under suitable conditions any relation satisfying (1)–(3)—any equivalence relation—will satisfy every axiom of the form (4_A). These conditions may be stated as follows. Given a relation $E(x,y)$, call a predicate P *E-blind* if $(x)(y)(E(x,y) \supset (P(x) \equiv P(y)))$. Examples of such blindness abound. Basketball coaches are interested only in

out what physical things they are identical to, we must formulate identity claims about the mind in a way which does not require that we now know a sortal that applies to mental and physical things.

[8] J. T. Stevenson says that PL is 'formulated in standard logic text books as $(x = y) =$ df. $(F)(Fx \equiv Fy)$' ('Sensations and Brain Processes: A Reply to J. J. C. Smart', in C. Borst, ed., *The Mind–Brain Identity Thesis* [St. Martin's, London: 1970], p. 88). The commitment of this second-order formulation to properties leads Stevenson's discussion of materialism into trouble: see sec. 4 below. It is not the standard form of PL in logic texts; see e.g. I. Copi, *Symbolic Logic*, 4th ed. (Macmillan, N.Y.: 1973), sec. 5.4.

the height of their men: if x and y are the same in height, then either can be a centre or neither can be a centre, and so on. Thus 'is a prospective centre' is blind with respect to 'is as tall as'. Suppose we have a language all of whose predicates are E-blind with respect to the equivalence relation E. Then E satisfies all the conditions of the form (4_A). In such a case, a relation which is not, intuitively, identity, acts like identity. The argument to show this proceeds by induction on $d(A)$, the number of occurrences of —, $\supset$, and universal quantifiers in a wff constructed by truth-functions and quantification from E-blind predicates. We may suppose x occurs free in A, and also that $E(x,y)$. If $d(A) = 0$, the result follows trivially, for then A is an E-blind predicate. Assume the result holds for $d(A) = k$ and choose an A for which $d(A) = k+1$. There are three subcases. (i) If A is $-B$, the result follows by taking negations on both sides of $B(x) \equiv B(y)$, which holds by the induction hypothesis. (ii) If A is $B \supset C$, clearly $d(B) \leqslant k$ and $d(C) \leqslant k$, and the result again follows by propositional logic. (iii) If A is $(z)B(z,x)$, then $B(z,x) \equiv B(z,y)$ by the induction hypothesis. We then get $(z)(B(z,x) \equiv B(z,y))$ by generalization, and finally $(z)B(z,x) \equiv (z)B(z,y)$, i.e. $A(x) \equiv A(y)$. The argument easily generalizes for languages with E-blind polyadic predicates.

Whenever an equivalence relation E which is not identity thus satisfies (1)–(4_A), we may say that it *simulates* identity. We have just seen how easy it is to simulate identity. Suppose x and y bear to each other a relation which simulates identity in our current conceptual framework. We now regard x and y as identical. How, in general, can we be sure that things we think are identical do not simply bear to each other a relation E to which all predicates in our current conceptual framework are blind? Perhaps some more inclusive framework contains a predicate which is not E-blind. We could ignore the mooted possibility only if we knew that all possible predicates are E-blind, but the notion of all possible predicates is obscure. Thus, while identity can be distinguished from its simulators from a point of reference outside a given set of predicates, there is no transcendent point of reference from which to discern identity *per se*. This might be reason to abandon the idea of strict identity and settle for a relativized notion.[9] Any sense of loss (it might be added) should be diminished by the thought that Skolem and others

[9] See W. V. O. Quine's *Philosophy of Logic* (Prentice-Hall, N.J.: 1970), chap. 5, for a view along this line.

take a similar blindness about cardinality in first-order logic to show that the notions of cardinality and set must be relativized.[10]

This position should be adopted only as a last resort. Whether George Washington was the first President of the United States does not seem to depend on the set of predicates one uses to describe American history. Of course, one's ability to discover or express such truths will depend on the richness of one's language, but this does not show that the truths themselves are relative to language.

A result of Gödel's suggests a safe passage between the Scylla of invoking all possible predicates and the Charybdis of relativizing identity: from any domain D in which a relation E simulates identity a domain D' and a relation E' defined on D' can be constructed such that E' is strict identity. More precisely: given a language L with domain of quantification D and E-blind predicates $P_1,...,P_n$, there is a domain D', a set of predicates $P_1',...,P_n'$ and a relation E' such that (1) for every element x in D there is a unique element x' in D', (2) for every predicate P_i defined on D there is a unique predicate P_i' defined on D', (3) for all $i \leqslant n$, $P_i(x) \equiv P_i'(x')$, hence (4) $E'(x',y') \equiv E(x,y)$, and (5) E' is identity. The proof consists in taking D' as the class of all equivalence classes induced in D by E: that is, $D' = \{x' \colon x \varepsilon D\}$, where $x' = \{y \colon y \varepsilon D \ \& \ E(y,x)\}$. Now define $P_i' = \{x' \colon P_i(x)\}$, and $E' = \{\langle x',y' \rangle \colon E(x,y)\}$. In particular, E' becomes identity. Suppose $E'(a,b)$, but a is not b. By the definition of E', a is x' and b is y' for some x', $y' \varepsilon D'$. If x' is not y', then there is some z which is, say, in x' but not in y'. (The identity of indiscernibles is not needed for this inference, which follows by the axiom of extensionality of set theory.) Since z is in x', $E(z,x)$ holds; but since z is not in y', $-E(z,y)$ holds also. But $E(x,y)$ by definition. Since E is an equivalence relation, $E(z,y)$ follows from $E(z,x)$ & $E(x,y)$, and this is a contradiction.

E' is not just an identity simulator on D'. For each x' is a set; as the identity of sets is exhausted by sameness of membership, and as $E(x',y')$ is tantamount to x' having the same members as y', E' is identity. Moreover, each x' collects all those objects previously indiscriminable from x; there is no independent reason to think that there are any more around. Thus, it never happens that *only* an identity-simulator holds in a domain. Whenever an identity simulator exists, identity itself can be defined in a closely related domain in

[10] See S. Kleene, *Introduction to Metamathematics* (Van Nostrand, N.J.: 1952), chap. XIV.

which the differences between indiscriminables are flattened out by membership in equivalence classes. One can round off the argument by reinterpreting the predicate '$E(x,y)$' as denoting the relation $x \varepsilon y$. True, this interpretation cannot be given in D and—if we want to think of the problem in these terms—speakers of the original language will not realize that 'E' is susceptible of this construal. But this has nothing to do with whether 'E' can be unmasked.

Identity is a relation that holds between objects. Not only is there no entity without identity, there is no identity without entity. We cannot seriously discuss the identity or diversity of items we are unwilling to admit into our ontology. This follows, indeed, just from the fact that bindable variables flank the identity sign. Identity involves us in construing the values of its variables as objects no more, but no less, than does any other predicate.[11] Sometimes, however, philosophers raise identity questions about items—properties and events—without an accompanying admission that they take such items as objects.[12] Identity for these items is often explained as the joint satisfaction of a special class of predicates admissibly ascribed to these items, with the accompanying proviso that other predicates cannot coherently be ascribed to the items in question. But if properties, events and states are nonentities, questions about their identity conditions altogether lapse. The predicament for one who would raise special questions about the identity of special entities is yet worse. Once properties (say) are reified so identity questions can be raised about them, the identity questions raised are the same as those raised about less problematic entities. For property P to be identical to property Q demands that every instance of the schema $A(P) \equiv A(Q)$ be true. For event e to be identical to event e', every instance of the schema $A(e) \equiv A(e')$ must

[11] For speculation about why Frege and others have missed this, see my 'The Extensionality of Causation and Causal-explanatory Contexts', *Philosophy of Science*, xliii (June 1976), 268–9.

[12] For recent discussions of property-identity, see P. Achinstein, 'The Identity of Properties', *American Philosophical Quarterly*, xi (1974); J. Kim, 'Causation, Nomic Subsumption and the Concept of an Event', *Journal of Philosophy*, lxx. (Apr. 1973), 217–36; and H. Putnam, 'On Properties', in N. Rescher, ed., *Essays in Honor of Carl G. Hempel* (Humanities, N.Y.: 1970). On event-identity, see D. Davidson, 'The Individuation of Events' in Rescher; G. Sher, 'On Event-Identity', *Australasian Journal of Philosophy*, lii. 1 (May 1974), 39–47; T. Nagel, 'Physicalism', in D. Rosenthal, ed., *Materialism and the Mind–Body Problem* (Prentice-Hall, N.J.: 1971). Davidson, for one, is clear about the ontological implications of identity questions.

be true. Philosophers who hold that two events are identical iff they have the same causes and effects (Davidson and Nagel) or that two properties are identical iff they are necessarily coextensive (Achinstein and Putnam) are best viewed as urging category doctrines about what traits it makes sense to ascribe to events or properties. The notion of identity which sameness of causal role (or necessary sameness of extension) is supposed to capture is the same notion of identity that applies to ordinary objects. These theories simply add a category doctine to restrict the substituenda for the schematic letter *A* in PL. There is no special question about what is required for properties or events to be identical.

Construing identity as holding only between objects, and holding the line on what objects there are, both simplifies and complicates the defining of reduction, and the reduction of the mental to the physical. The simplification is that we may ignore such ill-formed questions as whether all mental states are physical states and whether psychological properties are physical properties. The complication is loss of the intuitive distinction between merely coextensive predicates and coextensive predicates that pick out the *same* feature of their common extension. Jettisoning this distinction means that the strongest well-defined notion of reducing a feature of a system x is that of correlating that feature with features of x's constituents. Such a notion of reduction finds certain intuitively well-joined issues to be unintelligible. Thus, some dualists concede that all objects are material objects, but insist that some material objects have non-physical properties. We want to allow the dualist to say this, if only to disagree with him. Similarly, the most interesting kind of materialism holds that what we preanalytically identify as mental states and mental properties—indeed, properties of mental states—are really physical. Capturing these intuitions will require bestowing virtual objecthood on states and properties. But virtual objects are eliminable when the ontological chips are down.

3. *Ontology*

I have said that questions about the identity of events and properties make sense only if properties and events are construed as entities, or the questions are (re)construed to be about entities we are willing to countenance. But what is it to construe something as an entity? Determining the entities a body of discourse involves is the problem of finding a criterion of ontological commitment. The present section offers such a criterion, and the next argues that, under this criterion, the ontic prospects for properties and the like are dim.

Quine holds that the ontological commitment of a body of discourse *T* is the set of values of the variables of *T*. Let us call this 'Quine's criterion', or QC. QC, I think, is substantially correct, but it lends itself to two emendations. First, it is often convenient to give QC a metalinguistic twist: the ontological commitment of *T* is the set of values of the variables of the metalanguage in which the truth definition for (sentences of) *T* is given. Moreover, important distinctions between types of commitment and types of reduction become available if we supplement the metalanguage with the best available scientific account of the world. In short, I am suggesting that the ontological commitment of *T* is the set of values of the variables of a *scientific metalanguage M* for *T*. This is what *M* looks like. Just by being a semantic metalanguage, *M* contains names for all the sentences of *T*, translations of all the sentences of *T*, and the notion of satisfaction.[13] A typical '*T*-sentence' of *M* runs:

'*S*' is true iff *P*.

P is the *truth-condition* provided for '*S*' by *M*. A scientific metalanguage, using the best theory of the world at hand (or one of the best if there is a tie), not only supplies truth-conditions for sentences of *T* but gives those truth-conditions in terms of the best available scientific description.[14] *M* will also contain some account of the causal relations between speakers of *T* and the world, but this does not concern us for the moment. Thinking of the semantic definition of truth as a form of the correspondence theory that avoids the obscurities of 'fact' and 'correspondence', a definition of truth in a scientific metalanguage states what, by the best lights of science, is actually going on when a certain sentence is being used properly. It characterizes the reality a speaker of the sentence is noticing when he utters the sentence.

The truth of one's favourite ontology cannot be built into a criterion of ontic commitment that uses a scientific metalanguage. One piece of evidence against the omnicompetence of a given scientific theory would indeed be that no metalanguage augmented by it can yield truth-conditions for some body of discourse that

[13] Chapter 3 of Quine 1970 contains an accessible definition of satisfaction.

[14] J. Bennett alludes briefly to this possibility in *Linguistic Behaviour* (C.U.P., Cambridge: 1976), p. 267.

appears, on independent grounds, to have them. If, for example, it turns out to be impossible to state truth-conditions for sentences ascribing intensional states in a metalanguage supplemented by contemporary physics, and we also think those ascriptions do have truth-conditions, physics is not a complete account of the world. QC amended amounts to the suggestion that we construe the ontic commitment of a stretch of discourse as what, by our own best lights, is actually being talked about, even if this departs considerably from what users of that discourse may suppose they are talking about.

Waiving for a moment the scientific dimension, the rationale for a metalinguistic approach to ontological commitment emerges from the intuition Quine takes to underwrite QC: *T* is ontologically committed to whatever has to exist in order for *T* to be true.[15] It is natural, then, to take a sentence *S* of *T* to be ontologically committed to the things mentioned (i.e. quantified over) in the description of the truth-condition of *S*. Indeed, if we have not isolated *S*'s ontic commitment until we have the range of the bindable variables in *S* (as QC has it), we move in effect to a metalinguistic perspective anyway in saying 'The range of the variables used in '*S*' is . . .'. A metalinguistic criterion is thus guaranteed to do at least the work of QC. Three considerations suggest that such a criterion is at least more perspicuous than QC; and the third of these suggests that such a criterion should include appeal to empirical considerations.

(i) QC becomes entangled with the paradox of analysis. The paradigm of QC at work is the elimination of sakes. QC says that since

(1) Joe quit for Sam's sake

is equivalent to

(1′) Joe quit to help Sam,

and (1′) accommodates bindable variables at 'Sam' and 'Joe' while (1) (ostensibly) accommodates bindable variables at 'sake' as well, (1) is not committed to sakes. But if (1) is equivalent to (1′), why not put the argument in reverse: since (1′) is equivalent to (1), and 'sake' occurs at a bindable position in (1), (1′) is committed to

[15] Thus see *From a Logical Point of View*, 2nd ed. (Harper & Row, N.Y.: 1963), p. 103.

sakes.[16] Davidson actually uses this application of the paradox of analysis to avert the elimination of events (Rescher, p. 227). One defence available to the advocate of QC is to say that (1) is an abbreviation of (1′), and that 'sake' appears nowhere in an unabbreviated version of the object-language sentence in question. However, it is often reasonable to regard abbreviations of expressions of a given language *T* as expressions of *T*'s metalanguage which refer to expressions of *T*. To determine the ontic commitment of (1) in terms of (1′) thus construed is to shift to a metalinguistic criterion.

A metalinguistic criterion prevents exploitation of the equivalence of (1) and (1′) to frustrate ontic reckoning. Suppose *M* contains

(2) (1) is true iff Joe quit to help Sam;

suppose too that only 'Joe' and 'Sam' can be replaced by bindable variables in (2). On the face of it this is just to put '(1) ≡ (1′)' in a new guise. However, the truth-condition of (1) as given in (2) is a sentence of the metalanguage, which is expressively richer than its object-language. Thus, one cannot in general argue that truth-conditions like (1′), construed metalinguistically, are equivalent to the sentences of which they are truth-conditions. Ascent to the metalanguage disrupts the symmetry on which the paradox of analysis depends.

In some cases, to be sure, the truth-condition will be translatable into the object-language, and will there be equivalent to the sentence whose truth-condition it is. If for example this holds for (1) and (1′), the equivalence that led to the paradox of analysis reappears. But there is no pressure to move in that direction. Both (1) and (1′)—(1′) the homophonic descending translation of the truth-condition in (2)—can be given *T*-sentences with the *same* truth-condition: the truth-condition of (1′) will be its disquotation. One can concede that (1) and (1′) are equivalent in the object-language while insisting that all there need be for either of them to be true are Joe and Sam; for both are true iff Joe quit to help Sam.

Ascent to a scientific metalanguage blocks these troublesome equivalences in a stronger way. A scientific metalanguage, which employs resources that may have no counterpart in the object-language, provides its own description of the situations in which a

[16] Cf. W. Alston, 'Ontological Commitments', in P. Benaceraff and H. Putnam, eds., *Readings in Philosophy of Mathematics* (Prentice-Hall, N.J.: 1964), pp. 249–57.

given object-language sentence is true. We users of such a meta-language are free to draw our own conclusions about what is going on when the sentence is characteristically assented to. If (1)-like sentences are characteristically assented to when one person helps another, that is a sufficient description of truth for sentences like (1). Even if users of (1) are so locked into the 'sake' idiom they cannot paraphrase it away, *we* can do that by observing what they are talking about. Hence there is no presumption at all that a sentence and its truth-condition are equivalent in meaning. In fact, the application here of a scientific metalanguage to the paradox of analysis converges with Mackie's treatment of that topic.[17] Mackie suggests that an analysis can be true and informative if it is taken to report the unconsciously perceived *cues* that prompt the use of an expression. The analysis describes what the users of the expression were responding to when they used it. Such an account is informative because responding to a cue is a different matter from explicitly using it as a criterion. Mackie's suggestion also explains the sense of rightness one feels when presented with a correct analysis: it is the shock of recognition of the cues one has been unwittingly responding to. Mackie's account becomes the present one when the move to the metalanguage is made explicit, and made for the purpose of reckoning what entities a speaker is responding to.[18]

The limitations for ontology of the following strategy for handling the paradox of analysis wholly within the object-language suggest that an adequate treatment requires a (metalinguistic) theory of cues. Let us call the *ostensible* commitment of a sentence *S* the result of taking all nominal expressions in *S* to denote, and giving each a

[17] J. L. Mackie, *Truth, Probability, and Paradox* (O.U.P., Oxford: 1973), pp. 1–16.

[18] One is reminded here of Quine's long-standing view that only the stimulus meanings of a speaker's words are determinable at this stage, and that it is in principle impossible to attribute any one system of objective reference to a speaker. Quine holds that two scientific metalanguages *M* and *M′* can agree in the stimulus meaning they assign to every word of *T*, but disagree in the extensions they assign to at least some words of *T*. I have argued elsewhere that reference is not nearly so inscrutable as this; see my 'Length Relativity', *Journal of Philosophy* (March 1971): 164–74 and 'Relativity, Spatial and Ontological', *Nous* (Sept. 1975): 243–67; also H. Field, 'Quine and the Correspondence Theory', in *Philosophical Review* (April 1974): 200–28. My rejection of the inscrutability of reference does not involve jettisoning Quine's more attractive thesis that translation is indeterminate; see my 'Forcing and the Indeterminacy of Translation', *Erkenntnis*, forthcoming, for an example of indeterminacy which does not rely on inscrutability.

denotation. Sakes belong to the ostensible commitment of (1). Let [*S*] be the set of sentences equivalent to *S* in the sense of equivalence which generates the paradox of analysis. One sentence in [*S*] will have a minimal ostensible commitment (waiving refinements to deal with non-overlapping ostensible commitments). Call this the *minimal member* of [*S*]. We can identify the ontological commitment of *S* with the ostensible commitment of the minimal member of [*S*]. This is the pattern of reasoning employed whenever a philosopher says '*S* is not committed to *x* because there is a way of saying everything *S* says that is not committed to *x*', and it seems to be the rationale behind Quine's own use of QC to secure ontological economies. It is certainly object-linguistic and asymmetrical, since (1) and (1′) are both committed at most to what the less committal of them is committed to. None the less, this criterion of commitment will not always turn up the real, intuitive, ontic commitment of *S*. It might well happen that some misleadingly nominal phrase is so locked into an idiom that it does not paraphrase away. If this idiom is used in *S*, it will appear even in the minimal member of [*S*]. At this point we will have to use our own judgement about what there must be for any member of [*S*] to be true. We will have to cease moving laterally in *S*'s language and say something like 'Whatever *they* think is going on when they use *S* sincerely, the only things actually present are . . .'

(ii) A metalinguistic criterion sidesteps the puzzling intensionality of '*S* is ontologically committed to *x*'.[19] This latter does not entail '$(\exists x)$(*S* is ontologically committed to *x*)', for what *S* says there is may not exist. '*S* is ontologically committed to *x*' is thus opaque at '*x*'. Some writers take this to show that QC is a criterion for what sentences that use existential quantifiers *S* entails, rather than what *objects S* presupposes. One can then use QC without commitment to flying horses by saying that, according to QC, 'Pegasus is a flying horse' is committed to '$(\exists x)$ (*x* is a flying horse)'. But then QC ceases to be an altogether satisfying account of ontological commitment, for surely a criterion for ontological commitment should indeed determine what objects, not what sentences, 'Pegasus is a flying horse' is committed to.

The present account meets this challenge by moving the existential

[19] See M. Jubien, 'The Intensionality of Ontological Commitment', *Nous*, vi. 4 (Nov. 1972), 378–87; I. Scheffler and N. Chomsky, 'What is Said to Be' *Proceedings of the Aristotelian Society*, lix (1958–9), 71–82; also see D. Gottlieb, 'A Method for Ontology', *Journal of Philosophy*, lxxiii. 18 (Oct. 1976), 637–51.

sentence into the metalanguage and using it as (part of) a truth-condition. Sentence (3) will be entailed by a *T*-sentence for 'Pegasus is a flying horse':

(3) If 'Pegasus is a flying horse' is true, then $(\exists x)$ (x is a flying horse).

Since (3) is committed to the values of the variable x of its consequent, and this includes no flying horse (a scientific metalanguage knows horses don't fly), (3) is uncommitted to flying horses. (3) says that for 'Pegasus is a flying horse' to be true, one of the things there is, one of the members of x's domain, must be a flying horse—this is consistent with denying that there are such things. (3) does entail $(\exists x)$ ('Pegasus is a flying horse is true' $\supset$ x is a flying horse), but the latter holds only because its matrix has a false antecedent. All it requires is something that is a-flying-horse-if-P, with P false. Indeed, *any* arbitrary value of x is such. So (3) does not demand flying horses. The metalinguistic remark ' "Pegasus is a flying horse" is committed to flying horses' can, without yielding counterintuitive results, be understood as (3). A scientific metalanguage thus allows us to say, without concurring in, what a sentence falsely says there is—and it mentions the ontic commitment itself, not merely its name.

(iii) There is a tendency, when reflecting about ontological commitment, to concentrate on cases like 'sake'. Ontological commitment to a spurious entity is here averted by reconstruing the grammatical role of a word—contextually conjuring 'sake' away in the ascent to M. The question of what 'sake' denotes does not arise, M not needing a translation of 'sake' as a substituend for its bindable variables. Let us call such ontological trimmings *analytical eliminations*, and objects analytically eliminated through attention to logical form, *virtual entities*. Analytical elimination tends to be treated differently from cases in which an expression t is actually taken to denote, but no entities beyond those antecedently needed to supply the ontic commitment of t's context need exist for sentences using t to be true. Let us call such trimmings *identifications*. The metalinguistic approach offers a unified treatment of analytical elimination and identification, and treats the distinction between eliminating an entity and reducing it as a distinction between two kinds of identification.

Sometimes the determination of the entities a sentence is committed to depends on empirical discovery. If Sam happens to be Ralph, the sentence

(4) Joe did it for Sam and Ralph

is, intuitively, committed only to Joe and Sam, although this can't be demonstrated *a priori*. On the other hand, it is *provable* that

(5) $a \varepsilon \{a,b\}$ & $a \varepsilon \cup\{\{a\},\{b\}\}$

is, in the same intuitive sense, committed only to a and $\{a,b\}$ because it is provable that $\{a,b\}$ is the same as $\text{U}\{\{a\},\{b\}\}$. What (4) and (5) have in common is that reckoning what there must be for them to be true does not involve reclassifying expressions. Each contains a denoting expression which denotes the very thing denoted by another expression in the same sentence. If singular terms are explained away,[20] (4) and (5) correspond to open sentences with three free variables such that the only sequences that satisfy them agree in their second and third places.

Now a scientific metalanguage M yields ontic commitment for both (4) and (5) in just the way it yielded ontic commitment in cases of analysis: we read off the bindable variables in the truth-condition. M is allowed to use information in formulating truth-conditions, in particular that Ralph is Sam and that $\{a,b\}$ is $\text{U}\{\{a\},\{b\}\}$. The T-sentences for (4) and (5) are

(6) (4) is true iff Joe did it to help Sam

and

(7) (5) is true iff $a \varepsilon \{a,b\}$.

The truth-condition in (6) is not synonymous with (4), nor is (4) synonymous with the translation of the truth-condition in (6) into the object-language. I have already urged that this is an attractive as well as inevitable feature of using a metalanguage, and indeed thus unifying identification and analysis extends Quine's own ontological monism.

The foregoing exhibits how QC amended formulates ontological trimmings based on identification, but that does not amount to a criterion for identification (either of an object or the denotation of a term) itself. However, a metalinguistic criterion of identification

[20] See, e.g., Quine, *Word and Object* (M.I.T., Cambridge, Mass.: 1960), 176–86.

naturally suggests itself. The question 'What is *a*?' amounts to the question 'What does "*a*" denote?' This in turn is to ask for the object that satisfies '$x_i = a$'. Suppose (8) is a truth of *M*:

(8) '$x_i = a$' is satisfied by any sequence *s* whose *i*th member $(s)_i$ is *b*.[21]

We may say that (8) identifies *a*, or identifies *a* as *b*, or identifies what '*a*' refers to. (PL now becomes a consistency or adequacy condition on an identification.) What *b* is need not be strictly connected with what we meant by '*a*', or what we thought we were referring to by '*a*'. Rather, the right-hand side of (8) is the best account of what we were in fact talking about when we were using '*a*'. Reference, in fact, goes completely extensional: if b' is *b*, then if the *i*th member of sequence *s* is *b*, then the *i*th member of *s* is b'; so if (8) determines that '*a*' refers to *b*, then it determines that '*a*' refers to b'. (Note that '*a*' may refer to nothing at all—there may be no sequence that satisfies '$x_i = a$'.)

In one way this criterion does not amount to a *theory* of reference, but in another way it does. It says nothing about how to determine what '*a*' refers to—whether, e.g., a causal theory or a description theory is the correct account of reference.[22] It just says that if, e.g., science decides that what we were talking about all along when using 'water' was H_2O, water is H_2O. On the other hand, embedding (8) in an empirical theory of speakers and their causal relations to the world clearly favours taking 'what a speaker is referring to by "*a*"' as a more fundamental notion than 'what "*a*" refers to'. In Donnellan's language I am proposing a criterion for the referential (as opposed to attributive) use of terms; in Kripke's language, a criterion for speaker's reference as opposed to semantic reference.[23] This, I think, is proper. Certainly the most promising current accounts of reference—the Kripke–Donnellan and the Gricean approaches—appear to rest their accounts of semantic reference on speaker's reference.[24] Moreover, emphasizing what speakers are

[21] $\langle x_1, \ldots, x_n \rangle_i = x_i$.

[22] A causal theory says that '*a*' refers to the initial object in the right sort of causal chain which culminates in our use of '*a*'. A description theory says that there is some description '$P(x)$' such that '*a*' denotes $(\iota x)P(x)$.

[23] See K. Donnellan, 'Reference and Definite Description', in J. Rosenberg and C. Travis, eds., *Readings in the Philosophy of Language* (Prentice-Hall, N.J.: 1971); see S. Kripke, 'Speaker's Reference and Semantic Reference', *Midwest Studies in Philosophy*, ii (1977), 255–76.

referring to is more consonant with the treatment of elimination given immediately below. Finally, it is most pertinent when discussing the mind–body problem to determine what we are referring to by psychological terms. Suppose, to adapt one of Donnellan's examples, I see a rock at twilight and, mistaking it for a man with a stick, say 'The man with the stick is stooped'. *I* have referred to the rock as 'the man with the stick', although of course it isn't a man with a stick. It may be impossible to say what the words themselves referred to (especially if the semantic reference of expressions must be explained via speaker's reference), or we may decide they refer to nothing. Now the materialist thinks we stand to the mind (and other poorly understood phenomena) as I stand to the rock; whatever language I may use to describe it, what *I am talking about* when I use psychological language are physical phenomena. The materialist is not worried about what to construe my words as referring to if most of our beliefs about psychological phenomena are false. Since I think the materialist is right to put the problem this way, I am using a criterion for identification biased in favour of speaker's reference, or the referential use of terms.

Philosophers have sometimes written as if there were different kinds of identifications: identification *per se*, reduction, and elimination. In keeping with the broadly pragmatic notion of reference just canvassed, I propose that identification is primitive and that reduction and elimination are extra-systematic *interpretations* of identification. The distinction between a reductive and an eliminative identification becomes less a matter of the identification itself than of the attitude to take toward it. Suppose our discourse T has a meaning-postulate for the term 'a', such as 'a's are P'. (S is a meaning-postulate of T if any translation of a language T' into T which matched S with a sentence T'-speakers dissented from would *ipso facto* be a mistranslation.) Then an identification of a with b is an *elimination* just in case b is not P. Thus we say that there is no man with a stick upon identifying what, in the Donnellan example, we were referring to, since (presumably) it is a meaning-postulate of English that men with sticks are living things. This account fits typical cases discussed in the literature. It is said that we have

[24] For Kripke, see his 'Naming and Necessity', in G. Harman and D. Davidson, eds., *Semantics of Natural Language* (Humanities, N.Y.: 1972), p. 302; for a developed Gricean theory see Bennett, *Linguistic Behaviour*. Bennett takes semantic reference to arise when speaker's reference becomes conventional in the sense of D. Lewis.

eliminated witches by discovering that what the residents of seventeenth-century Salem were talking about when they used the word 'witch' were just psychotic old women. However, when it was discovered that 'lightning' denotes (or that we use 'lightning' to denote) a stream of electrons, it was said that what was discovered was what lightning was. The difference between the two cases seems to be that 'A witch consorts with the Devil' is a meaning-postulate for 'witch' that the psychotic women in question did not satisfy, while there are no parallel postulates about lightning that streams of electrons fail to satisfy. This is why we say, on the basis of our identification of witches, that there were no witches at all.

It is, to be sure, awkward to say both that rock *r* satisfies 'x_i = the man with the stick' (or that Sara Good satisfies 'x_i = Wanda the witch') and that there is no man with a stick (and no witch Wanda). This awkwardness can be mitigated by taking '*a*' as it occurs in '$x_i = a$' as having its purely referential use, and '*a*' as it occurs in 'There are no *a*s' to be the '*a*' of meaning-postulates governing '*a*'. Indeed, it seems to me that the only sort of account that makes sense of such remarks as 'It turned out that there were no witches, witches being only psychotic women' is that the first 'witch' is that of 'witches consort with the Devil', and the second 'witch' is that of ' "witch" was used to refer to psychotic women'. Such remarks may appear solecistic, but we must make sense of them if we are to make sense of the elimination of entities.

One corollary of this account of elimination is that the question of whether an identification is an elimination can only be settled by linguistic survey. This has application to the mind–body problem. Suppose sensations turn out to be brain processes (allowing processes to be entities); that is, that 'sensation' refers to brain processes. Whether we have thereby eliminated sensations depends on whether 'Sensations are non-physical' is a meaning-postulate of English that governs the word 'sensations'. If it is, we have discovered that there are no sensations. If, however, the only meaning-postulates governing the ordinary use of 'sensation' are, like 'Headaches are unpleasant', neutral with respect to physicality, the identification would not show that there are no sensations. Indeed if, as sceptics about the notion of meaning might maintain, the semantic status of 'headaches are non-physical' is indeterminate, no clear sense at all attaches to the identification *versus* elimination issue. These considerations diminish the importance of whether materialism is construed as an identity thesis or as an eliminative thesis in intent or upshot: from a logical point of view, it is just a thesis about what we use 'sensation' to refer to.

I have neglected for the last two pages another kind of identification philosophers of science commonly refer to: reduction. Part at least of what they mean is this: entity a is *reduced* when (1) a is identified with a set of objects $b = \{b_1,...,b_n\}$; (2) this identification is not an elimination; and (3) all the properties of b are reducible to the properties of the b_i. In general, a is reduced when every sentence '$P(a)$' has as truth-condition an expression of the form $R(b_1,...,b_n)$.

This definition obviously awaits an explanation of property reduction, a matter postponed until after the discussion of the ontological status of properties in the next section. Pending satisfactory resolution of these complications, however, certain comments are in order. Condition (2) should be taken as a verbal stipulation; we might call cases satisfying only (1) and (3) 'eliminative reductions'. The need for condition (1) in explicating reduction is shown by the case of the morning star and the evening star. We have identified the two, yet why do we not say that the morning star has been reduced to the evening star? The reason seems to be that, for all relevant purposes, both are single objects. Reduction goes from the individual to the ensemble. It might be said that we have not reduced the morning star to the evening star because any argument to this effect could be matched by a parallel argument to the effect that we have reduced the evening star to the morning star. But this suggestion just assumes that reduction is or ought to be asymmetrical without explaining why, whereas (1) contains the asymmetry we evidently have in mind—the asymmetry in direction between objects and sets.

Both reduction and elimination decrease the number of objects we say there are: if a is eliminated as a misunderstood b, or reduced to b, our estimate of the cardinality of any set $\{a,b,...\}$ shrinks by one. In the reductive case, we say things like 'a is nothing over and above the b_i'. The b_i need not be antecedently familiar. It is conceivable, for example, that mesons turn out to be clouds of previously unknown particles with previously unknown properties that explain the observed properties of mesons. The theory of these particles would be developed *ambulando*. In that case mesons would surely have been reduced to these new particles even though these particles played no role in physics until it was discovered that we were calling clouds of them 'mesons'.

4. Some Nonentities

Identity, reduction, and elimination have so far been defined only for entities. This section rejects the claims to entityhood of events, states, processes, and properties: truth-conditions can be given for statements that ostensibly refer to these objects that do not involve variables ranging over them. Since certain intuitions are lost if one cleaves too firmly to the analytical elimination of properties, and since the definition of reduction in section 3 requires some notion of property reduction, derivative sense to identity questions about properties is assigned in section 5.

Consider event *e*, the ignition of match *m* at t'. To say there is such an event as *e* is to say that $(\exists t)(\exists t')(t < t'$ & $-(m$ is afire at $t)$ & m is afire at $t')$. Similarly, it would seem, any context '$F(e)$' in which *e* appears is true just in case $F^*(m,t,t')$, in which only *e*'s constitutive continuants and temporal bounds appear. Davidson (Rescher, p. 227) rejects this fact as sufficient for the elimination of events on the grounds that, if $F(e)$ and $F^*(m,t,t')$ are truly equivalent, they have the same ontological commitment. This is, transparently, an application of the paradox of analysis to the assessment of ontological commitment. On Davidson's reasoning, the equivalence of 'John did it for Joe's sake' to 'John did it for Joe' is no ground for saying that there are no sakes. Anyway, as I stressed in the previous section, this deployment of the paradox of analysis is circumvented by taking $F^*(m,t,t')$ as the truth condition for '$F(e)$'. Since Davidson seems willing to grant the equivalence of $F(e)$ to $F^*(m,t,t')$ he can have no objection to this move.

It has also been argued that treating causation as an extensional relation requires reference to events in truth-conditions for causal statements.[25] I have argued elsewhere[26] that this is a confusion: the extensionality claim is preserved if we recognize that the contexts which replace '*c* caused *e*' and '*c* caused *e* because *c* is *D*', when events are analysed away, are themselves extensional. Davidson also argues (in the same article) that supplying truth-conditions for sentences with adverbs requires reifying events since 'Joe walked

[25] Cf. D. Davidson, 'Causal Relations', *Journal of Philosophy*, lxiv. 21 (Nov. 1967), 691–703.

[26] 'The Extensionality of Causation and Causal-Explanatory Contexts.'

slowly' entails 'Joe walked', and the only way to represent this as an instance of the first-order logical truth $(\exists x)(W(x)\ \&\ S(x)) \supset (\exists x)W(x)$ is to construe 'a walk that Joe took' as a subject of the predicates 'taken by Joe' and 'slow'. This argument moves too quickly. If 'Joe walked slowly' is given the logical form $W(j)$ and 'Joe walked' the logical form $W'(j)$, the mooted entailment can be explained in terms of the meaning-relations between the two predicates W and W'. The relation can be construed as like the one between 'x is a man' and 'x is human', even up to the typographical accident that both contain 'man'. The entailment can be construed as holding in virtue of meaning, not logical form. This approach multiplies the number of predicates in natural language (although Quine's '-ly' operator that maps predicates to predicates would keep this multiplicity down); but better to multiply predicates than objects. But wouldn't this multiplicity of predicates make the acquisition of language by children impossible? I take up another application of this language-learning argument in chapter V, and would transfer what I say about it there to this application, *mutatis mutandis*.[27] I see no reason, then, to admit events as any part of the furniture of the world.[28]

Processes go the way of events. Talk of a process p is talk of a series of events $\langle e_1,...,e_n\rangle$; when reference to the e_i is explained away, so is reference to p.

The nominalist has a number of reasons for dismissing properties, and replacing talk of them by talk of predicates. The most compelling, perhaps, is this. Reifying properties is tantamount to construing predicates as denoting expressions; but if predicates were denoting expressions, it becomes hard to see how there could be any *sentences*, how it would be possible to assert anything. If a predicate were a name, a sentence would be a list. It is clear that a paradigm list like 'Joe, Sam, 37' *asserts* nothing. If 'is tall' were the name of the property of tallness, 'Joe is tall' would be the list 'Joe, tallness'; and that is not an assertion. The Platonist only evades this difficulty if he downplays the analogy he has created between sentences and lists—if he says, for example, that predicates *con*note properties, or that subjects and predicates are connected by a copula. Either

[27] Also see my 'Explanation and Prediction in Grammar (and Semantics)', *Midwest Studies in Philosophy*, ii (1977), 134.

[28] T. Horgan has recently elaborated this position in 'The Case Against Events', *Philosophical Review*, lxxxvii. (Jan. 1978), pp. 28–47—but his elimination of events makes rather free use of non-truth-functional sentential connectives.

connoting is like naming, and the original difficulty reappears; or connoting is not like naming, and the Platonist has abandoned his position. Either the copula names a relation between subject and property, and the original difficulty reappears; or the copula names nothing, and the Platonist has abandoned his position. It is similarly unhelpful to say with Strawson[29] that a predicate is related to its subject by a 'non-relational tie', for this is to explain the obscure by the more obscure. It is helpful to remember that the role of predicates is to *describe* objects identified by terms. An assertion is the application of a description to an already identified object. Assertion is not a matter of picking an object out by a term, and then picking some other object out by another term.

Such uncompromising nominalism is often challenged to make sense of 'natural recurrence', i.e. such patent facts as the existence of many yellow things.[30] This highly ambiguous challenge disintegrates as one attends to its various possible interpretations. It might mean that nominalism cannot *express* the facts of natural recurrence. But surely the nominalist can express the recurrence of yellow as the fact that many things are yellow—i.e. that many things satisfy the predicate '*x* is yellow'. He need not even deny that there are things exactly similar to each other. What he finds unnecessary is the move to an object that exactly similar things share. If the objection is that the nominalist cannot *explain* natural recurrence, this too is unwarranted. The nominalist defers to the physicist in his explanation of the existence of many yellow things: he points out that there are many things which reflect light of certain wavelengths only. The phenomenon of yellowness, in so far as it is explicable, is explained by science. The nominalist simply does not see how the existence of many yellow things can be explained by saying they all have yellowness, even if he could understand this suggestion. Finally, the objection from natural recurrence might be that the nominalist cannot explain why objects satisfy the predicates they do. But explanations of just the sort the Platonist finds lacking are available to the nominalist for a large class of predicates, in fact any predicate whose satisfaction condition is not a primitive predicate of the metalanguage. Take Uncle Joe, who satisfies the

[29] *Individuals* (Methuen, London: 1959), pp. 170ff. He eventually settles on 'attributive tie', a term he credits to Cook Wilson.

[30] See C. Landesman, *Discourse and Its Presuppositions* (Yale U.P., New Haven, Conn.: 1972).

predicate 'x is an uncle'. The Platonist says the nominalist can make no sense of the natural explandum, *why* Joe satisfies 'x is an uncle'. (The Platonist's explanation, of course, is that Joe has unclehood.) The nominalist replies with this explanation: since sequence s satisfies 'x_i is an uncle' iff $(\exists y)(\exists z)(y$ is a parent of z & y is a sibling of $(s)_i$ and $(s)_i$ is male), Joe satisfies 'x is an uncle' because he is the male sibling of a parent. Presumably the Platonist and the nominalist agree that explaining why Joe is an *uncle*, how Joe got to be an uncle, involves biology and family history. The satisfaction condition for 'x is an uncle' is established by empirical observation of the users of the predicate 'x is an uncle' supplemented by our own best analysis of the situations in which they use it. True, when one comes down to a primitive predicate such as (say) 'x is yellow', the only explanation of why an object satisfies 'x is yellow' is that it is yellow. This is thin, but no thinner than the Platonist's 'Because it has the simple property of yellowness'.

Once properties are eliminated, so are states. The state σ of an object x during the interval Δt is, intuitively, the set of properties x has during Δt. Now we are left with just the set of predicates x satisfies during Δt, and indeed Quine and Smart simply identify σ with the Δt time-slice of x.

I have attacked Platonic realism at length because a quite popular objection to materialism tacitly rests on it. Suppose we have discovered empirically that some entity a is identical to entity b. One standardly explains that this is an *empirical* discovery by saying that while 'a' and 'b' denote the same thing, each is associated with a different description. The term 'a' means or was introduced as 'the thing which is F', and 'b' means or was introduced as 'the thing which is G'; the empirical discovery is that the unique F is the unique G. But, the argument goes, this means that even if $a = b$, there remains a duality of properties, F and G, which a $(=b)$ has. And this duality of properties haunts the materialist. Thus J. Stevenson:

> [According to materialism, T]he properties which are connoted by 'brain process' and also those that are connoted by 'sensation' are possessed by one and the same thing. . . . Thus *we have not got rid of the danglers*. . . . [I]t turns out that brain processes are danglers, for now brain processes have all those properties which made sensations danglers. . . . [W]e are *now* to say that a brain process has P-properties if and only if it has certain M-properties. But it is still a contingent matter of fact . . . we

have to deal with certain properties of sensations rather than sensations themselves. We might try to conjure away P-properties by claiming 'All P-properties are identical with certain M-properties. . . .' Thus the new danglers would be properties of P-properties.[31]

Popper deploys what may be the same argument, although his failure to explain 'language' leaves his argument unclear:

if . . . two languages are not inter-translatable, then they deal with different kinds of facts . . . once the two languages (of physics and psychology) are admitted not to be translatable into each other, they cannot any longer be said to talk about the same facts, and must be admitted to talk about different facts.[32]

Stevenson's argument, then, is this. Allowing processes to be entities, suppose 'my backache' denotes what 'the firing of neuron #37' denotes; let their common denotation be x. If this is an empirical discovery like the discovery that lightning = electrical discharge, the property by which x was identified as a backache is a psychological property which differs from the physical property by which x was identified as a neural process. Consequently, identifying mental and physical entities precipitates a dualism of properties—psychological and physical. Even if mental entities are physical entities, the dualist can claim the day. The regress Stevenson mentions is this: if one claims that psychological properties are identical to physical properties (to regain the day for the materialist), then the second-order properties by which a psycho-physical property was initially identified as psychological must differ from that by which it was initially identified as physical, and dualism breaks out again.[33]

The weakness in Stevenson's argument is its tacit shift from the difference in sense of the two descriptions associated with co-referring terms to a difference between the *properties connoted* by these descriptions and possessed by their referent. This move converts the uncontroversial truth that any empirically discovered identity presupposes a *duality of predicates* that the entities in

[31] 'Sensations and Brain Processes,' pp. 89–91. Stevenson says several times that singular terms connote properties; I noted earlier his use of the second-order form of PL, p. 7 above.

[32] *Conjectures and Refutations* (Basic Books, N.Y.: 1965), pp. 294, 300. It is astounding that a man who has declaimed endlessly on the irrelevance of issues about language to philosophy, should put so much stock in a point about translation.

[33] R. Bernstein also appeals to this argument in 'The Challenge of Scientific Materialism', in Rosenthal, ed., *Materialism and the Mind–Body Problem*, p. 208.

question must satisfy into the more consequential claim that any empirically discovered identity precipitates a duality *in re* of the properties of the thing(s) identified. In fact, the materialist can say with entire consistency that x was initially identified as 'my backache', and it has come to be known that x is also describable as 'the firing of neuron #37'. Nothing interesting follows from this duality in language that the physicalist presupposes. A dualism *in re* can be induced only by enlisting properties to explain this duality. Similarly, accusing the physicalist of attributing both mental and physical features to x either harmlessly repeats the facts about the language the physicalist is happy to admit, or illegitimately reifies features as stand-ins for properties.

Some philosophers do write as if a duality in the predicates used to describe conscious beings sufficed to establish a more substantial dualism between conscious beings and merely physical things. Strawson, for example, holds that 'persons' form a primitive ontological category on the grounds that there are two independent kinds of *predicates* ascribable to persons, while only one kind is ascribable to physical objects.[34] But even Strawson is not consistent in using this as the basis for his dualism. When he is not officially formulating his doctrine as one about predicates, Strawson lapses into formulating it as the claim that there are two different kinds of characteristic, or even things[35] that we ascribe to persons as opposed to only one kind of characteristic for merely physical things. So perhaps a Stevenson-type argument lies beneath Strawson's 'person' theory, a conjecture that coheres well with Strawson's neo-Platonic view of properties (see p. 25 above).

It is instructive to note that Stevenson's reification of properties leads his argument to violate the stricture of section 1 against proving too much. Reasoning entirely parallel to Stevenson's 'proves' that the identification of lightning with streams of electrons leaves us saddled with a residual dualism. 'Bolt of lightning' has been discovered to refer to what 'stream of electrons of type #38' refers to. This cannot establish that lightning is nothing but electron stream #38, however, for 'bolt of lightning' means 'flash in the sky' and 'electron stream #38' is introduced by some physical description (perhaps 'electron stream #38' itself). These descriptions connote different properties: even if bolts of lightning are streams of electrons,

[34] *Individuals*, pp. 100 ff.

[35] See especially ibid., p. 83.

we are saddled with a duality of *properties* that lightning bolts have; those physical properties that allow them to be identified physically, and those that allow them to be identified as lightning bolts. There is a duality *in re* between the lightning properties of (some) electron streams, and the general physical properties all electron streams have. We even have dangling correlations: why do some electron streams have lightning-properties while others do not? And if we say that lightning-properties are identical to certain electrical discharge-properties, a regress ensues. If this is a scientific discovery then lightning properties must first have been identified by second-order properties, properties of lightning-properties, which differ from the second-order properties by which these same lightning-properties were identified as physical, electrical discharge-properties.

Anyone growing impatient with this attempt to parlay a difference in how lightning and electricity were first encountered into an ineluctable lightning-electricity dualism ought to grow equally impatient with Stevenson's argument; it's the same one. This is not, of course, to deny the possibility that, given the notion of property-identity introduced below, mental-state and brain-state properties will turn out to differ. It is only to say that the duality of predicates Stevenson cites is no guarantee of this.

Stevenson might reply[36] that the lightning/electrical discharge and mental state/brain state situations differ. The contingency of the former discovery is explained by saying that lightning appeared to differ from electrical discharge, and this appearance was misleading. But this explanation backfires in the mind–body case. It requires mental states to appear to differ from brain states, saddling the materialist with *appearances* of brain states—mental phenomena that escape the materialist's net.

Such a rejoinder equivocates on 'appear'. Sometimes, to be sure, talk of how an object x appears involves some connection between x and the sensory states of percipients; as in 'the barn had the visual appearance of a church'. But talk of how x appears may simply refer to the *opinion* that someone holds of x, as in 'it appeared that ZF entailed GCH until Paul Cohen came along'. In this latter sense we can say that something appears a certain way without at all referring to appearances in the former sense, without referring to sensory states. ('Impression' is similarly ambiguous; as in 'having a visual

[36] Cf. T. Nagel, 'What is it Like to be a Bat?,' *Philosophical Review*, lxxxiii (Oct. 1974), 445.

impression' and 'forming an impression'.) But surely it is the second sense of 'appearance' that is at work when the contingency of $a = b$ is explained by saying that a appeared to be different than b. One need not mean that a created two different sensory states. To say that Clark Kent appeared to be too weak to be Superman is only to say something about beliefs that were formed about Clark Kent. Without further argument we may take it that this is the sense of 'appear' at work in the remark that brain processes appear to differ from mental processes: people *think* they differ. One need not postulate two different kinds of sensory states that brain processes give rise to, sensory states to embarrass the materialist.

5. *Properties: Their Identification and Reduction*

Simply dismissing identity questions about properties excludes too much. There is intuitive sense to the idea that being temperature T is the same property of collections of gas molecules as having mean kinetic energy E. Intuition opposes this case to cases in which two distinct properties are constantly conjoined—Putnam's example is the temperature and conductivity of a metal. The physicalist and his opponent want to argue about which of these two sorts of cases subsumes being in pain and being in brain state #37; as things stand their conversation cannot get started. If the predicates '$P(x)$' and '$Q(x)$' are allowed to 'express properties P and Q' at all, the strongest relation between P and Q so far available is extensional equivalence, induced by extensional equivalence of '$P(x)$' and '$Q(x)$'.[37] Nor will it do to define '$P = Q$' as the synonymy of '$P(x)$' and '$Q(x)$'; if one takes property identity seriously, one will want to take seriously the idea of two properties being empirically discovered to be identical. This requires one and the same property to be 'expressed' by non-synonymous predicates.

The metalinguistic apparatus of section 3 admits properties in special contexts as entities expressed by predicates and supplies, in those terms, a natural criterion for property identity. Call the sentence

a satisfies '$P(x)$' iff . . . a . . .

of M for discourse T, M's *satisfication clause* for '$P(x)$'. The right side of the biconditional is M's *satisfaction-condition* for '$P(x)$'. If a property is conceived as the state of affairs which a predicate expresses, which legitimates the use of a predicate, a natural candi-

[37] Cf. Putnam, 'On Properties', p. 246.

date for the property (of being) P is the satisfaction-condition for the predicate '$P(x)$'. This suggests the convention that property P = property Q if '$P(x)$' and '$Q(x)$' have the same satisfaction-condition in M.[38]

The satisfaction-condition of '$P(x)$' is, informally, the feature of the world '$P(x)$' describes or expresses. M supplies the features of things described by predicates of discourse T just as it supplied the objects T presupposes. When it does so, it identifies properties. Speakers of T use '$P(x)$' in certain typical situations; some constellation of features cues it. Users of '$P(x)$' need not know what its cue is, nor employ its cue as their criterion for applying '$P(x)$'. A child may be trained to identify objects as 'red' without realizing that he is responding to a certain kind of radiation. But the presence of that radiation counts for M as the satisfaction condition of '$P(x)$' for the child and his linguistic community. Classical examples of scientific property identification fit this pattern. Objects are called 'hot' when they cause pain, when they have been rubbed, and when they alter thermometers. (These clauses need not be taken as the *meaning* of 'x is hot'.) We subsequently discover that the motion of molecules plays this causal-explanatory role; we have discovered what phenomenon 'x is hot' is geared to.

The cue/criterion distinction I am pressing so hard is paralleled by Leibniz's confused knowledge/distinct knowledge distinction:

> When I recognize a thing among others, without being able to say in what its differentiae or properties consist, the knowledge is *confused*. It is thus that we sometimes know . . . without being in any way in doubt, whether a poem or a picture is good or bad, because there is a *je ne sais quoi* which satisfies us or offends us. But when I can explain the marks which I have, the knowledge is called *distinct*. And such is the knowledge of an assayer, who discerns true gold from false by means of certain tests or marks which make up the definition of gold. [Leibniz adds that] when everything that enters into a definition or into distinct knowledge is known distinctly, down to the primary notions, I call this knowledge adequate.[39]

The main difference between Leibniz's idea and the present one is that for Leibniz 'adequacy' is based on ever deeper logical analysis, while here it is based on empirical investigation of the conditions under which a predicate is employed.

[38] Sameness for satisfaction-conditions is the '=' of PL, satisfaction clauses being ultimately expressions (of M).

[39] *Discourse on Metaphysics*, trans. P. Lucas and L. Grint (Manchester U.P.: 1953), XXIV.

The present method of introducing properties treats predicates as analogous to names. Taking M to be supplemented by science allows M's satisfaction condition for a predicate '$P(x)$' to be remote from what, intuitively, its users mean by it. Determining what '$P(x)$' expresses is thus much like determining the speaker's reference for a term (see pp. 19–21 above). (So M may identify the properties expressed by nonsynonymous predicates.) The meaning of '$P(x)$' is best construed, I think, as that paraphrase most T-speakers would give for '$P(x)$'. If, as some think, the notion of meaning is empty, satisfaction-conditions remain as the only reasonable objects of inquiry. Either way, M is not a theory that gives the meaning of expressions of T. Here I differ from Davidson, who regards an adequate semantics for a language as a theory of meaning for that language.[40] M is, however, an empirical theory—as Davidson takes a truth theory for a language to be—and M and a Davidsonian semantic theory for discourse T are (if I understand Davidson correctly) testable in quite similar ways. The primitive clauses of the satisfaction definition for predicates of T are obtained by noting correlations between the verbal behaviour of T-speakers and features of their environment. These correlations are supplemented by a theory of stimulation (although I am not sure Davidson would agree to this proviso). The truth definition for the sentences of T, and particular satisfaction-conditions for particular predicates, form an empirical conjecture derived from projectible regularities. It can be tested by predicting the environmental features that will elicit assent to a sentence or the use of a predicate. One makes similar predictions about predicates the theory constructs by truth functions and quantifiers from the satisfaction clauses for simpler predicates. There are well-known difficulties in all this—how, if at all, to isolate pure truth condition from collateral belief? I suspect these problems press harder on Davidson than me, for he wants truth- and satisfaction-conditions to be, in some recognizable sense, meaning. I do not, being content to take predicates on the analogy of names. My argument also avoids the objection[41] that adding an arbitrary true conjunct 'C' to selected satisfaction-conditions for predicates of T will result in a truth definition that systematically entails only true

[40] See his 'Truth and Meaning', in Rosenberg and Travis, *Readings in the Philosophy of Language*.

[41] See J. Foster, 'Meaning and Truth Theory', and B. Loar, 'Two Theories of Meaning', both in G. Evans and J. McDowell, eds., *Truth and Meaning* (O.U.P., Oxford: 1976).

T-sentences, yet yields truth-conditions which by no stretch of the imagination amount to meanings. Since my metalanguage *M* will be an empirical theory about what is going on when . . . , considerations of simplicity dictate deletion of such otiose clauses even though they are compatible with all the data. Davidson hamstrings himself when, in 'Truth and Meaning', he erroneously claims that adherence to Tarski's convention *T* will rule out all such pathological constructions. There is, finally, the problem of how a *falsehood* could ever be attributed—since any utterance could simply be taken as further information about the objects of a speaker's reference and the satisfaction-conditions of his predicates. Perhaps the answer lies in our well-entrenched beliefs that the speaker would have spoken differently if (say) his spatial orientation had been different or his line of sight clearer. What all this shows is that most of the interesting work will be done in the development and verification of *M*, something I am presupposing already accomplished. But a *definition* of property identity should not by itself be competent to decide what properties are what. It merely provides a metaphysically responsible framework in which such decisions can be formulated.

My appeal to features does not reintroduce properties surreptitiously, nor does it even take features themselves seriously. Talk of features, in the limited way so far explained, is replaceable by talk of satisfaction clauses: ' "$P(x)$" expresses feature ...' is, in Goodman's phrase, slang for '*a* satisfies "$P(x)$" iff ...*a*...'. Indeed, we could well have treated '$P = Q$' as an unanalysable whole, defined directly as sameness of satisfaction-conditions for '$P(x)$' and '$Q(x)$'. No further contexts $A(P)$ for P itself have so far been explained. Suppose, in general, that '$A(x)$' has a satisfaction clause in *M*. It is tempting to explain $A(P)$ as: the satisfaction clause of '$P(x)$' satisfies '$A(x)$'. But this confuses satisfaction clauses as linguistic entities with satisfaction clauses as, literally, features of the world. Satisfaction clauses may be values of *M*'s variables in the former sense, not in the latter—but they can provide sense for $A(P)$ only if taken in the latter sense. To see this, suppose (1) and (2) (made trivial to diminish complications) are theses of *M*:

(1) *a* satisfies '*x* is red' iff *a* radiates light of 4027μ
(2) *a* satisfies '*x* is interesting' iff *a* is interesting.

(1) and (2) do not yield

(3) 'Redness is interesting' is true iff radiates light of 4027μ is interesting,

since

radiates light of 4027μ

is not a value of *M*'s variables. (3) is gibberish. If *M* has quotation-names for its satisfaction conditions, the right side of (3) can be turned into the sensible statement

(4) 'radiates light of 4027μ' is interesting.

But (4) is a statement about an expression of *M*, not the feature of the world picked out by it, or by 'x is red'.

We have, thus, stipulated a sense for the identity of properties, but none for any other attribution of properties to properties except '. . . is picked out by predicate – – –'. We cannot yet apply PL to properties, since the consequent of PL thus applied is ill-formed, and the '=' of the antecedent of PL is merely homonymous with the '=' of '$P = Q$', however natural its definition. Anticipating some account of the consequent of $P = Q \supset (A(P) \equiv A(Q))$, however, let us call this formula PL_P, or PL relativized to properties. It must again be emphasized that however PL_P is eventually specified, it is not a corollary of PL. In fact, one begins to perceive an analogy between properties and those other virtual objects, abstracted classes.[42] It sometimes proves convenient to introduce the class $\{x: F(x)\}$ into some standard system of set theory (ZF, say), but not as a value of the variables of the axioms and definitions of ZF. This being so, identity for abstracts must be explicity defined even though identity for sets is antecedently understood. In particular, if x and y are real sets, $x = y$ iff $(z)((z \varepsilon x \equiv z \varepsilon y) \;\&\; (x \varepsilon z \equiv y \varepsilon z))$; but '$\{x: F(x)\} = \{x: G(x)\}$' must be *given* a sense, standardly '$(x)(F(x) \equiv G(x))$'. This stipulation treats '$\{x: F(x)\} = \{x: G(x)\}$' as an unanalysed whole, and, like our stipulation for '$P = Q$' leaves $A(\{x: F(x)\})$ unexplained, where $A(x)$ is any other predicate of ZF. As with identity itself, the meaning of '$A(...)$' for abstracts must be stipulated even if $A(x)$ is well defined for real sets. Thus $x \subset y$ means $(z)(z \varepsilon x \supset z \varepsilon y)$, but it must be explained anew for $\{x: F(x)\} \subset y$; the intuitively natural explanation, of course, is $(x)(F(x) \supset x \varepsilon y)$. There is no *a priori* requirement that sense be given to every such

[42] Cf. the discussion of 'wffs in the wider sense' in G. Takeuti and W. Zaring, *Introduction to Axiomatic Set Theory*, vol. i (Springer-Verlag, N.Y.: 1970); and Quine's *Set Theory and Its Logic*, 2nd ed. (Belknap, Cambridge, Mass.: 1969), pp. 9–46.

context, nor is there any *a priori* guarantee that all theorems of ZF will hold when wffs of ZF are replaced by 'wffs in the wider sense'.

The situation is the same with properties: we must stipulate, for any given context $A(P)$, what is to count as '$A(P)$''s being true. Nothing demands that a stipulation be provided for every context; the most that can be said is that some stipulations are natural. It is natural, for example, to define '$\{x_1,...,x_n\}$ is the extension of P' as: according to M, each and only the x_i satisfies '$P(x)$'. As a by-product, this stipulation partially defines the consequent of PL_P: PL_P now says that, if $P = Q$, P and Q have the same extension. Another natural class of contexts to define for properties are those describing their causal powers. We can for example define $A(P) \equiv [y$ is R because x is $P]$ as: the explanatory argument whose conclusion is '$R(y)$' contains '$P(x)$'.[43] This natural stipulation deepens PL_P, which now requires that if $P = Q$, $[y$ is R because x is $P] \equiv [y$ is R because x is $Q]$. When all appropriate causal contexts are similarly defined, PL_P asserts in part that if $P = Q$, everything which holds in virtue of a thing's being P holds in virtue of that thing's being Q. There is, of course, no a priori requirement that only causal-explanatory contexts are worthy of stipulative definition for properties.

Suppose we have assembled all the well-defined contexts $A(...)$, so that PL_P is fully defined. There are two ways to interpret PL_P. PL_P can be taken as a consistency requirement on M's assignment of satisfaction clauses to predicates; as part, that is, of how M determines which satisfaction clauses to assign. It says, for given $A(...)$, that '$P(x)$' and '$Q(x)$' can be given the same satisfaction clause only if $A(P) \equiv A(Q)$. This is not trivial, for, thus interpreted, PL_P is a record of *what* facts about a predicate determine its satisfaction clause. The stipulations lately mentioned, for example, determine that M's assignment of a satisfaction clause to a predicate will be sensitive to its extension and its causal-explanatory role. These decisions, of course, do not *define* identity for properties: that has already been defined. One can see, though, why philosophers have thought there was a special problem about what property-identity is. Specifying the $A(...)$ fleshes out what properties are and, concurrently, the chief constraints on what properties are in fact identical. Genuine entities require no such stipulative enrichment, so it seems that identity for properties has a special *meaning*.

[43] For a proof that $(x)(P(x) \equiv Q(x))$ does not entail $A(P) \equiv A(Q)$, see my 'The Extensionality of Causation', pp. 269–71.

A quite different approach would be to interpret PL_P, first fleshed out by the stipulations discussed above, as implicitly defining '$P = Q$'. This would help unify the formal treatments of real and virtual identity—the difference remaining that PL requires no parallel stipulations. (This would yield a nice explanation of what philosophers who worry about the meaning of identity for properties dimly perceive: that PL_P without the stipulations (or 'category doctrines') is inadequate even as an implicit definition). Call property-identity thus implicitly defined '$=_i$', and let '$=_e$' be property-identity explicitly defined as above. I have emphasized $=_e$ because it facilitates talk of identifying the property a single predicate expresses: in fact $=_e$ and $=_i$ come down to the same thing. Suppose $P =_i Q$. By definition $A(P) \equiv A(Q)$ for all well-defined contexts $A(...)$. We can take $A(...)$ to be $... =_e Q$, which is well defined in terms of predicates and satisfaction. Then $P =_e Q$. Suppose $P =_e Q$. All well-defined contexts $A(...)$ are explained via the satisfaction condition for '$P(x)$'; so if '$P(x)$' and '$Q(x)$' have the same satisfaction condition, we always have $A(P) \equiv A(Q)$. So $=_e$ *satisfies* the implicit definition of $=_i$; and it is not easy to contrive another definition of property-identity which satisfies PL_P, keeps properties virtual, and does not amount to the synonymy of predicates.

Maintaining the parallel between predicates and names suggests the following definition of property reduction. Suppose P holds of x, and x is identified with the set $\{x_1,...,x_n\}$. P is reducible to the properties $\{Q_1,...,Q_n,R\}$ if the satisfaction-condition for '$P(x)$' in M is: $Q_1(x_1)$ & ... & $Q_n(x_n)$ & $R(x_1,...,x_n)$. (Let us abbreviate this conjunction as $Q'(x_1,...,x_n)$.)[44] Suppose P is a property of $x = \{x_1,...,x_n\}$: if there is some set of properties to which P is reducible, P is *reducible*; if not, P is *emergent*. (Intuitively, P is emergent if the strongest connection between P and microproperties of the constituents of x is correlation.) We say, for example, that the surface tension of a volume of liquid v is reducible to the electrostatic attraction between v's molecules because those phenomena in virtue of which we say v has such-and-such surface tension have turned out to be aspects of the electrostatic attraction between some of v's molecules. v bulges over the lip of its container

[44] To avoid complications I am using the same style of variable and predicate letter in both the object-language and the metalanguage.

and *v* supports light objects. It turns out that light objects don't penetrate *v*'s surface because the molecules at the surface, being electrostatically bound, won't get out of the way. It was these phenomena that we were calling 'surface tension' all along.

This account of property reduction contrasts instructively with B. Enç's.[45] Enç holds that property *P* is reducible to property *Q* when *Q* produces *P* but *P* does not produce *Q*. One of Enç's illustrative arguments for this proposal is that science identifies the pressure of a gas with *dp*/*dt*—*p* the momentum of the gas's molecules—because *dp*/*dt* generates the force on the walls of the gas's container, and 'force is an essential component of the concept of pressure'. But this proposal allows a theory to identify attributes that the theory itself entails are distinct. For if *dp*/*dt causes* the pressure, it surely cannot *be* the pressure, causation holding only between distinct existences. Indeed, this example fits better into the present framework. It is intuitively plausible to identify *dp*/*dt* with pressure because *dp*/*dt* has turned out to be the cause, not of pressure, but of what pressure is supposed to cause. Pressure is the cause of there being a force exerted on the walls of the container, a force which varies with temperature and volume. 'The pressure of the gas' is introduced to refer to whatever *accounts for* this force and its laws. Deeper investigation shows that the force and its laws can be accounted for by *dp*/*dt*—the causal properties of pressure turn out to be the causal properties of *dp*/*dt*. The momentum of the gas molecules is what we were calling 'pressure' all along.

There are two natural objections to the present definition of property reduction. In the first place, there is no well-formed contrast between identifying (the presence of) a property *P* of *x* with microproperties of *x*'s constituents and correlating *P* with those microproperties. If, for example, 'gives rise to a whole with property *P* when combined with $x_2,...,x_n$ in relation *R*, where x_i is Q_i, $i = 2,...,n$' counts as a property of x_1, it would seem that *P* becomes trivially reducible. To dismiss the cited property as spurious is *ad hoc*: reducibility is in fact relative to an antecedent specification of admissible microproperties and microrelations.[46] Even given such

[45] 'Identity Statements and Microreductions', in *Journal of Philosophy*, lxxiii. 11 (June 1976), 285–306.

[46] Cf. P. Henle, 'The Status of Emergence', *Journal of Philosophy*, xxxix. 18 (Aug. 1942), 486–93; C. Hempel, *Aspects of Scientific Explanation* (Free Press, N.J.: 1965), pp. 260–1. Henle and Hempel formulate this objection in a way designed to frustrate definitions of reduction in terms of the *entailment* of the

a specification S, whether P is emergent is further relative to the theoretical part of M. According to theory T, $P(x)$ may follow from $Q'(x_1,\ldots,x_n)$ for some Q' given by S; while according to another theory T', $P(x)$ does not follow from $Q'(x_1,\ldots,x_n)$. Whether P is reducible to $\{Q_1,\ldots,Q_n,R\}$ depends on one's background theory. (This latter point may be harmless, since choice of M already involves a choice of background theory.)

The second objection is that no reduced property P can literally be identical to $\{Q_1,\ldots,Q_n, R\}$, since the extension of P differs from that of the Q_i, of R and of Q'. P's extension includes x, while the extensions of the Q_i include only the x_i; P is also diverse from R and Q' since P is monadic and R and Q' n-adic.

These objections suggest that (theory-relative) correlation is the strongest well-defined relation between a reduced macroproperty and the reducing microproperties. The best way to evaluate these objections is to consider an alternative account of reduction inspired by them and based on theory-relative correlation, the classic statement of which is chapter 11 of E. Nagel's *The Structure of Science*.[47] Nagel takes reduction to be a relation between theories: instead of speaking of properties being reduced, Nagel takes as primitive the idea of theory T_1 being reducible to theory T_2. This holds, in particular, when T_2, supplemented by 'bridge laws' correlating the 'notions'[48] of T_2 with those of T_1, entails T_1. Bridge laws are needed because, the vocabulary of T_2 typically not containing that of T_1, T_2 by itself cannot entail T_1. Suppose, for example, that T_2 is classical mechanics and T_1 is phenomenological thermodynamics. T_2 does not entail T_1 because the function symbol '$t(x)$' = 'the temperature of x' occurs in T_1 but not T_2. However, T_2 and the bridge law $B = (x)(k\cdot t(x) = 2/3 \cdot$ the mean kinetic energy of $x)$ does entail T_1. One might now define a derivative notion of property reduction: P is reducible to Q if P-theory is reducible to some Q-theory. (Note that some other theory T_2' which shared the vocabulary of T_2 might *not*, when supplemented with B, entail T_1; whether temperature is reducible to mean kinetic energy is relative to choice of mean kinetic energy-theory.) Nagel's main point, though, is that bridge laws express contingent correlations between the notions they

reduced property by the reducing, but presumably they would adapt their point as done here.

[47] Harcourt, Brace and World, N.Y.: 1961.

[48] See, e.g., p. 345.

nvolve. The reducibility of T_1 to T_2, for example, does not mean that x's having a temperature of $n°$—as determined by some appropriate test—*is* x's molecules having average mean kinetic energy E; there is just a constant conjunction between these two independent phenomena. Indeed, Nagel cautions against construing a reduction as showing that a reduced entity is 'merely an appearance': we must not 'wipe out or transform into something insubstantial or "merely apparent" the distinctions and types of behavior which [T_1] recognizes' (p. 366). Thus, the reduction of psychology to physics would amount to no more than a correlation between (say) the presence of headaches and physical conditions: 'The [reduction in question] will consist in stating the conditions, formulated by means of the primitives [of physiology], under which, as a matter of sheer contingent fact, a determinate psychological phenomenon takes place' (p. 366). Let us refer to this conception of reduction as *N*-reduction.

The reasons for Nagel's weak interpretation of bridge laws are unclear. It sometimes seems traceable to an unwillingness on Nagel's part to reify properties; but at other times Nagel speaks freely of the 'attributes' and 'traits' discussed by a theory. He says, for example, that bridge laws establish 'relations between whatever is signified by "A" [an expression of T_1] and traits represented by theoretical terms already present in [T_2]' (p. 354). Sometimes Nagel claims that raising the issue of property identity leads to entanglement in the pseudo-problem of essence (p. 365); but Nagel never defends this claim and, intuitively, the issues seem to be distinct. Anyway, by claiming that reduced attributes are always distinct from reducing ones, Nagel is tacitly allowing that reasoned judgements of property identity can be made.

A more positive reason for rejecting *N*-reduction as an adequate explication of reduction in science is that under it a quite weak form of determinism entails the *N*-reducibility of all macroproperties to microproperties. It is intuitively unacceptable that so weak a form of determinism should guarantee so strong a conclusion. Thus, imagine that every property of a whole x were correlated by law with some properties of x's constituents: for any property P, some bridge law B gives necessary and sufficient conditions for P in terms of x's microproperties, so that P-theory is reducible to the correct theory of x's microproperties. But this would hardly guarantee universal reducibility of the sort achieved for surface tension and hardness. Indeed, if the microproperties $\{Q_1 \ldots Q_n, R\}$ cause P, Nagel must still say that P was reducible to $\{Q_1,\ldots,Q_n,R\}$ —the implication that scuttled Enç's proposal. Even if macro-micro determinism were true, we would surely want to preserve the distinction between discovering that $Q'(x_1,\ldots,x_n)$ is the occasion for P and discovering that calling x 'P' amounted to noticing that Q' held of $\{x_1,\ldots,x_n\}$. The passages cited above from Nagel, p. 366 suggest that identifying reduction with N-reduction begs the mind–body question against materialism. The mere N-reducibility of psychology to physics will not satisfy the materialist, who will find little comfort in the assurance that no stronger notion of reduction is definable.

These difficulties should prompt re-examination of the significance of the points on which Nagel bases N-reduction. The contingency of bridge laws, for one, proves nothing. The logical truth that a reducing theory must be supplemented by factual bridge laws if it is to entail the reduced theory shows only that the correlated properties are identified independently. This no more shows that the properties themselves are diverse than the fact that Lois Lane independently identifies Clark Kent and Superman implies that the two are diverse. That temperature is operationally 'defined' by operation O, and mean kinetic energy by operation O', is compatible with O and O' being tests for the same thing (as there are different ways of measuring the property of height). Indeed, one could take the fact that there is some theory T_2 which, when supplemented by bridge law B, reduces theory T_1, to confirm the conjecture that the two 'notions' correlated by B are the same.

Consider the second argument on p. 38 and the two citations from Nagel, p. 366. Must we really accept the dilemma of either merely correlating P with microproperties or rejecting P as merely apparent? This dilemma plays off a true but trivial fact about predication against a more interesting but unsupported claim about properties, a move encouraged by the ambiguity of the word 'notion'. Nagel in effect argues from the undoubted fact that the ascription of the predicate 'P' to x is sometimes true to the diversity of the property P from x's microproperties. A reduction of P to microproperties should certainly not imply that x is not the proper subject of predication for 'P', nor should it transform the P/not-P distinction into something merely apparent. How could it, when to do so would be to destroy the very phenomenon being reduced? Now these are facts about the *predicate* '$P(x)$': a reduction of P must be compatible with the distinction between correctly and incorrectly applying the *predicate* 'P' to the object x. But these requirements can be met even if the use of the predicate in question is explained in terms of the properties of x's constituents. Nagel's facts about predication entail that such an explanation is incorrect only if every predicate of the relevant body of discourse expresses a distinct property. If we drop this assumption, we can preserve the P/not-P distinction while identifying a macroproperty of x with a microrelation Q'.

It will prove useful to examine in detail an important typical case of this circumstance. Suppose $x = \{x_1,...,x_n\}$, and each x_i is in the domain of some function f_i (which need not all be distinct). Let $R(f_i)$ be the range of f_i. It may happen that there is a proper subset V of $R(f_1)$ X...X $R(f_n)$ such that x satisfies the predicate '$P(x)$' iff $\langle f_1(x_1),...,f_n(x_n)\rangle \varepsilon V$. In such a case we may call V the P-range of the f_i. In other words, x's being P amounts to the values of certain parameters of x's constituents lying within certain limits. We may also suppose for convenience that there are sets $V_i \varepsilon R(f_i)$ such that $\langle f_1(x_1),...,f_n(x_n)\rangle \varepsilon$ the P-range of the f_i iff for all i, $f_i(x_i) \varepsilon V_i$. (Natural language may well, in that case, contain predicates Q_i such that $Q_i(x_i)$ iff $f_i(x_i) \varepsilon V_i$; in that case the satisfaction definition for '$P(x)$' has the form shown on p. 36.) For example, it might turn out that we call something 'hard' just in case the masses and electrostatic forces of its constituent molecules fall within certain limits. The masses (for example) of the molecules of a hard object are only a proper subset of the masses that molecules may have: the hardness-range of mass and electrostatic attraction is a proper subset of R (mass of x), where the function 'mass of x' is homogeneous throughout its range from the point of view of physics alone. In such cases, the P/not-P distinction is the distinction between V and $R(f_1)$ X...X $R(f_n) - V$, and is not 'merely apparent'. That 'hardness' names a class of mass-states that men have found especially salient (for reasons ultimately given by psychology) no more relegates hardness to the merely apparent than it does the distinction between the hardness-range of mass and the range of mass.

The apparatus of functions just introduced helps deal with many otherwise clear cases in which not only is the grammatical subject of predication the object x, and not x's constituents, but in which the reduced predicate expresses a property of x that is merely correlated with properties of x's constituents. For these cases, it might seem,

N-reduction is the correct account. Consider mass, which proponents of a strong reducible/emergent distinction usually cite as a paradigm of a reducible property, since the mass of x is 'nothing but' the sum of the masses of x's constituents. In fact, however, the mass $m(x)$ of x is clearly distinct from the masses $m(x_1),\ldots,m(x_n)$ of its constituents, and it is implausible to say as we did with hardness that referring to $m(x)$ is a way of referring to any concatentation of the $m(x_i)$. The mass $m(x)$ is merely correlated with the $m(x_i)$; and this shows the bankruptcy of the intuition that the mass of an object is 'nothing but' the masses of its constituents, while (say) consciousness is novel relative to the properties of the constituents of a conscious being. But even in cases like the mass case, however, there may be warrant for claiming that something stronger than N-reduction is available, and hence for retaining the contrast between reduction and correlation. The contrast can be made in terms of the distinction between determinables and determinations. A *determinable* is a property than can be instanced in different ways, each way being one of its *determinations*. Colour is a determinable, red and green two of its determinations. A function like $m(x)$ is a special kind of determinable, each member of its range yielding a different determination. To see this, first define '$M(x,y)$' to mean 'y is a mass of x', where y is a real number. Clearly $m(x) = y$ is equivalent to $M(x,y)$ & $(x)(y)(z)((M(x,y)$ & $M(x,z)) \supset y = z)$. Now the dyadic predicate $M(x,y)$ can be decomposed into $2^{\aleph_0}$ predicates $M_y(x)$, each ascribing the property of being y-massed. Each predicate $M_y(x)$ is a determination of the determinable $M(x) \equiv x$ has a mass, since $M(x) \equiv (\exists y)(m(x) = y) \equiv (\exists y)M(x,y)$. The basis of the intuition that the mass of x is not wholly independent of the masses of the x_i is evidently that $M_{m(x)}$ is a determination of the same determinable—M—of which x's constituents have other determinations. (Clearly, $(x)M_{m(x)}(x)$.) The microconditions for x having a given determination of the determinable M are determinations of the same determinable. The determinable is predicated at both macro- and microlevel; what is predicated at the macrolevel only is a specific determination, in point of empirical fact the arithmetical sum of the microdeterminations. Whether $M_{m(x)}$ is a property of x merely correlated with the masses of the x_i thus turns on an ambiguity in 'mass' that affects all functions. The mass of x is independent iff the particular *determination* $M_{m(x)}(x)$ is meant; the mass of x is the same property as occurs at the microlevel if the *determinable* $M(x)$

is meant. But surely those who hold consciousness (say) to be emergent and merely correlated with suitable microproperties would take their thesis to be *false* if consciousness turned out to be a determination or range of determinations of otherwise identifiable physical determinables. (Similarly, those who hold wetness or colour to be emergent[49] would not be satisfied if the viscosity of a fluid were an additive function of the viscosity of the fluid's constituents.) K. Campbell, for example, seems to be contrasting awareness with the shape of a magnetic field in terms of the independent identifiability of the relevant determinables:

> The great difference between the novelty of shaped magnetic fields and the novelty of awareness . . . is this: the properties of simple material particles which cooperate in forming the first can be investigated in isolation. . . . But properties cooperating in . . . awareness are accessible only in the complex manifestations.[50]

The determin*able* mass is, thus, reducible to microdeterminations in a sense stronger than N-reducibility. A natural specification of the sort demanded by Hempel (cf. p. 37 above) is that the reducing microproperties be determinations of the same determinable the N-reduced macroproperty is a determination of.

If claims of independence are construed as theses about determinables, there is no distinction between *additive* functional determinables, like mass, and determinables whose macrodeterminations are non-additive functions of microdeterminations. Thus consider a system $\langle x_1,x_2,p\rangle$, where x_1 and x_2 are exerting forces $f(x_1)$ and $f(x_2)$ on point p. The force $f(\langle x_1,x_2\rangle)$ exerted on p by the 2-body system $\langle x_1,x_2\rangle$ is not $f(x_1)+f(x_2)$, but the vector sum of $f(x_1)$ and $f(x_2)$. It would be a mistake, based on the common tendency to take arithmetical addition as a 'natural' mode of compounding determinations, to regard the determinable mass as 'more reducible' than the determinable force. But the arithmetical additivity of mass is just as contingent a fact as the vector additivity of force.[51] If the N-reducibility of $M_{m(x)}(x)$ to the $M_{m(x_i)}(x)$ supports the stronger reducibility of mass itself, so precisely does the N-reducibility of $f(\langle x_1,x_2\rangle)$ to $f(x_1)$ and $f(x_2)$ support the stronger reducibility of force.

[49] See e.g. C. D. Broad, *The Mind and Its Place in Nature* (Littlefield, Adams & Co., N.J.: 1960), chap. II; K. Lambert and G. Brittain, *An Introduction to the Philosophy of Science* (Prentice-Hall, N.J.: 1970), chap. 6.

[50] *Body and Mind* (Anchor, N.Y.: 1970), p. 122.

[51] Cf. the brilliant discussion of this point in N. Campbell, *Foundations of Science* (Dover, N.Y.: 1957), pp. 279–88.

6. *Why Consciousness seems Emergent*

There is a link between reducibility intuitions and certain linguistic phenomena, the rationale for which is provided by the apparatus of the past few pages. This link in turn provides some insight into the strength of the intuition that consciousness cannot be reduced to physics.

I suggested that in some cases of reduction the reduced property amounts to some proper subrange of a range of possible micro-properties. (This dovetails with the asymmetry of reduction: the reduced property is an instance of a more general, independently describable, phenomenon.) We might put this loosely by saying that a characteristic feature of property reduction is that an apparent difference in kind—the difference between the reduced property P holding and not holding of some object x—is explained as a difference in degree (at the microlevel). Thus when P is reducible we should expect certain behaviour on the part of the predicate '$P(x)$', and, contrapositively, when it seems that '$P(x)$' could not exhibit this behaviour, we tend to suppose that what '$P(x)$' expresses is emergent. In particular, when P is reducible we should expect there to be actual or possible borderline cases between P and not-P, cases that are objectively indeterminate with respect to '$P(x)$'. These will be cases in which the microstates of an object x's constituents are such that a *linguistic decision* about whether to *extend* the predicate '$P(x)$' will be the only way to answer the question of whether x is P, there being no objectively correct answer. In case the satisfaction-condition for '$P(x)$' is given in terms of the P-range V of a set of functions (see p. 41 above), x will be a borderline case, if, say, $V = V_1 \text{ X...X } V_n$ and $f(x_1) \varepsilon V_1,...,f_{n-1}(x_{n-1}) \varepsilon V_{n-1}$, but $f_n(x_n) \notin V_n$.

Consider by way of example the phenomenon of life. It is now believed that 'x is alive' expresses a complex constellation of chemical transactions, including self-replication and assimilation of environmental substances. These processes are special cases[52] of processes that occur in non-living nature. As this is so, one would expect there to be describable configurations of molecules that meet only 50 per cent of the scientifically determined satisfaction-condition of 'x is alive', configurations whose claim to being alive would be indeterminate, a matter of linguistic decision. And indeed the

[52] A phosphate ion must be present, for example.

tobacco-mosaic virus is precisely this sort of case: scientists regard the question of whether this virus is *really alive* as meaningless.[53] The existence of such borderline cases confirms the thesis that life is a specialization of parameters that characterize non-living nature.

This suggests, conversely, that one will regard P as irreducible if the predicate '$P(x)$' appears to admit of no borderline cases. On the present conjecture it is a mark of an irreducible, or at most N-reducible, property that the predicate expressing it always applies or fails independently of any linguistic *decisions*. The question of *extending* such predicates does not arise: they are globally well defined. Emergent properties strike us as simple and homogeneous, completely applicable or completely inapplicable. We may not *know* if they apply, but we never doubt that there is a fact to be known. In this light, consider consciousness, a trait that strikes many philosophers as irreducible to properties of non-conscious entities. Why does it seem so? I would suggest that the root of this conviction is the apparent inconceivability of an *intermediate case* between consciousness and non-consciousness, a thing about whose sentience there is no objective fact. Even if degrees of consciousness are introduced to capture the difference between the mental lives of men and ants,[54] there remains the strong impression that the feeblest grade of consciousness is discontinuous with what lies outside the series of degrees. One simply *cannot imagine* anything standing to the sentient/insentient distinction as the virus stands to the living/non-living distinction. According to NASA the on-board computer of Viking I has the capacity of a small insect. Since small insects are presumably conscious, does it follow that Viking I is? Whatever we conclude, one thing that seems certain is that we will either be *right* or *wrong*. Saying that the issue can be settled by a stipulative extension of 'conscious' to Viking I has, I think, all the plausibility of saying that the issue of the height of Wilt Chamberlin can be settled by a stipulative extension of '7 feet 2 inches' to Wilt Chamberlin. What could be a more natural counterpart to the virus than Viking I? Yet, upon reflection, it fails to fill the role of a borderline case. This is why, I suggest, it is so hard to suppose that 'conscious' is a name we have given to a special case of *something else*. Often, when thinking about consciousness, the best we can do

[53] See G. and M. Beadle, *The Language of Life* (Anchor, N.Y.: 1967), p. 225.

[54] See e.g. K. Sayre, *Consciousness: A Philosophic Study of Minds and Machines* (Random House, N.Y.: 1969), p. 148.

is: many nerve cells come together and—experience! The break is sharper than the (potentially blurry) break between a range and a subrange. This intuition evidently lies behind K. Campbell's reluctant adoption of

> the doctrine of real novelty. Let us label this doctrine *Emergence*. Emergence the orymaintains that the appearance of non-physical properties in neural systems is not a co-operative effect of properties of simpler parts. It is a quite new phenomenon, which just emerges in a certain sort of physical system.[55]

While acknowledging the force of this intuition, I would also stress two points. The first is that men once entertained similar intuitions of discontinuity about life. It is said that Leonardo da Vinci despaired of finding the principle of life however diligently he investigated the innards of men and beasts, and he concluded that life is a miracle wholly distinct from the principles by which bone and muscle move once life is present. He would have dismissed as absurd the thought that life is no single thing but an arrangement of the same sorts of things and processes he saw in non-living nature, or in dead creatures that once lived. Leonardo would have been unable to conceive something like the virus, half-way between life and non-life: to live is to have the life principle, which is either present or absent. The suggestion that there were things such that whether to call them alive was *up to us* would have puzzled Leonardo, just as the same suggestion about the consciousness of Viking I puzzles us. Leonardo's views, then, should make us wary.

The natural reply to this cautionary tale is that Leonardo had, after all, made a fundamental category mistake. He thought that 'life' referred to an ingredient—he would have been unable to conceive borderline cases of life because an *ingredient* is either present or absent. But had Leonardo reflected on the meaning of 'x is alive', he would have realized that 'life' refers to a range of processes and their causes, and that the search for a (miraculous) ingredient was conceptually confused. With the right conceptual preliminaries he would have been able to comprehend borderline cases and the possibility that life is a special case of some broader familiar phenomenon. But surely, the reply continues, unless analytical behaviourism is true (see II.2 below), we are *not* making a similar category mistake about consciousness. We know exactly what we

[55] *Body and Mind*, p. 123.

are talking about when we refer to awareness, and there is neither need nor room for the sorts of conceptual clarification that pave the way from life to physics. We are directly acquainted with consciousness, and can see that it forbids the sort of intermediate cases that mark reducibility.

This reply assumes that all re-evaluation of the logical behaviour of concepts proceeds *a priori*. My second point is that this assumption is false. That a belief is a category mistake; that a concept admits borderline cases; that a word refers not to a thing but to a state: all these can be discovered empirically. An example from the history of science shows this. It was thought before Rumford that heat was a fluid, a kind of stuff, dubbed 'caloric'. Physicists reasoned that since heat can leave one object and enter another, it had to be a substance. But the caloric theory could not explain how two things rubbed together can both become hot: the caloric theory implied, contrary to the conservation of matter, that friction created matter. Rumford refuted the fall-back hypothesis that friction lowers specific heat by showing that metal filings produced by a high-friction process raise the temperature of a given amount of water the same amount as do ordinary filings at the same temperature. Rumford concluded that

> anything which any . . . system of bodies, can continue to furnish *without limitation* cannot possibly be a *material* substance; and it appears to me . . . impossible . . . to form any distinct idea of anything, capable of being excited and communicated, in the manner [of] Heat . . . except it be MOTION.[56]

Rumford had discovered empirically that heat was a state of entities rather than an entity itself, a special case of a phenomenon (motion) found in situations not involving heat. Rumford's discovery shows that even strong irreducibility and category intuitions are empirically revisable.

Note also that only after Rumford had shown that heat *was* other than a material substance did it become clear how heat *could be* other than a material substance. Rumford answered the 'how possible' question by answering the 'how actually' question. Thus the present impossibility of describing a borderline case for consciousness does not preclude the possibility that some day a correct reductive account will give, as a corollary, an explanation of how

[56] Quoted in J. Carney and G. Scheer, *Fundamentals of Logic*, 2nd ed. (Macmillan, N.Y.: 1974), p. 326.

this is possible. There are in fact many 'how possible' questions about the reducibility of consciousness we cannot now answer.[57] But as the Rumford case shows, they may be, or have to be, answered by inferences *ab esse ad posse*.

[57] T. Nagel worries extensively about such how-possible questions in 'What is it Like to be a Bat?'

II

The Mind–Body Problem

1. The Possible Positions

THE foregoing chapter suggests several ways of formulating the mind–body problem. One way is to ask about mental entities: what kinds of things are mental phenomena? The two most conspicuous answers to this form of the mind–body problem are Cartesian dualism and substance-materialism. Cartesian dualism is the claim that the universe consists of two kinds of entities, physical objects and minds. Materialism as an ontological thesis is the denial that there are any things but material things. Perhaps the materialist owes us some account of what makes a thing material, but he can say at this point that this is just the other side of the dualist's obligation to say what makes an object mental. The materialist can use the dualist's characterization of immateriality (lack of spatial extension, say) to assert that what the dualist thinks is immaterial is material, or just that there simply are no things of the sort the dualist imagines.

But the mind–body problem can also be formulated as a problem about properties. There are even reasons for preferring such a formulation. Suppose Cartesian dualism were false, not because there are in fact no mental entities in the way there are no unicorns but because what we loosely call mental phenomena are states or properties of entities. To repudiate laziness is not to deny a certain range of phenomena, it is merely to say that laziness is a virtual entity with the phenomena in question being lazy people. There might be no perceptions because perceptions are virtual entities. If so, the *problem* of perception becomes the problem of what happens when people perceive: but this is not to say that the problem has been resolved. In fact, I argue in chapters IV and V that such entities as perceptions are in fact virtual.

Formulating the mind–body problem as a problem about properties has obvious attractions for the materialist. Leibniz complains that however closely we examine a brain, we never see a perception.

No wonder, replies the materialist: perceptions, being merely virtual, are not there to be detected. Perceiving is something nervous systems do, the *problem* being what the process is. This approach also has advantages for the dualist, for it accommodates dualistic intuitions even if the ontological version of dualism fails. It allows the dualist to concede that there are no mental entities while maintaining that there is a basic difference between mental and physical—a difference in the kinds of properties things have. It would be premature for the materialist to claim victory if all mental entities are virtual. Virtual entities are explained away in terms of the ascription of predicates to genuine objects, but if psychological predicates do not express physical properties, dualism has, intuitively, won the day. And certainly if what the Cartesian takes to be mental substances are in fact physical objects, the possibility remains open that these physical objects have non-physical properties.

There are, then, three basic positions on the mind–body problem:

(1) There are both mental and physical entities.

(1) entails

(1*) There are non-physical, psychological, properties.

It would be absurd to adopt (1) without endowing non-physical substances with some non-physical properties. We will consider shortly whether (1*) entails (1). The denial of (1)—which we take here to be the claim that there are only physical entities—can be specified in two incompatible ways. These specifications are the second and third basic positions:

(2) There are only physical entities but some physical entities have both physical and non-physical, psychological, properties.

(3) There are only physical entities, and all properties of physical entities are physical.

Theses (2) and (3) are versions of *substance monism*: (2) is *property dualism*[1] and (3) is *property monism*. When I use 'materialism' or 'physicalism' or 'the identity thesis', I shall normally mean (3).

Someone might complain that (2) is self-contradictory and (3)

[1] E. Nagel, for example, appears to adopt property dualism in 'Are Naturalists Materialists?' in *Logic Without Metaphysics* (The Free Press, Glencoe, Ill.: 1956).

redundant on the grounds that a thing with non-physical properties cannot be a material thing.[2] This complaint can be interpreted in two ways. It might mean that, given antecedent specifications of 'physical object' and 'non-physical psychological property', it can be shown that no physical object has non-physical properties. Alternatively, the complaint could amount to the stipulation that anything with a non-physical property (whatever the criterion for that is) not be *called* a physical object. That is, if it turned out that the nervous system were what is sentient, and sentience is a non-physical property, it would follow *ex vi terminorum* that the nervous system is not physical. It must be this latter interpretation which is being suggested here, for on the former interpretation (2) would not be contradictory nor (3) redundant—they would be synthetic, their respective falsity and truth corollaries of the demonstration that a thing with non-physical properties is (also) a non-physical thing. Now one may adopt this stipulation, but the results it achieves are as empty as any won by verbal manœuvre. If the brain were sentient and in this sense non-physical, the proponent of the stipulation would still have to admit that something *B* exactly like a brain but insentient would be physical. The brain and *B* are made of the same stuff and have the same physical properties. But then (i) 'a brain is a sentient physical thing', and (ii) 'a brain is non-physical because it is sentient', differ only verbally. Anyone who insists on (ii), while granting that the brain is otherwise physical, invites the question: what *else* is a brain? It would seem, *prima facie*, that we already know what a brain is: its physical description is as fundamental as we want. Do we have any idea of a more fundamental what-it-is level of description at which to place brains, for the positive description of the brain the stipulation demands?

Since, however, this stipulation may prove tempting, let us go along with it for a while. I noted in passing that property dualism can be formulated even if the stipulation is in force, as the claim that everything is either physical or exactly like something physical except for having psychological properties. In fact, each of (1)–(3) survives as recognizable, coherent, and distinct when adapted to the stipulation. (This, perhaps, should diminish its appeal.) To formulate these adapted versions, first let M be the class of mental properties and P the class of physical properties. Next, we adopt a slightly

[2] Cf. J. Cornman and K. Lehrer, *Philosophical Problems and Arguments*, 2nd ed. (Macmillan, N.Y.: 1974), pp. 308–10.

weaker version of the troublesome stipulation in the guise of convention (C):

$(x)[(\exists M)(M \varepsilon \mathrm{M} \ \& \ x \text{ has } M) \supset x \text{ is a mental entity}] \ \&$
$(x)[(\exists P)(P \varepsilon \mathrm{P} \ \& \ x \text{ has } P) \supset x \text{ is a physical entity}].$

Let $M^*(x)$ mean that x is a mental entity, i.e. $(\exists M)(M \varepsilon \mathrm{M} \ \& \ M(x))$, and $P^*(x)$ mean that x is a physical entity, i.e. $(\exists P)(P \varepsilon P \ \& \ P(x))$. (C) is compatible with a single object x having some property from M *and* some property from P; (C) then rules that x is both a mental and a physical entity. Perhaps some argument might show that the intersection of the union of the extensions of the M and the union of the extensions of the P is empty—but in any case the contested thesis of property dualism is just the claim that this intersection is non-empty. The three positions on the mind–body problem can now be stated modulo (C). (1) becomes the claim that there are mental entities, there are physical entities, and some mental entities are not physical entities:

(1′) $(\exists x)P^*(x) \ \& \ (\exists x)(M^*(x) \ \& \ -P^*(x))$.

(2) is the claim that there are mental and physical entities, that every mental entity is also a physical entity, but that not all psychological properties are physical properties:

(2′) $(\exists x)M^*(x) \ \& \ (\exists x)P^*(x) \ \& \ (x)(M^*(x) \supset P^*(x)) \ \& \ \mathrm{M} \not\subset \mathrm{P}$.

(3) is the claim that not only are the first three conjuncts of (2′) true, but that all psychological properties are physical properties:

(3′) $(\exists x)M^*(x) \ \& \ (\exists x)P^*(x) \ \& \ \mathrm{M} \subset \mathrm{P}$.

(3′) entails $(x)(M^*(x) \supset P^*(x))$. (2′) and (3′) are distinct from the eliminative claim that there are no psychological phenomena:

(4) $(x)P^*(x) \ \& \ -(\exists x)M^*(x)$.

The distinction between (2′) and (3′), on one hand, and (4) on the other, is an instance of the distinction made in I.3 between the semantic notion of identification and the pragmatic notion of elimination. *If* ordinary usage forbids a mental entity or property from being physical, the proper gloss to put on the third conjunct of (2′) is that there are no mental entities, and the proper gloss to put on the last conjunct of (3′) and its corollary is that there are no mental entities or psychological properties. (3′) would then entail (4) or some version of (4). I will, however, treat (2′) and (3′) in entire independence of (4), and not only because the material of chapters IV and V wars with the mooted claim about ordinary usage. Even if that claim were true, the basic options on the mind–body problem should not be hostage to sociolinguistics.

No special slot has been left for the 'double aspect' theory because this popular view is best construed as a version of (2). To fix our ideas, suppose that *A* is having a yellow after-image; let '*m*' denote (the state of *A*'s having) the yellow after-image. The double aspect theory maintains that while *m* may be a physical state (a brain state, say), there is a difference in how *m appears to A* and how *m* appears to anyone else. To *B*, *m* appears as the firing of nerve cells. On the other hand, *m* appears to *A* to have certain phenomenal properties; *m* presents a certain phenomenal appearance to *A*. Now if, as he typically does, the double aspect theorist goes on to say that this shows that option (3) omits something, he must be treating 'appears in such-and-such way to *A*' as a (non-physical) property of *m*, and hence advocating a version of (2). Thus Bernstein writes:

> these two sorts of knowledge are irreducible . . . even if the neuro-physiologist of the future could completely describe and explain brain processes—what these *same* brain processes are 'acquaintancewise' is left open. . . . In short, instead of an ontological dualism between two irreducibly different types of entities, we are left with an epistemological dualism between two irreducibly different types of knowledge. . . . I may agree that 'sensations' turn out to be brain processes. But if I am to describe these brain processes as *I experience* them then I must use phenomenal predicates to describe them.[3]

Bernstein is claiming that 'appears such-and-such to *A*' is a property of *m* that eludes the physicalist's net. The double aspect theory does *not* require that *m* actually have the phenomenal properties it appears to have for *m*'s appearance to block physicalism; all *m* has to have in reality is that appearance. This replacement of phenomenal properties by the seemingly weaker and more plausible notion of phenomenal appearance may explain why many philosophers take the double aspect theory to be a distinctive position on the mind–body problem. It is, indeed, a sufficiently specialized form of property dualism to require special discussion.

The properties quantified over in (1′)–(4) are of course virtual.

[3] In Rosenthal, ed., *Materialism and the Mind–Body Problem*, pp. 206–18.

The same holds for the property identities implicit in (2′) and (3′)—which become explicit when $x \subset y$ is construed as $(z)(z \, \varepsilon \, x \supset (\exists w)(w \, \varepsilon \, y \, \& \, w = z))$, a natural construction if $x \subset y$ is an empirical discovery. These parsings, of course, have nothing to do with the properties in question being *mental* properties. Finally, the claim that certain ostensible mental entities (perceptions, pains, sensations) are virtual, and to be exchanged for mental properties, is an independent thesis that will require independent support.

2. Other Positions

(1)–(3) are not the only well-formed positions on the mind–body problem. We have neglected idealism, for one, another interpretation of the denial of substance dualism. Idealism holds that there are only mental entities. It is tempting to overrule idealism at once on the grounds that in philosophy as elsewhere we are allowed to use what we know, and we know that rocks are not minds or states of minds. But we needn't go to this length, short as it is. It suffices to remark that the idealist must, like anyone else, acknowledge and provide for the difference between a conscious being and a rock. He must reintroduce, in new and paradoxical terms, the very distinctions and options registered in (1)–(3). For the idealist, all things are created mindlike, but some things are more mindlike than others. Whatever its attractions, idealism does not even address the mind–body problem.

James and Russell held that there are neither mental nor physical entities, both minds and material objects being constructed out of a single kind of 'neutral' stuff. Minds and material objects are just different ways of putting these primordial ingredients together. An example helps clarify this somewhat obscure position, Suppose minds $m_1,\ldots,m_n$ perceive tables $t_1,\ldots,t_m$. Let us call these *nm* states of awareness *percepts*, and denote m_i's percept of t_j by 'p_{ij}'. According to 'neutral monism', what really exists are the percepts $p_{11},\ldots,p_{ij},\ldots,p_{nm}$. These percepts are neither mental nor physical, and both the minds m_i and the tables t_j are virtual entities, different ways of arranging the p_{ij}. Thus, m_i is $\{p_{i1},\ldots,p_{im}\}$, and t_j is $\{p_{1j},\ldots,p_{nj}\}$: a mind is all its percepts, and a material object is all the percepts of it.

One trouble with neutral monism is that percepts are not neutral enough. On the account it gives of them, percepts are much more mental than they are physical. If 'percept' is given its most natural interpretation, neutral monism is a brand of idealism. Neutral monists sometimes plead that they call the p_{ij} 'percepts' because this is the best they can do in a natural language ill-equipped to express an ontology more fundamental than minds or bodies. But apart from the implausibility of the doctrine that languages have built-in prejudices and limitations (cf. V.3), this plea still leaves percepts unexplained. If a percept is not mental, what is it? Second, it is embarrassing that p_{ij} has to be introduced as 'm_i's perception of t_j', which refers to entities supposedly constructed, in part, out of p_{ij}. The neutral monist cannot simply wish away the impredicativity of introducing percepts in terms of what is perceiving and what is perceived as an atavism of natural language. So even if the obscurity and mentalistic bias of 'percept' are ignored, neutral monism is circular.

It is not an altogether antiquarian exercise to dismiss neutral monism, for the 'neutral theory' broached by Cornman and Lehrer[4] may be a version of it. According to the 'neutral theory', mind and matter are identical, but mind is not reducible to matter. Mental entities and certain physical entities, rather, are both (identical to) some third thing which is neither. If this is *not* neutral monism, then perhaps Cornman and Lehrer are urging that we not *call* the brain physical if it is also the mind. In terms of convention (C), they won't call something 'physical' if it is M^* and P^*. But then we are back to the stronger ill-motivated convention scouted earlier.

3. *Behaviourism*

Behaviourism is absent from this survey of mind–body options because, given the several ways it is normally understood, it is not a distinguishable theory of the mind at all. Either it is not a thesis about mental phenomena at all, or it is a version of materialism. Which it is depends on which side of the well-worn but sound distinction between methodological and analytical behaviourism one is attending to.

Methodological behaviourism is the precept that only the behaviour of organisms is a fit subject for science, since only this subject offers publicly available evidence. Whatever its merits, this precept has no bearing on phenomena other than the behaviour of bodies. Methodological behaviourism can admit they exist while still favouring public data exclusively, insisting only that such phenomena are

[4] *Philosophical Problems and Arguments.*

scientifically suspect because irrelevant to the prediction of behaviour, or that non-behavioural phenomena be admitted only via postulates about the behavioural differences they make. Methodological behaviourism, then, is not a thesis about mentality but a recommendation to scientists about what to study.

It is worth noting parenthetically that methodological behaviourism does not warrant the bad press it receives in some philosophical circles. Many seem to hold it as obvious that unless intra-organismic factors are taken into account, no interesting correlations can be found between stimulus and response.[5] But surely this is a matter to be adjudicated empirically. The behaviourist programme seems to this layman to have had marked success in a number of areas, despite the assurances that this is impossible.[6] Suppose the same stimulus provokes the same response over a wide range of internal states of a given organism. Response will be uniquely correlated with stimulus throughout this range, even though the formal representation of the functional dependence will mention internal states. Such a pseudo-function can even express time-lag and storage, phenomena sometimes held to be incompatible with behaviourism.[7] Additionally, the basic law of conditioning—that reinforcement increases probability of response—is not the truism that what increases probability of response increases probability of response. The law becomes testable if one specifies independent hypotheses about what stimuli are in fact reinforcers, what stimuli in fact increase the probability of the responses they are associated with. If no such specification is at hand, the empirical core of this law becomes the claim that *there are* reinforcers, and the search for those stimuli that, in point of fact, increase the probability of responses they are associated with. In just this way the law $f = ma$ has hard empirical meaning because one can either independently specify a force function, or determine experimentally what influences in fact increase acceleration inversely with mass.

[5] The locus classicus for this view is N. Chomsky's review of B. F. Skinner's *Verbal Behavior*, in *Language* xxxv. 1 (1959), 26–58.

[6] P. Meehl rightly notes 'the unblinkable fact that Skinner's epoch-making book *The Behavior of Organisms* . . . gave rise to a technology of behavior control which has, to an unprejudiced mind, no real competitors' ('Psychological Determinism and Human Rationality', in *Minnesota Studies in the Philosophy of Science*, iv. ed. M. Radner and S. Winokur (U. of Minnesota Press, Minneapolis: 1970), p. 311).

[7] See e.g., R. J. Nelson, 'Behaviorism is False', *Journal of Philosophy*, lxvi. 14 (July 1969), 417–52.

Analytical behaviourism claims that what we call 'mental states' are dispositions of bodies to behave and, perhaps, the occurrent physical microstructures that underlie these dispositions. This view is usually presented as an analytical elimination. Analytical behaviourism is thus a version or subthesis of materialism, since it holds talk of the mental to refer to the physical. Its main distinctive contribution is the suggestion that, since mental 'states' are really nomologically connected clusters of dispositions, it is natural that some mental-state ascriptions pick out no single discriminable occurrence. Improperly understood, this fact has been taken to show that the mind–body problem is ill-posed.

The specific claims of analytical behaviourism tend to be conflated with quite general points about dispositional explanation, conflations encouraged by some features of Ryle's pioneering work *The Concept of Mind.*[8] For one thing, a dispositional analysis of psychological terms need not be behaviouristic: one can maintain for example that a motive is a multi-tracked disposition to behave in certain ways *and* to have certain feelings, where feelings are occurrent mental states. Even if it is a 'category mistake' to construe motives as cause-events, analytical behaviourism might be false.

A second, subtler, confusion is this. Ryle writes as if (i) the dispositionality of vanity (greed, frustration, ...) has something to do with the fact that 'vanity' belongs to the vocabulary of psychology; and (ii) the fact that

(1) He did it because of his vanity [greed, X-ness]

is a dispositional explanation has something to do with the fact that 'vanity' ('greed', 'X-ness') belong to the vocabulary of psychology. These are mistakes. *Any* explanation of the form

(2) Event *e* happened because of *A*'s X-ness [or: because *A* is X]

must be dispositional. What triggers the occurrence of *e* must, tautologically enough, be an event. Since X-ness, or *A*'s X-ness is a state, not an event, it follows from the logical form of (2) that (2) is not a causal explanation whatever X-ness is. It is irrelevant whether 'X-ness' is a psychological term. In particular, the dispositionality

[8] Hutchinson, London: 1949. R. Carnap anticipated much of Ryle's work in his 1932 paper 'Psychology in Physical Language' (trans. G. Shick) in A. J. Ayer, ed., *Logical Positivism* (Free Press, N.Y.: 1959), and 'Testability and Meaning', in H. Feigl and W. Sellars, ed., *Readings in Philosophical Analysis* (Appleton-Century-Crofts, N.Y.: 1949).

of (1) follows from the fact that (1) is an instance of (2), from the fact that 'vanity' is a noun and 'vain' an adjective, not from the fact that (1) is a *psychological* explanation. The great distance between the general point about dispositional explanation that Ryle uncovered and analytical behaviourism becomes clear with the observation that (2) is usually co-ordinate with a sentence which cites the event that triggered *e*. This trigger, for all that (2) or (1) dictate, can be an event of any sort. Ryle usually *assumes* that the triggering event for the explanandum in (1) will be some environmental event (a remark about him made within earshot), but nothing in the logic of (1) bars the trigger from being a change in the subject's mental state (his *becoming aware* that a remark has been made about him). It is a matter of grammar, having nothing to do with the nature of psychological explanation or psychological concepts, that *vanity* cannot *cause* behaviour—a matter of grammar compatible with the cause being an impulse to shine.

Two things can be said on behalf of Ryle, if not his exorcism of the Cartesian ghost. First, he brought it vividly to the attention of philosophers than an object's predispositions may be more helpful in explaining what becomes of it than are triggering causes. (Whether this is especially so in psychology is less evident.) Second, he made it clear that dispositional explanations need not be as circular as they sound. 'The glass broke when struck because it was fragile' seems to get nowhere if '*x* is fragile' means, in part, 'under normal conditions *x* will shatter if subjected to moderate stress'. But there is always lurking in the background some vaguely formulated but still definite antecedent notion of what counts as 'moderate' stress and 'normal' conditions. This is why it does not do to say that the hull shattered when the iceberg struck it because the hull was fragile: conditions were abnormal and the impressed force immoderate.

While analytical behaviourism is not a distinct option on the mind–body problem, it is worth remarking that arguments commonly taken to show that it is *obviously false* are in fact inconclusive. As with its methodological cognate, reports of its demise are premature.

The standard grounds for rejecting (analytical) behaviourism are the presumed facts that (i) the behavioural manifestations of a mental state can be duplicated with unlimited accuracy in the absence of the mental state itself; and, conversely, (ii) a mental state can be present and make no behavioural difference.[9] This 'can' expresses

[9] See K. Campbell, *Body and Mind*, pp. 72–4.

empirical possibility: since one can *in fact* imitate a man in pain without being in pain, pain is not the disposition to act as a man in pain does.

The Stanislauski 'method' of acting, and the observations that evidently suggested it, seem to me to call these presumptions into question. Stanislauski taught that the only way to act convincingly as if you are angry is to *become angry*. One should, when trying to duplicate angry behaviour, remember an episode in which one was genuinely angry.[10] This is the 'Stanislauski Method', behind which is the philosophical message that the inner and the outer are firmly connected. The empirical truth of the matter may well be that the behaviour appropriate to a mental state can be completely 'simulated' only if the mental state itself is present. At least, no one has ever verified the glib claim that *of course* one can act as if one is angry—and over a good long stretch—when one is not. If Stanislauski is right,[11] one cannot act exactly as one who is angry unless one is angry. The onus of proof, surely, is on the anti-behaviourist.

Similarly, the possibility of mental states that make no difference in behaviour becomes less plausible under scrutiny. K. Campbell says 'A slight glow of well-being may have no behavioral manifestations at all, yet still exist and be felt',[12] but just asserting this begs the question. Surely there will be *some* difference; in gait, muscle tone, posture, diction, or pupil diameter. It is a commonplace of psychology that people respond 'intuitively' to each other's moods by subliminally registering such cues. One's mental state may, of course, lead to no *action*; but that is a very different matter.

The anti-behaviourist may retreat to the claim that it is conceivable that one be in a mental state without showing any signs of it, or that there be an 'imitation man' or zombie who acts just as we do but lacks an inner life.[13] This would be to reconstrue the 'can' of p. 58 as the 'can' of logical possibility, a move governed by ground rules of notorious unclarity. The anti-behaviourist might

[10] Cf. Konstantin Stanislauski, *The Actor Prepares* (trans. E. Hapgood) (Theatre Arts Books, N.Y.: 1936), esp. chap. 9.

[11] Laurence Olivier has reported that he constructs a character 'from the outside in .... What I've just said is ... absolute heresy'; quoted in H. Burton, ed., *Great Acting* (Bonanza, N.Y.: 1967), p. 23.

[12] *Body and Mind*. I ignore here a point to be stressed in IV: glows of well-being are not felt—they *are* feelings.

[13] Thus see R. Kirk, 'Sentience and Behaviour', *Mind*, lxxxiii. 329 (Jan. 1974), 43–60.

sharpen his revised claim to be that the relation between the inner and the outer is tightly causal—so that even if the two cannot be separated, talk of mental states is not just talk of behaviour. In fact, I eventually adopt a version of this view in chapters IV and V, and thereby implicitly reject analytical behaviourism. But I have not been defending behaviourism in these recent paragraphs; just cautioning against arguments commonly thought to demonstrate the falsity of behaviourism to a moral certainty.

4. *Matter*

Something must be said about what matter (material objects, physical properties) is if our three positions are to be considered well defined. I mentioned in I.1 that relativizing the characterization of matter to the current state of physics, conceived as the omnicompetent account of the world, risks converting materialism into a trivial truth. If 'physical' means 'whatever physics appeals to', and some day physicists had to attribute sentience to electrons to explain some experimental result, sentience would become a physical property by definitional fiat. The materialist must have something more ambitious in mind when he claims that sentience will turn out to be physical, so more has to be said about matter.

Perhaps we are moving too abruptly. Reluctance to transfer the problem of defining matter to physics may be branded unreasonable on the grounds that it is extremely *unlikely* that intuitively psychological properties will turn out to apply to the particles of physics. Whatever currently unknown property θ explains the currently puzzling behaviour of elementary particles, θ is not likely to be sentience. Letting physics determine physicality does allow the logical possibility that sentience, as an unexplained primitive, might end up physical. Perhaps an ideal definition of 'physical' would forbid this. Still, letting physics be the guide leaves materialism well-posed because there is practically no chance this possibility will be realized.

This argument can be backstopped by an account of *why* elementary particles are unlikely to have intuitively psychological properties. Psychological properties are properties of complex things—organisms with nervous systems—and they apply to such complexes because of their complexity. It seems likely that they are at least *N*-reducible to the microproperties of the complexes they hold of. There are, to be sure, determinable properties like mass that apply to complexes and their constituents—call such properties 'distributive'. But there are differences between psychological properties and properties like mass that suggest that the former are not distributive. First, distributive properties like mass hold of objects at every level of complexity: if $x = \{x_1,...,x_n\}$ and $x_i = \{y_1,...,y_m\}$ and $M(x)$ and $M(y_j)$, we have $M(x_i)$ (for $i = 1,...,n$ and $j = 1,...,m$). Galaxies, atoms, and everything between have mass. Psychological properties, however, are not instanced by the molecular components of nervous systems; as no known distributive property skips levels, it is unlikely that psychological properties reappear at a level more fundamental than that of the constituents of nervous systems. Connected with this is the fact (see pp. 42–43) that the macrodeterminations of a distributive determinable like mass are typically arithmetical functions of the microdeterminations of the same determinable. It seems altogether inconceivable that my awareness of a tomato should turn out to be a function of the awarenesses of things that compose me.

These considerations may well justify passing the definitional buck to physics, conceived as the limit toward which inquiry is moving. But two countervailing considerations seem to me to favour a drastic curtailment of this programme—even to the point of defining materialism in terms of *present-day* physics. The first is that such a curtailment guarantees materialism its proper measure of falsifiability. Since materialism advertises itself as that account of mental phenomena most consonant with modern science (see IV.1), it should share with modern science the trait of falsifiability; it should, ideally, be *as* falsifiable as modern physics. Now let $P(H)$ be the probability of H, $P(H/H')$ be the probability of H given H', and let f be a monotonically increasing function. It is clear, in general, that $P(H_2) = f(P(H_1))$ entails $P(H_2/H_1) > P(H_2/-H_1)$. But the materialist says the antecedent holds if H_1 is modern science and H_2 is materialism. He is thus committed to saying that materialism is disconfirmed if modern physics is. But if materialism is true iff some extension of modern physics is, it is not clear how, if at all, the probability of materialism would be affected by the demise of modern physics. Suppose we list the independent primitives of current physical theory. The success of this list in reducing other domains is what makes materialism plausible, or so materialists argue (see IV.1). If so, that makes it likely that *this list* will eventually reduce mental phenomena. Indeed, the thesis that some extension or revision of this list will do the job is not only not as falsifiable as modern physics, it may not be falsifiable at all.

Does tying the concept of matter to current physics construe 'matter' and materialism too narrowly? It is surely easy to imagine the current list of primitives being inadequate for explaining mental phenomena, but that the augmentation of this list by a new primitive θ did the job. Would it not be reasonable to say that even if materialism in my highly restrictive sense were false, at least materialism $+\theta =$ materialism$'$ were true? Surely the augmentation of contemporary physics in such a way ought to be allowed to vindicate materialism.

We have already seen, however, that not *any* extension of physics is a materialistic extension. The new primitive θ must be *similar* enough to the primitives on the current list to count as a *physical* primitive. Now the second reason for confining 'physical' to present physics is that the notion of similarity needed here is completely undefined. What are the criteria for a new primitive of physics being *like* the old ones, or *sufficiently* like them to render the new theory an extension of physics? The present list of primitives is small, and it will not be easy to extract even a family resemblance to serve as a criterion for 'being a physical property'. That scientists took Maxwell's theory of the electro-magnetic field to be 'in the spirit' of Newton's mechanistic physics—so that today's physics is still 'mechanistic'—offers insufficient guidance. The intuitions at work in that case could only be reapplied if our hypothetical θ stood to contemporary physics more or less as Maxwell's electric field strength **E** and magnetic field strength **H** stood to Newton's: and what 'more or less' means here is the very problem before us pushed back a step. That 'physicalistic' is ill-defined means that less sense than meets the eye attaches to the claim that a physicalistic extension of physics will turn out to be an adequate account of the world. Nobody knows how to distinguish a physicalistic extension from a non-physicalistic one.[14]

It is thus tempting to conclude that materialism must be relativized to present physics: if mental phenomena are not identical to physical phenomena as present physics describes 'physical', materialism is

[14] An illustration of this problem turned up in *New York* magazine. This magazine has a contest section. One of the contests it ran was to parody a section of *New York*, and, predictably, someone parodied the contest section: 'Contest: Give a theory of Relativity. 1st prize: A. Einstein, for $E = mc^2$. 2nd prize: Dan Greenberg, for $E = mc$.' What is *a* theory of relativity?

false, whatever *else* mental phenomena turn out to be. There may be one way to loosen this narrow conception somewhat.[15] We might allow that a new parameter p of objects is a physical parameter if p is implicitly defined *via* a force-function; if, that is, $p(x)$ is introduced by way of a specification of the force x exerts on some appropriate physical system s. A force on s, in turn, must be specified in terms of the time-rate of change in s's momentum, where momentum reduces to the operationally definable notions of mass (see III.7), time, and distance. It is in this essentially Newtonian conception of a force-function that our old conservatism comes in. On this specification, then, a physical property is a property that makes a difference in the motion of masses, a property that figures in a (broadly) mechanistic explanation.

[15] The rest of this paragraph leans heavily on the classic discussion of mechanism in Nagel, *The Structure of Science*, especially pp. 169–70.

III

Substance Dualism

1. Types of Dualistic Arguments

MANKIND'S official view of itself is dualistic. The literary masterworks and conventional precepts of every culture distinguish a spiritual element in man from its bodily container. This spiritual element is taken to be the locus of value, the virtues of the spiritual part being more important than those of the physical. This is true even of world-views which are often thought to be explicitly non-dualistic (Buddhism, for example), a fact obscured by special conditions that may be placed on the individuation of spiritual parts. It may be held, for example, that the non-physical component of a man is no discrete thing, but part of some larger cosmic whole. But the cosmic whole is normally conceived as different in kind from physical wholes.

The attractiveness of dualism is easy to understand. Joy wants forever, as Nietzsche said, while material things eventually disintegrate. Death is rightly considered a great evil. Immortality being impossible if we are our bodies, we come to hope that we are not. Hope leads to belief. But whatever its non-rational origins, substance dualism has traditionally found extensive support among philosophers. Three kinds of argument are commonly used to defend it. The first cites a variety of sophisticated traits exhibited by men that, it is said, only a non-physical thing could exhibit: love, creativity, speech, imagination, intrinsic moral worth. This is the 'argument from man's higher nature'. The second concerns a variety of traits which, while not so elevated, are thought to be intrinsically non-physical: consciousness, intentionality, after-imaging, self-awareness. The third type of argument is epistemological. The way in which the self is known appears to differ from the way in which other things are known. I can conceive my body not existing, but not myself not existing. This marks a difference between myself and my body.

This chapter concentrates on the epistemological argument (sections 2–4). The alleged irreducibility of sensations, intentionality, etc., would in any case be insufficient to establish substance dualism. It is most effective, if effective at all, against property monism. As noted in the previous chapter, the physicalistic inexplicability of sensing would show only that sensing is not a physical state of a senser, not that the senser is non-physical. I will defer the initial type of argument to the next two chapters. There are two reasons for bypassing the higher-nature argument. First, it assumes that a physical system could not exemplify a certain range of traits; if a physical system could exhibit such traits there would be no need to posit anything further. I try to undermine the problematic assumption later in this book: chapter VI sketches an account of how a computer could recognize patterns and fall in love, and chapter VII argues that a material object can have free will and intrinsic moral worth.

The other difficulty for the higher-nature argument is that, even if its main assumption is true, it is not clear that this aids dualism. The argument itself fits a familiar pattern: other things being equal, if hypotheses H_1 and H_2 are competing to explain data E, and H_1 fails to explain E, choose H_2. The dualist wants to instantiate this pattern with man's higher nature for E, substance monism for H_1, and substance dualism for H_2. But conformity to this pattern justifies choosing H_2 only if H_2 does explain E, or comes closer to explaining E than H_1. Otherwise, the rational course is to reject both H_1 and H_2 or remain agnostic between them. But this appears to be the situation in the present case. Even if substance monism cannot explain creativity (say), it is hardly obvious that we have a clear idea of how a *non*-physical entity could create. This trouble is not due to any pervasive obscurity in dualism; to the charge of obscurity the dualist could reply that the truth may *be* obscure. The trouble is that even if dualism were clear, how it would explain creativity is not. Creativity must be to some extent mysterious if the higher-nature argument is to get any purchase; if creativity is not somewhat mysterious why should it be thought that materialism cannot explain it? Let us suppose (contrary to fact, I believe) that a creative act cannot be governed by causal laws. If physical determinism is true, no physical system can be creative. But for all we know non-physical systems are governed by causal laws of their own (although not mechanical laws). If its incompatibility with determinism is why creativity rules out substance materialism, its incompatibility with determinism is an equally good reason why creativity rules out substance dualism. The dualist may respond by attributing secret powers to non-physical entities, but he must permit the materialist a similar response. Once again we have a draw, and a draw nullifies the higher-nature argument.

2. The Epistemological Argument

This leaves the epistemological argument as the best bet for the substance dualist (or 'Cartesian'). More specifically, the Cartesian argues as follows: (1) I may be systematically mistaken about physical objects. I can conceive that no physical object exists; I can imagine being wrong in believing there are any physical objects. (2) These are not possibilities when the subject is myself; I cannot be wrong in thinking I exist. (3) Hence I have a property which physical things lack: being indubitably existent to myself. By PL I am not a physical object.

A. Plantinga[1] and others take this argument to establish the *necessary* diversity of self and body as well, using the notion of necessity explicated in Kripke semantics. But necessity so explicated requires that *all* identities and diversities be necessary, so nothing is really added by the essentialist's extra step; consequently, I will ignore it here.[2]

This is also not the place for an extended discussion of scepticism. Consider how many problems irrelevant here are raised by the short statement 'The existence of the external world is dubitable'. Is global doubt coherent? Is '-able' meant epistemologically? metaphysically? logically? Are the classical sceptical arguments from dreaming, illusion, and evil demons cogent? Does 'knowledge' have a built-in justification requirement that leads any knowledge claim to a vicious regress? In view of this, I will simply state, perhaps a bit dogmatically, how I see the situation. Thus scanting scepticism does no injustice to the epistemological argument, because its most interesting features appear in connection with steps (2) and (3); and I concede enough to the Cartesian to allow him to get to these steps.

The standard sceptical arguments fail because they rely on distinctions which make no difference, and a distinction which makes no difference is no real distinction. The possibilities the sceptic opposes to commonsense realism and challenges us to refute—that

[1] See A. Plantinga, 'World and Essence', *Philosophical Review*, lxxix. (Oct. 1970), 483–6.

[2] I criticise the essentialist approach to dualism at greater length in 'Kripke's Argument against the Identity Thesis', *Journal of Philosophy*, lxxii. 6 (Mar. 1975), 149–67. For a discussion of Kripke semantics, see S. Kripke, 'Semantical Considerations on Modal Logic', *Acta Philosophica Fennica* (1963).

we are being systematically deluded by our senses, by a lifelong dream, or by a demon—are indistinguishable from the 'possibility' that the world is about as we think it is. It is a commonplace to complain that this criticism relies on the oft-discredited verification principle, but this complaint is ill-founded. The relevant form of the verification principle ran: a distinction is no real distinction unless it makes an experiential difference, a difference specifiable in a language of observation predicates. The maxim I am deploying is much more general: a distinction which makes no difference specifiable in any language at all is no distinction. It is this maxim that the sceptic violates when he says, for instance, that maybe the demon is making it appear as if my wife is cooking lunch—'my wife cooking lunch' is not an expression of any observation language. The most devastating criticisms of the positivist's verification principle aimed, accurately, at the connection it established between meaning and the existence of evidentially relevant *observations*. These criticisms never neutralized the intuition that a sentence *p* is devoid of sense if *nothing at all* is allowed to count as evidentially relevant to *p*. This intuition is common coin even among philosophers who repudiate positivism. Thus generalized, verificationism is sufficiently forceful to banish as empty the 'possibilities' brandished by the sceptic.

Despite this, the Cartesian has a right to claim that it is conceivable to him that the physical world does not exist. It is logically possible—and in that sense conceivable—that there are not now, and never have been any, material objects. The existence of a physical world is not entailed by a complete description of my present experiences (see IV.4), hence the non-existence of the physical world is conceivable in the somewhat stronger sense of 'compatible with my present experiences'. This claim obeys the strictures of generalized verification: one could acquire evidence that there are no, and never have been any, material objects. Imagine that, for fifty years, there was a voice that occasionally popped into your mind and correctly foretold all your sensations for the coming week. It also announced solutions to complex mathematical problems that you subsequently verified. One day it announced that there are no physical objects. This would surely be evidence relevant to 'There are no physical objects'.[3] (Of course, none of this will happen.)

[3] This argument adapts one of E. Erwin, in his 'The Confirmation Machine', in *Boston Studies in the Philosophy of Science*, viii, eds. R. Buck and R. Cohen, (Humanities, N.Y.: 1971), 306–21.

Conceding the Cartesian his first step offers no aid or comfort to the sceptic. This is especially clear under the following (sort of) analysis of knowledge, which I take to be correct: *A* knows *p* iff *p* and *A* was caused to believe *p* by a process that usually results in true belief. If *p* is true and *A* was caused to believe *p* in the right way, *A* knows *p* even if it is possible that $-p$, and even if *A* concedes that it is possible that $-p$. *A* knows *p* even if some actual or hypothetical *B* believed a false p' as a result of the same causal process that led to *A*'s belief that *p*. Even if *A* cannot distinguish his state from *B*'s, *A* can know *p*. The sceptic contests my claim to know that physical objects exist because their non-existence is logically compatible with my present experiences (and because I cannot *prove* that the evidence described a paragraph ago will not start flooding in tomorrow). But suppose I believe that physical objects exist on the basis of experience, and that *in fact*, *sub specie aeternitatis*, most beliefs formed on the basis of experience are true. Then I *know* that physical objects exist. Granted, I may not know that, in general, beliefs formed on the basis of experience are true. But all this shows is that I don't *know that I know* that material objects exist. I might have to wait until the end of time to rate the reliability of the process that caused my belief. But this is compatible with its actually being a reliable process, and hence with my knowing the beliefs it causes me to have. Perhaps I will never know whether I know that material objects exist—for all that, I can still know that material objects exist.[4]

The Cartesian, then, does not need scepticism to sustain his first premise. And so far as I can see scepticism is sufficient for his first premise only because a falsehood is sufficient for anything.

3. *My Own Existence*

The Cartesian claims to be unable to suppose that he does not exist. He must exist if *he* is supposing that he does not exist, or how could *he* be supposing anything? Even if he is a figment of someone else's imagination he still exists—as a mental entity, a figment. No matter what, the Cartesian believes at least that he is supposing something, and you cannot believe that you suppose something unless you exist.

[4] These remarks have assumed away the requirement that *A*'s belief that *p* be *reasonable*; in V.4 the present argument is extended to cover holding beliefs reasonably. Also, 'usually' cries out for specification (that's why the analysis offered here is a *sort*); but the concept of knowledge may be as vague as 'usually'.

There is thus an absurdity about 'I do not exist' that does not hold of 'material objects do not exist'.

The inference from 'I think' to 'I am', the *cogito*, is often held to be trivial or circular. Any object that satisfies any predicate must exist. One could as easily argue 'I walk, therefore I am'. There is nothing especially existing-certifying about thinking—and to assume 'I think' as a premise is already to assume my existence. Some philosophers[5] take the *cogito* to be, not an argument, but a self-certifying performance: I demonstrate my existence by saying 'I think' as I might demonstrate my presence by saying 'I'm here'. This is an interpretation of the *cogito* the Cartesian should by-pass. If 'I necessarily exist' is not true, it cannot serve as a premise for the application of PL. There is a sense in which I have to be present if I successfully say 'I'm here'; but even if I do, it does not follow that I am necessarily here. My body doesn't have to be present, but my success in saying 'I'm here' does not show that I am not my body. 'I necessarily exist' as the performative account construes it is too weak for the epistemological argument.

The Cartesian should also by-pass the non-standard logics often connected with the performative account, logics which either abandon existential generalization or deny the full force of existence to the existential quantifiers. The Cartesian accomplishes nothing if he proves his existence in a sense of 'existence' this weak.

The most natural defence of the *cogito* is that 'I think' is itself certain, while the premise of the '*ambulo*' is not. I can doubt that I am walking, but not that I am thinking. Is 'I think' certain (in the same sense of 'certain' used in premise 1))? Well, 'I am thinking' is self-guaranteeing, where a sentence *p* is self-guaranteeing if '*p* is doubted' entails *p*, and a valid argument is self-guaranteeing if its premises are. A self-guaranteeing sentence cannot be rationally doubted. No one could doubt it successfully, although an unreflective man might believe that he could. The *cogito* is self-guaranteeing, since 'I doubt that I am thinking' entails 'I am thinking'; clearly, the *ambulo* is not self-guaranteeing. In this sense, the premise and conclusion of the *cogito* are certain. Beyond this, however, there is nothing necessary about self-guaranteeing sentences. It may be uncertain in just the way the existence of the material world is

[5] See J. Hintikka, 'The Cogito: Inference or Performance?' in W. Doney, ed., *Descartes* (Anchor, N.Y.: 1967); A. J. Ayer, *The Problem of Knowledge* (Penguin, Harmondsworth: 1971).

uncertain. If it is known that someone doubts the premise of a self-guaranteeing argument, we know that its premise and conclusion are true. If I know I am doubting, I know I exist. But surely if we know that someone is walking, we know he exists. The *cogito* is still no stronger than the *ambulo*. Performativists like Ayer rightly insist that in themselves, 'I think' and 'I exist' are no more necessary than 'I walk'. Replace the 'I' by 'Levin' in these sentences. The results are obviously dubitable—there can be evidence against a self-guaranteeing sentence. It seems, indeed, that whether my non-existence is conceivable to me depends on how I refer to myself—a daunting qualification on the Cartesian's second step.

The Cartesian will reply that this is the wrong conclusion to draw from the behaviour of '*x* exists' when 'Levin' replaces 'I', and that Ayer's argument in fact equivocates on two different referents of 'Levin'. If 'Levin' designates, say, the man born at such-and-such place and time, it is clear even to me that Levin might not exist. But if 'Levin' refers to the subject of this present act of thinking, I cannot imagine that Levin does not exist. And this is what I am referring to when *I* use 'I'. It only seems that I can suppose this thing not to exist because the term by which I refer to it is taken to refer to a different, public object known by a description I can imagine applying to nothing. The thing *I* refer to as 'Levin' is something I cannot doubt exists.

This reply has the odd consequence that only the person acquainted with his present act of thinking can understand the use of his name appropriate for the epistemological argument. *A* cannot exhibit the denotation of '*A*' for himself, a key component of *A*'s *cogito*, to anyone else. The soundness of an argument is not usually thought of as person-relative; yet *A*'s *cogito* is cogent only for *A*. *A* can prove to himself that his existence is indubitable but he cannot prove it to anyone else; nor can anyone else prove the indubitability of his existence to *A*.

The Cartesian will find this consequence nothing worse than uncomfortable. In fact, his use of PL will require an additional doctrine about the intimacy of each man with himself.

4. *Application of PL*

I have been lenient with the Cartesian in anticipation of the popular view that the major difficulty with the epistemological argument is that open sentences involving epistemic locutions cannot replace the schematic letter in PL. PL works only with *extensional* predicates, those that permit the truth-preserving substitution of co-referring terms, and permit existential generalization on their instances. Intuitively, ascriptions of belief, conception, etc., fail these tests. Jocasta is Oedipus' mother, even though

(1) Oedipus believes Jocasta is his wife

is true, while

(2) Oedipus believes Oedipus' mother is his wife

is false. Unfortunately, '*A* conceives ... not to exist' is such a locution, so

(3) A can conceive that $-(\exists x)(x = A\text{'s body})$

and

(4) A cannot conceive $-(\exists x)(x = A)$

do not show that *A* is distinct from his body.

As it stands, this argument is circular. PL is restricted to extensional predicates, which in turn are explained as predicates that offer no counterexamples to PL. PL, in other words, applies to what it applies to, and shows objects to be diverse just in case they are inequivalent with respect to a predicate inequivalence with respect to which implies diversity. Fine, but which predicates are they? Nor can Quine's notion of 'purely designative occurrence' be used to identify the range of application of PL, since for Quine a term occurs purely designatively in a context if that context conforms to PL. No independent reason has yet been given for not concluding that Jocasta $\neq$ Oedipus' mother from (1) and (2). This inference is not faulty because 'Oedipus believes ... is his wife' is non-extensional, or because '...' does not occur purely designatively; these are just other ways of saying the inference does not go through. One must eventually fall back on one's logical intuitions about when a term occurs purely designatively, or a predicate is extensional (i.e. satisfies PL).

The Cartesian can now counterattack by observing that there are cases in which belief contexts are extensional. Suppose I see a man robbing a showcase at Tiffany's. I say to myself, 'That man is a thief'. I believe, of that man, that he is a thief. Suppose, further, that unbeknownst to me that man is the Transylvanian Ambassador. Is it not appropriate to say that it is the Transylvanian Ambassador that I believe to be a thief? It is the man himself about whom I have the belief, and if the man is in fact the Transylvanian Ambassador, then it is of *him* that I have the belief. In such a case, 'is believed by Levin to be a thief' can replace $A(x)$ in PL.

One distinctive mark of this case is that the x about which I hold the belief actually exists. It is tempting to say that if A believes x to be P, 'is believed by A to be P' is extensional if x exists. But this condition is insufficient. Suppose we are standing on the corner and I assure you 'The next bus will be along in 5 minutes'. Suppose also that the next bus is Charlie, and sure enough it comes along in 5 minutes. Did I believe that *Charlie* would come along in 5 minutes? No. What I believed was: 'Whichever bus is the next one—and I have no idea which it is—it will be along in 5 minutes.' So just because I hold a belief about the next bus, and the next bus exists, it does not follow that 'is believed by me to be about to arrive' is a property of the entity which is the next bus.

But suppose, instead, I peer down the street and see Charlie emerging from the garage. I judge, from the premonitory rumblings of its engine, that this very bus will be the next one. Then I say 'The next bus will be here in 5 minutes.' In that case it does seem appropriate to say that Charlie has the property of being believed by me to be about to arrive. Thus, if A believes x is P, there are two conditions jointly sufficient for the belief ascription to be extensional. One is that x exists—which accommodates the need to support existential generalization. The other is that A bear a *direct epistemic relation* to x.[6] There may be no way to define 'direct epistemic relation' beyond indicating such examples as perceiving and remembering. One might partially define 'R is a direct epistemic relation between A and x' by: $R(A,x) \equiv ((A$ believes x to be $P) \supset (x = y \supset A$ believes y to be $P))$. This renders tautological the remark that if A has a direct epistemic relation to x then 'x' occurs extensionally in 'A believes x to be P'. The point of so defining it would be to emphasize that there *are* such relations. Note, inci-

[6] D. Kaplan ('Quantifying In', in L. Linsky, ed., *Reference and Modality* (O.U.P., Oxford: 1971), pp. 112–44) suggests the condition that A have a vivid name for x. This may be sufficient, but it is not necessary; I might not dub Charlie anything. J. Hintikka has developed the hint that in the first case 'the next bus' is an accidental designator, while in the second case 'Charlie' is a rigid designator.

dentally that 'x' occurs extensionally in 'A stands in a direct epistemic relation to x'.

The two conditions of the last paragraph are satisfied by A's self if the *cogito* is correct. It is plausible, if the *cogito* is correct, that A has a direct epistemic relation to A—A cannot even doubt his own existence, and if that is not a direct epistemic relation, what is? Thus 'is believed by A to be P', when applied to A as the object of the belief, is the ascription of an extensional predicate to A and the application of PL proceeds as before. Standing in a direct epistemic relation to x is of course no guarantee that a belief held by A about x is *true*. A might bear a direct epistemic relation to himself and form the *erroneous* belief that he is not his body. But all the Cartesian needs to deploy PL is that a direct epistemic relation guarantees his belief to be relational.

This Cartesian move rests on the distinction between '*de re*' and '*de dicto*' belief. If the two conditions just discussed are met, A stands in a genuine relation to x. If, however, A believes that x is P but does not bear a direct epistemic relation to x, A's belief is not a relation between A and x but the satisfaction by A of the monadic predicate 'is a $P(x)$-believer'.[7] The idea that there are both kinds of belief blunts a paradox that threatens belief contexts construed extensionally, and motivates some useful apparatus. Suppose Wolfgang composed the *Jupiter* and Ludwig believes that Wolfgang is in Vienna. So:

(5) Wolfgang is believed by Ludwig to be in Vienna.

Suppose too that Ludwig has seen Wolfgang close up, so Ludwig bears a direct epistemic relation to Wolfgang. So L = 'is believed by Ludwig to be in Vienna' holds of Wolfgang extensionally. But suppose Ludwig does not know that Wolfgang composed the *Jupiter* and in fact believes that the composer of the Jupiter is not in Vienna. Thus:

(6) (The composer of the *Jupiter* is believed by Ludwig to be in Vienna.)

Hence Wolfgang is L, the composer of the *Jupiter* is not L, L is extensional, and consequently Wolfgang did not compose the *Jupiter*.

[7] I follow Quine, *Word and Object*, sec. 44 in construing *de dicto* belief monadically; for more on this, see V.4.

This paradox can be avoided with the aid of two conventions. First: when a belief of *A* about *x* is extensional, express it as:

(E) *x* is believed by *A* to be *P*.

In terms of (E), (5) correctly describes Ludwig's belief about Wolfgang. Since Wolfgang *is* the composer of the *Jupiter*, (6) is considered false. Instead

(7) The composer of the *Jupiter* is believed by Ludwig to be in Vienna

is to be considered true, as per my encounter with the Ambassador. Using identity statements to warrant across the board substitution into the extensional belief contexts, (E) turns the tables on spurious proofs of counteridentity *via* extensional belief contexts. 'Wolfgang' occurs extensionally in (5) because Ludwig stands in a direct epistemic relation to the composer of the *Jupiter*. So, if Ludwig's direct epistemic relation to Wolfgang induces extensionality in Ludwig's belief about Wolfgang, the same belief of Ludwig about the composer of the *Jupiter* must be extensional, since, by the extensionality of 'stands in a direct epistemic relation to', Ludwig stands in a direct epistemic relation to the composer of the *Jupiter*.

What of the fact that Ludwig believes that the composer of the *Jupiter* is not in Vienna? The chief warrant for saying this is that Ludwig would assent to the sentence 'The composer of the *Jupiter* is not in Vienna'. This is the *de dicto* notion of belief. The second convention stipulates that *de dicto* beliefs, resistant as they are to substitution and quantification, be rendered

(I) *A* believes *x*-to-be-*P*.

Thus:

(8) Ludwig believes: the-*Jupiter*-composer-not-to-be-in-Vienna.

Making the situation as difficult as possible, let us allow that Ludwig recognized Wolfgang when he saw him, and (9) is also true:

(9) Ludwig believes: Wolfgang-to-be-in-Vienna.

No paradox arises from the joint truth of (8) and (9), since (8) is not a substitutional variant of (9).

Since Ludwig stands in a direct epistemic relation to Wolfgang, and Wolfgang *is* the composer of the *Jupiter*, the composer of the

Jupiter is believed by Ludwig to be in Vienna whether Ludwig realizes it or not. This is no more puzzling than the fact that one can become a grandfather without realizing it. But Ludwig also assents to the sentence 'The composer of the *Jupiter* is not in Vienna'. (E) and (I) drive the wedge of non-entailment between the two. In general, (E) and (I) are compatible but neither entails the other. Indeed, while A would have to be irrational for

(10) A believes $x \neq x$

to be true, it can happen that

(11) x is believed by A not to be x.

(11) is what happens when someone is directly epistemically related to something whose identity he has got wrong.

Even though the Cartesian is entitled to appeal to PL, his argument stalls right there. Anyone who holds that A is A's body will simply contend that, perhaps surprisingly, if (4) is true, then A's body cannot be conceived by A not to exist. A's asseveration that he can conceive this would be explained as his willingness to assent to the *sentence* 'My body might not exist'. *Since* he is his body, the anti-Cartesian says, and since 'is believed by me not to exist' is extensional, then *whether he knows it or not*, the Cartesian cannot believe his body not to exist. The very facts which render the relevant belief context extensional, and hence permit appeal to PL, make it impossible for the Cartesian to establish anything stronger than the conditional: if his body can be believed by A not to exist and A cannot be believed by A not to exist, then A is not A's body. Unfortunately for him, it is the consequent he wants.

5. *The Elusiveness of the Self*

The Cartesian has twice had to claim that each man has a special epistemic link with his self. This invites a broad objection to substance dualism: not only does a man not have a direct epistemic relation to himself, the self is not an object of awareness at all. Hume held that the very idea of a thinking substance distinct from various thoughts and feelings is empty:

For my part, when I enter most intimately into what I call *myself*, I always stumble on some particular perception or other, of heat or cold, light or shade, love or hatred, pain or pleasure. I never can catch *myself* at any time without a perception, and never can observe anything but the perception. (*Treatise:* I. iv. 6.)

Hume has a point. If my *self* is the ground of the identity through time of all my mental states, it is strange that I never detect it apart from those states for whose identity it is supposed to be the ground. Even waiving Hume's stringent demand that every idea must arise from some one impression, the fact is that we never do detect a bare thinking substance.

One point about Hume's objection should be noted. Despite his ironic suggestions to the contrary, it is unlikely that Hume and the Cartesian disagree because their introspective experiences differ. They both know and agree on what it is like to be cold. Their dispute is about how to describe such conscious states. The Cartesian describes the experience of being cold as '*my* experience of cold', while Hume holds that, strictly speaking, the most we are entitled to call it is '*an* experience of cold'.

Descartes anticipated Hume's objection and proposed a suitable reply. Descartes reflects that a piece of wax may change all its sensible properties—all the ways it is 'distinctly known' to him—and yet he retains, possibly groundlessly, the idea of the piece of wax as a self-identical entity throughout these changes. In so far as Descartes' point is about concept formation, it is that the idea of a self-identical material thing comes neither from the senses nor the imagination. It is a 'perception of the understanding'. Thus, it is a mistake to contrast awareness of the self with awareness of material objects in point of self-identity, for the idea of a self-identical material substance could as little be supplied by any kind of awareness as the idea of a self-identical thinking substance:

[I]t is at present manifest to me that even bodies are not properly known by the senses nor by the faculty of imagination, but by the understanding alone; and since they are not known in so far as they are seen or touched, but only insofar as they are understood by thinking, I see clearly that there is nothing easier for me to understand than my mind. (*Meditation* III).

This is a brilliant riposte, but Hume would call the victory more forensic than real. It is true, Hume might agree, that the ground of identity through time of material properties is no clearer than that for mental states; but this shows that the whole idea of identity through time for any set of properties or states in any *kind* of particular, material or mental, should be abandoned. The idea of a self is, perhaps, not *especially* unclear: the ideas of self and body are *both* unacceptable.[8] Selves are sets of conscious states, and bodies are sets of properties.[9]

One is tempted to join Hume in throwing in one's hand here because the stakes have been raised too high. Once selves and bodies are introduced as posits, it is as easy to let them fall together as to let them support each other. But there is no need to divide the idea of a particular x, mental or physical, into the idea of a property P of x and the posit of x for P to apply to. If we do this, we can disregard the posit as superfluous and construe 'x' as referring to P and the rest of (what we usually call) x's properties. But we need not, indeed cannot construe the idea of x this way. Consider what is required if x is to be analysed as a set of abstracta: instances of physical properties if x is a body, particular mental states if x is a self. Let x_1 be a black plastic telephone. x_1 cannot just be {blackness, plasticity, ...} since there are other black, plastic, ... things about, such as the black plastic calendar x_2 nearby. We have to specify *which* instances of blackness, plasticity, ... constitute x_1. The object x_1 must be a set of individuated property-instances; even if we disregard the problem of similar objects, we must be able to rule out such Goodmanesque entities as {the colour of the wall, the plasticity of the cup, ...}. Individuating properties by where and when they are instantiated[10] leaves space-time points as particulars—and if we allow these (odd) particulars, why not allow material and mental objects? The same moral applies to construing minds as sets of mental states. If I am to be a perception of pain, an awareness of cold, ..., I must be some *instance* of the generic state 'awareness of pain', the generic state 'awareness of cold', ... The problem, then, is to determine which instance of blackness B_1 is to be a member of

[8] This is Hume's tack in 'Of Scepticism with Regard to the Senses' in the *Treatise*. Much of his argument against Descartes seems to be a corollary of his *global* rejection of identity through time having little to do with the nature of the self.

[9] The doctrine of the impossibility of self-identical particulars is independent of phenomenalism, although historically there has been a tendency to merge the two. The claim that a thing is a set of properties does not entail that a thing is a set of *phenomenal* properties; even if theoretical properties are allowed, there is still the problem of what they are properties of: cf. J. Bennett's distinction between the 'predication problem' and the 'veil of perception problem' in his *Locke, Berkeley, Hume* (Clarendon Press, Oxford: 1971).

[10] As Russell does in *Inquiry into Meaning and Truth* (Penguin, Baltimore, Md.: 1940).

x_1 and which instance of blackness B_2 is to be in x_2. It is clear that the only way to pick out B_1 is as 'x_1's blackness'; and, similarly, B_2 is identified as x_2's blackness. When it comes to picking the particular mental states my mind is to be the set of, there seems to be no other way of identifying the perception of cold to put in my bundle than as the one which is *my* perception of cold. So Descartes was right and Hume wrong when Descartes characterized an experience as 'my perception of cold' and Hume characterized it as 'a perception of cold'. Hume has to tell us which experience of cold he is talking about, and he can't do this without overt or covert reference to the experiencer.

This discussion has not relied on the question-begging dictum that every property must belong to a substance. The point is that individuated property-instances require a principle of individuation, and the only one there is appeals to the particulars property-instances apply to. Nor does this discussion leave the topic of particulars and substance hanging in limbo, because these notions never were in limbo. There is no problem of substance, nor of the concept of a thing. These are tangles that can be unravelled by a tautology, the only problem being to see that the tautology is all that needs be said. Let the telephone on my desk be a working example of a substance. The problem of substance, when stripped of phenomenalist accretions, is: what has all the properties of the telephone? The answer to this is quite straightforward: the telephone. What *else* could have all and only the properties of the telephone? The telephone, logically enough, is what has all the properties of the telephone. The question of substance is baffling because it is so often posed in a way which rejects its only answer: 'What is it, *other than the telephone*, which has the properties of the telephone?' Well, there is no other thing, by stipulation. We are told to look beyond the tautological answer, but there is no other answer. Similarly, the answer to the question 'What thinks my thoughts?' is *me*. What else could think the thoughts *I* think?

6. *Thinking Things?*

Substance dualism has proved tenacious. The Cartesian has not established it, but we have so far found no reason to reject it. It is time now to examine two such reasons. One is the familiar difficulty of mind–body interaction. First, however, I want to take a closer look at the self. The sailing here is not quite as clear for the Cartesian as I made out in the previous section. Despite the fact that the entityhood of the self is as defensible as the entityhood of material things, a suspicion lingers that in some way the latter is clearer than the former. One would expect that a proper explication of this suspicion would also explain why philosophers are more troubled by their inability to detect a bare self than their inability to detect a bare material substance.

The trouble, I suggest, is this: we can say what sort of stuff a material thing is an individuated piece of, while no one has any idea of the sort of stuff a self is an individuated piece of. We can say what a piece of wax or a rainbow are *made of*, but not what even those selves we can identify are made of. In addition to describing a seal as a fragrant thing and a yellow thing, we can describe it as a piece of wax. 'Wax' is a stuff-word; it is what some things are made of. In general, the result of applying a term of individuation ('piece', 'glass of') to a stuff-word specifies a kind of thing, what the thing is made of, and the kind of thing it is. 'Pail of water' tells us, of a thing, that it is water and a pail's worth. The stuff-words of English are not the last word on stuff: physics has reduced water to hydrogen and oxygen, bronze to copper and tin. But whatever the ultimate stuff is—energy, space-time—we tend to say that we know *what* a thing is when we can refer to it as a P of S, where 'P' is a term of individuation and 'S' is a stuff-word.

It is in this sense that it is impossible to form an idea of what the substance dualist's self is. While there are descriptions that can identify a self, we cannot refer to it as a P of S, for we do not know and evidently cannot imagine the *stuff* it is a piece of, or the sort of piece it could be. Simply positing an x retaining its identity through time while successively satisfying predicates is useless unless one of the predicates is 'is a piece of ...'. Without this, we don't know what x is. This, perhaps, is the genuine problem toward which the pseudo-problem of substance is a gesture: what stuff is a given thing, or things generally, made of? This reconstructed substance problem can be partially answered for material objects.[11] But no one has the faintest idea of the stuff selves are made of. True, the question 'what is it?' is not always explicitly about stuff; it may be relative to context, purpose, the presumed knowledge of one's interlocutor, and so on. But the 'what is it?' problem that nags philosophers about the

[11] Perhaps completely answered: see G. Feinberg, 'Physics and the Thales Problem', *Journal of Philosophy*, lxiii. 1 (Jan. 1966), 5–17.

self *does* seem to be a question for which only a 'stuff' answer would be satisfactory (perhaps because, unlike the other cases, there is no presumption that the stuff—'what is it?' question can be answered).

Here, I suspect, is the source of the mysteriousness of substance dualism, and it is a most serious difficulty for the substance dualist. At best, he leaves completely open the question of what selves are made of. All the Cartesian has had a right to claim since the epistemological argument broke down was that something thinks and perceives, and that this may as well be called the mind. But this is compatible with the mind turning out to be a material object. Even if thinking and perceiving turn out not to be physical states, it would not yet follow that the thing that thinks is non-physical. As we have seen, this would only establish property dualism.

7. *Interaction*

The anti-Cartesian now turns to the traditional stumbling-block of substance dualism and many forms of property dualism, the interaction of mind and body. Substance dualism is *prima facie* incompatible with, or renders unintelligible, a wide range of familiar facts. If I bang my toe, I feel pain; if I decide to take a walk, my body moves. How can things as dissimilar as minds and bodies are supposed to be, interact? The dynamic features of the mind—motives, resolves—seem entirely different from the dynamic forces of physics. Since these latter forces are the paradigm ways of getting bodies to move, it is hard to see how the *self*, or changes in the self, can do so.

Hume is the substance dualist's best ally. Hume's famous analysis of causation implies that the sense of difficulty is caused by an inflated notion of what interaction is. According to Hume, there really is no such thing as causality, if '*c* caused *e*' means *c made e* happen, or *c necessitated e*. The only relation *c* has to *e* when *c* causes *e* is that $\langle c,e \rangle$ exemplifies a constant conjunction between *c*-like and *e*-like events. The something more we feel connecting *c* and *e* is the feeling of expectation *in us* created by (i.e. regularly following) the perception of the constant conjunction of *c*-like and *e*-like events. There can be no necessary or *a priori* connection between distinct existences, and the constant conjunction of *c* and *e* must be purely contingent. No *a priori* argument can determine what kinds of things can enter into causal relations: any two substances may turn out to interact, including the most intuitively dissimilar. Indeed, the rational core of causality being just constant conjunction, the interaction of physical objects is no more metaphysically intelligible than the interaction of minds and bodies. *Why* any two kinds of event are constantly conjoined is ultimately inexplicable. (Hume vacillates on whether this is because we can never *find out* why they are conjoined, or because—all why-questions being at bottom requests for the appropriate constant conjunction—ultimate why-questions are meaningless. But this does not affect his defence of the possibility of interaction.)

The anti-Cartesian is ill-advised to call Hume's durable analysis into question. For one thing, he has no guarantee that mind–body interaction will be incompatible with any non-Humean replacement. Take this counterfactual analysis: '*c* caused *e*' means 'if *c* had not happened, *e* would not have happened'.[12] Whatever its other merits, this variant has no bearing on the present issue. Why should it not be true that *if* I had not wanted to take a walk yesterday I would not have moved; and *if* the hammer had not fallen on my toe I would not have experienced pain? Nothing in the counterfactual analysis of causation rules out the interaction of dissimilar substances. The anti-dualist, then, might as well formulate the interaction objection within a Humean framework (where this includes appeal to acceptable counterfactuals).

One such reformation is this: as a matter of empirical fact, the cause of any bodily event is always some other physical event. The notion of '*the* cause' of an event has a sufficiently wide preanalytic currency to justify invoking it here. When we say that event *c* is the cause of event *e*, we mean that *c* contains all the necessary conditions for *e*, and that, given *c*, *e* had to occur. (The second clause is necessary because, if determinism is false, the first clause may hold but not the second. Talk of 'necessity' here is to be understood as, in the previous paragraph, consistent with the Humean analysis.) A *description* of *c* will refer to only some of *c*'s traits, and this has led some philosophers to suppose that 'the cause' of an event is simply the most distinctive causally relevant preceding event. This is a mistake: *c* itself is the (entire) preceding event, although it may be the cause only in virtue of some of the descriptions it satisfies. Understood thus, a given event has only one cause. If *c* is the cause

[12] Cf. D. Lewis, 'Causation', *Journal of Philosophy*, lxx. 17 (Oct. 1973), 556–67.

of e, then no event c' can be the cause of e, and no part of c is dispensable.

Armed with this notion, the anti-dualist presses what appears to be the empirical fact that for every physical event e involving a human body, there is some preceding physical event which is *the* cause of e. As far as anyone knows there are no gaps in the sequence of bodily events to be bridged by a mental event, or into which a mental event might slip. There is no physical event whose cause is mental, in the dualist's intended sense.

The dualist might take issue with the notion of 'the cause'. Many thinkers take seriously the possibility of causal overdetermination; perhaps preceding bodily events and mental events are multiple causes of bodily events. But the notion of 'the cause' rules out the possibility of causal overdetermination—a counterintuitive consequence. It goes against Freud, for example, who speaks of the overdetermination of dreams, and against such commonsense judgements as 'A combination of overwork and worry killed Jones'. The anti-dualist must deny that both overwork and worry killed Jones: only one must be the cause. The anti-dualist can reply that ostensible cases of overdetermination can be analysed harmlessly. He construes 'c and c' caused e' as: c (say) was the cause of e, but had c not occurred, c' would have caused e or an event e' very similar to e. To say that a dream was overdetermined by an Oedipus complex and a heavy dinner means that had the dreamer not had an Oedipus complex, the heavy dinner would have the caused the same dream or a similar one. But the Oedipus complex was in fact the cause of the dream. The case of Jones might be analysed this way, or it might require this refinement: *the* cause was the composite event $c+c'$ (=overwork+worry); but had only c or c' occurred, Jones would have died, and died a death very similar to the one caused by overwork and worry. These points also apply to explanation. Given an event e, there is exactly one argument which is *the* explanation of e, which completely accounts for e's occurrence. Sometimes, to be sure, there seem to be several basic co-existing explanations for the same phenomenon, as when the oboe cadenza in Beethoven's Fifth Symphony is explained causally (events in Beethoven's brain [or air passing along a reed]) and aesthetically (the cadenza enhances the tension). But the aesthetic explanation does not purport to tell why the cadenza occurs, but why its occurrence is aesthetically satisfying. The causal explanation is *the* explanation of (the existence of) the cadenza.[13]

The dualist can also reply that the causes of some bodily events are not purely physical. His argument here is reminiscent of a standard defence of epiphenomenalism, the thesis that some physical events cause mental events but mental events have no causal efficacy of their own. Epiphenomenalists reply to the charge that their theory makes mentality causally superfluous by observing that if mental event *m* had not occurred the physical event *b* that caused *m* would not have occurred, nor any further physical events *b* was the cause of. Similarly, replies the dualist, suppose that when I form the intention (event *m*) to move my leg (event *e*), and thereafter move it, neural event *c* causes *e*. Assuming that the formation of an intention is an event, both *c* and *m* are necessary for *e*. Had I not intended to move my leg, it would not have moved. Consequently, *c* does not contain all the necessary conditions for my leg's moving and is not the cause of my leg's moving.

The anti-dualist might deny that *m* is part of the cause of *e*, saying instead that *c* is the cause of both *m* and *e*. Since this would require that *c* have simultaneous and non-simultaneous effects, a a position not without problems, he might refine his reply to be that there is another physical event *c′* which immediately precedes *c* and causes both *c* and *m*. This proposal is open to the familiar objection that anyone who rejects the action of mind on body ought to be equally puzzled by physical events bringing about mental events. More seriously, as the recently noted defence of epiphenomenalism brings out, it is hard to see a difference between the anti-dualist's suggestion and the admission that *m* was part of the cause of *e*.

Some writers[14] try to explain this difference—to explain, that is, what it means to call *m* causally superfluous or epiphenomenal—in this way. Given the way the laws of nature actually are, *c′* will never happen unless followed by *m*, and *m* will never happen unless preceded by *c′*. But if, *per impossibile*, *c′* were to happen without causing *m*, *e* would happen anyway, while if *m* happened without *c′*, *e* would not happen. And in fact we do in ordinary life make judgements of causal superfluity of just this sort. Suppose two factories let out for lunch at 12.01 and 12.02 respectively when a

[13] See p. 132 below.
[14] e.g. Lewis, loc. cit.

central whistle blows at noon. The 12.01 workers then consume all the roast beef in their commissary at 12.03. Even though in fact the workers at the 12.01 factory will never break for lunch unless the 12.02 workers do a minute later, we permit ourselves to reason counterfactually about what would happen if the 12.01 workers broke and the 12.02 workers did not. If the whistle blew and the 12.01 workers left, the roast beef would have been eaten anyway. Contrariwise, if *per impossibile* the whistle blew, the 12.01 workers stayed put, and the 12.02 workers left, the roast beef would not have been eaten. Hence the 12.02 workers leaving is epiphenomenal to the causal sequence resulting in roast beef consumption. However, one condition required for construing the $\langle c',c,m,e\rangle$ sequence on the model of the ⟨whistle, 12.01 workers breaking, 12.02 workers breaking, roast beef consumed⟩ sequence is that we have some idea of how each of the two events regularly preceding the fourth event can be isolated from each other, so that their independent contribution to the fourth event can be assessed. If both are—as in these two cases—the results of a common cause, it must be possible to interfere with this branching causal tree to allow just one path to be realized. Thus, if the consumption of roast beef is regularly preceded by two lunch breaks, one can try to make each break occur without the other and see in which case, if either, the roast beef is consumed. If this is not possible—as perhaps it might not be, by definition, if the branching causal structure is dictated by natural laws—one must be able to reason by analogy from similar situations in which interference is possible. But in the mind–body case no one has the faintest idea how to create each of c and m in isolation. Nobody knows how to get a leg to be raised in the way it is when it is raised intentionally without getting someone to intend to raise his leg. Even if general sense can be made of causal superfluity, there is no warrant now for saying that intentions are superfluous, nor is it clear that we could ever be in a position to do so. One needs another argument to show that the action of a mind could not be part of the cause of a bodily event.

Another traditional argument, however, does seem to show decisively that the causal relations between the mind as the dualist conceives it and the body are impossible. Originally my leg, which has mass w, is motionless. Then it moves distance d. Enough work was done to move a mass w a distance d. Where did the energy come from? It is an empirical fact, the law of the conservation of energy, that the energy had to come from somewhere, and not only does it come from some preceding physical event, no immaterial substance could possibly supply mechanical energy. The mind can apply no physical force to the leg, while the contraction of the hamstring muscle supplies just the right amount—and the bodily event just *is* the motion of an object of mass w through distance d. Thus the contraction of the muscle is *the cause* of e. If there were non-physical causes of physical events, the energy in the universe would increase.

Broad cites, on the dualist's behalf, systems whose parts are causally related but which, allegedly, exchange no energy. The state of the bob of a pendulum is constantly changing, yet the shaft applies no force to the bob.[15] This analogy is misguided in several ways. When my leg moves a force *is* being applied to a physical object; energy is being transferred. Since all the requisite force is supplied by a change in another physical object, any change in any other (especially immaterial) object is superfluous. The pendulum case is at best a precedent for a very limited number of mind–body interactions. More damaging is the fact that energy is actually being exchanged in the pendulum case. The shaft is exerting centripetal force on the bob, and the bob is exerting centrifugal force on the shaft; and at different positions the bob is exerting and bearing different amounts of both. The potential and kinetic energy of the bob are constantly changing.

The dualist may complain that this appeal to the conservation of energy reifies energy as a kind of stuff passed from object to object, whereas legitimate talk of energy (and mass) is shorthand for facts about acceleration.[16] The conservation of energy in particular is shorthand for an empirical fact about constancies in such ratios. But even if energy is analytically eliminable, the present objection stands. Suppose we 'operationlize' energy and mass, explaining the mass of a body as its (constant, additive) tendency to induce acceleration. My leg, which has a constant additive tendency to induce acceleration w, moves with average velocity v during time-interval Δt. It is a hard empirical fact that some object with a

[15] *Mind and Its Place in Nature*, pp. 104–9.

[16] See Hume's *Enquiry Concerning Human Understanding*, VII. ii, fn. 1; Mach's *The Science of Mechanics* (Open Court, La Salle, Ill.: 1960), trans. T. McCormack, esp. p. 368. The definitive discussion of the empirical core of Newton's third law—the basis of the conservation of energy—is Nagel, *Structure of Science*, pp. 192–6.

constant additive tendency w' to induce acceleration must have moved with such an average velocity v' during Δt that $\int^{\Delta t} \frac{1}{2}wv^2dt = -\int^{\Delta t} \frac{1}{2}w'v'^2dt$. Since (see II.4) immaterial objects have no tendency to induce acceleration, it cannot have been an immaterial object that slowed down. But *the cause* of my leg's moving was the slowing down of the object with mass w'.

Only materialism, it seems, is compatible with mind–body interaction. Not only must the mind be a physical thing, but mental events must be changes with respect to physical properties. If not, mental events could not be involved in changes in acceleration, and at most epiphenomenalism would be true. We turn, then, to materialism, the view discussed, and eventually advocated, in the next two chapters.

IV

Materialism, 1

1. Plausibility and Simplicity of Materialism

MODERN science brings with it a picture of the universe from which everything but matter is excluded. So far as we know, everything, except possibly the psychological states of sentient beings, is physical. The laws of nature, whose predictive and explanatory power has been repeatedly vindicated, are couched wholly in non-psychological terms. As the evidence accumulates, it becomes ever harder to suppose that future discoveries will radically alter this world-picture.

Such large scale considerations[1] have convinced many philosophers that mental phenomena too will eventually be incorporated into physical theory. Views with a family resemblance to materialism have been urged since antiquity, but more as programmes than theories; it is only in the last century that materialism has become plausible. Unless a case can be made for such subsidiary mental entities as pains, hopes, etc., the falsity of substance dualism leaves property dualism and property monism the only alternatives on the mind–body problem, and it is simply more reasonable to think that the properties expressed by psychological predicates will turn out to be physical. Given that most of the universe is explicable physicalistically, the view which least multiplies independent principles is that the entire universe is explicable physicalistically.

The simplicity of materialism is sometimes put this way:[2] Most phenomena in the universe fall into nomological networks; the same explanatory principles are used to explain events throughout a network, and every node in a network is linked by law to other nodes. Astronomical phenomena form such a network: similar principles are used to explain the behaviour of all stellar systems.

[1] See J. Smart, 'Philosophy and Scientific Plausibility', in *Mind, Matter and Method*, eds. P. Feyerabend and G. Maxwell (U. of Minn. Press, Minneapolis: 1966), pp. 377–90.

[2] See J. Smart, 'Sensations and Brain Processes', in Rosenthal; ed., *Materialism and the Mind-Body Problem;* H. Feigl, *The 'Mental' and the 'Physical'* (U. of Minn. Press, Minneapolis: 1967).

(Ultimately, says the materialist, one network will cover everything.) But suppose that property P were a node in a nomological network, and that some property P' were correlated with P but nothing else in P's network; and that the law connecting P' to P was nothing like the laws connecting P with the rest of the network. P', or the law connecting P' to P, would be a 'nomological dangler'. An account of the world which includes nomological danglers is more complex, hence less desirable, than one which omits them. A nomological dangler leaves such questions as 'Why is P' correlated with P? Why not P''?' unanswerable.[3] Answering them would involve further information about the kind of property P' is and how it is related to other things than P, but by hypothesis P' is unconnected with the rest of the world.[4] Property dualism, which claims that mental states are correlated with the states of certain physical systems, apparently treats mental states as nomological danglers and thus violates precepts that control theorizing elsewhere.

The proscription against complexity does not require omission of patently real phenomena If the evidence warrants it, we will have to accept property dualism, danglers and all. Rather, the principle of parsimony tells us to choose the simpler of two hypotheses equally competent to account for all available data. Another point to be clear on in passing is that two kinds of simplicity may come into play. A hypothesis H is *ontologically* simpler than H' if H posits fewer entities, or fewer different kinds of entities, than H'. H is *ideologically* simpler than H' if the predicates H applies to their common domain are less outlandish than those of H'. A particular case of ideological simplicity is that the predicates of H form a proper subset of the predicates of H'. I will argue in section 3 below and V.3 that pains and other such mental entities are analytically eliminable. Since Cartesian egos were scotched in the last chapter, the materialist must be claiming, specifically, that his view is ideologically simpler than property dualism. Given their common ontologies, materialism countenances fewer properties for things to have than does property dualism. This refinement, however, is ignored in what follows, which applies to both ontological and ideological simplicity. (Also: H may posit more entities than H', but

[3] See H. Putnam, 'Psychological Predicates', in W. Capitan and D. Merrill, eds., *Art, Mind and Religion* (U. of Pitt. Pa.: 1967), p. 40.

[4] This also violates M. Slote's 'Principle of Unlimited Inquiry': see his *Reason and Scepticism* (Humanities, N.Y.: 1970), *passim*.

fewer kinds of entity. A full treatment of the matter would define the natural partial ordering of hypotheses with respect of both kinds of simplicity, and finally simplicity *per se*.)

It is natural to ask why the principle of simplicity should be adopted. A natural answer is that a simpler theory is preferable to an otherwise satisfactory but more complex one because the simpler theory is more likely to be true. Being simpler, less can go wrong with it. Indeed, that simplicity is plausibility is the account of simplicity the materialist must give. Why, asks D. Gunner, a critic of the identity thesis, should the simplicity of a theory make us think the theory is true?[5] If the value of simplicity lies not in the plausibility or 'safety' it confers but in some *sui generis* 'aesthetic' property (as Goodman believes), the simplicity of H over H' ceases to be a reason for *believing* H, although it may be a reason for *using* or *expounding* H rather than H'. The materialist needs a stronger justification of parsimony if he is to parlay this methodological feature of materialism into a claim about reality.

The nature and justification of simplicity is the subject of a vast technical literature. My review of the claim that simplicity boosts safety must be brief and, perhaps, inadequate. To begin with, there is a clear intuitive link between the two in many cases. Suppose two murders are committed within a single hour at opposite ends of Manhattan. In both cases a copy of Spinoza's *Ethics* is left on the victim's chest. Kojak considers these two hypotheses:

(H_1) There are two murderers, each a devotee of Spinoza, who, independently of each other, struck, within a single hour.
(H_2) There is one Spinoza devotee who used the subway.

Intuitively, H_2 is simpler and preferable. Why? Because H_1 is subject to refutation in more ways than H_2. If there are fewer than two murderers, H_1 is false; while H_2 is true if there is one murderer. H_1 requires belief in the existence of two highly improbable beings, H_2 only one. The probability that both exist is too small for H_1 to be rationally credible. Here, then, the simpler hypothesis is preferable precisely because it is more probable.[6]

[5] 'Professor Smart's "Sensations and Brain Processes" ', in C. Presley, ed *The Identity Theory of Mind* (U. of Queensland Press, St. Lucia, Qld: 1967).

[6] J. Kemeny is able to *prove* that, in certain cases, the simplest hypothesis is very probably the true one ('The Use of Simplicity in Induction', in M. Foster and M. Martin, eds., *Probability, Confirmation and Simplicity* (Odyssey, N.Y.: 1966), pp. 309–22). R. Ackermann ('Inductive Simplicity', ibid., pp. 322–31)

Popper, as is well known, holds that simplicity is desirable just because the simpler a hypothesis is the more risky it is—and the scientific value of a hypothesis is inversely proportional to its probability. But when Popper praises 'risky' hypotheses, he seems to confuse two things. The first is a hypothesis which is implausible relative to current evidence. The second is a hypothesis which probabilifies a prediction whose probability on any competing hypothesis is very low. Popper's views make good sense if 'risky' is interpreted the second way, and very little when interpreted the first way. But a hypothesis can be risky in this second sense and *still be very plausible*. So even if Popper is right about the value of simplicity, this is no reason to suppose that simplicity is not a matter of safety.

Goodman[7] proposes this counterexample to identifying the two. Consider the hypotheses

(H_3) All elm trees are deciduous.
(H_4) All elm trees, except possibly those on Main St., are deciduous.

H_3 is simpler than H_4, but H_4, being less adventurous, is safer than H_3.

One might reply to Goodman that the relative simplicity of two hypotheses H and H' cannot be gauged just by comparing them with each other, but against some background theory T whose augmentation by H or H' is under consideration. If, in Goodman's example, T entails that elms are a natural kind—so that all elms have the same flowering properties—the possibility introduced by H_4 can be discounted. Relative to T, H_3 is simpler and no less safe than H_4. Equivalently: relative to T, H_4 is as simple as H_3. It is not clear, then, that $\langle H_3, H_4 \rangle$ prevents the identification of simplicity with safety.

Thus relativizing simplicity has, to be sure, some inconvenient consequences. H may be simpler than H' relative to T, but less simple than H' relative to T'. Also, H and H' cannot be compared for simplicity if we propose to augment two independent theories T and T' by H and H' respectively. (This may be the most troublesome

---

points out some technical limitations of Kemeny's result; but a result with even a very restricted scope must be considered important here.

[7] 'Safety, Strength, Simplicity', in P. Nidditch, ed., *The Philosophy of Science* (O.U.P., Oxford: 1968), pp. 121–4.

problem, since we do *apparently* make intuitive simplicity assessments without benefit of background theory.) Finally, suppose that one of T and T' must be rejected, but that we can save T by adding H or save T' by adding H'. If T and T' have done equally well in the past, it is impossible to assess the relative simplicity of the two moves unless we can compare T & H and T' & H' against some further background theory T''—and what guarantee is there that such a T'' exists?

These consequences are not, I think, fatally counterintuitive. After all, what *a priori* guarantee do we have that any two hypotheses can be compared with respect to simplicity?—although of course one can stipulate a sense for 'is simpler than' which is well defined for all pairs of hypotheses. In sum: it is far from self-evident that simplicity is a virtue of theories because simpler = more plausible. Nevertheless, the position can be defended, and the materialist is therefore entitled to call the argument from simplicity a *plausibility* argument.

The materialist's appeal to simplicity need not be so global as Smart and others sometimes imply. Simplicity considerations may favour a materialistic interpretation of specific empirical situations that bear on the mind–body problem. Suppose we have reduced the question of what pain is to the question of what property a speaker is expressing when he ascribes 'x is in pain' to himself. Suppose further we discover that this verbal response is a function of a neural event; the speaker can be conditioned to assent to this ascription precisely when this neural event occurs. Suppose, even, we find a causal chain from the neural event through a 'speech centre' to the verbal behaviour. We can say either that what the speaker is responding to—what the satisfaction condition for 'x is in pain' is—is the neural event, or that it is a private phenomenal event accompanying the neural event. Simplicity considerations evidently dictate that what the speaker is responding to is the neural event itself, not a non-physical accompaniment.

2. *Why Materialists Argue as They Do*

Materialists often spend more time formulating what they want to say and defending it against objections than presenting explicit arguments in its favour. Smart's classic 'Sensations and Brain Processes', for example, consists mainly of answers to eight objections. It is now clearer why materialists take such a negative approach. The main positive evidence for materialism is the global considerations discussed in section 1.[8] Materialists take these considerations to make materialism *obvious*: it need only be well defended to be accepted.[9] It is the disparity in scale between the considerations favouring materialism that can create the illusion that materialism has no *powerful* arguments in its favour, that it is just a consistent promissory note.

In fact, a major part of the job of defending materialism is formulating it properly. (There are obviously good general reasons for presenting materialism 'at its best'.) This is because many arguments against materialism claim, on *a priori* or quasi-*a priori* grounds, that materialism is incoherent or incompatible with obvious facts. Consequently, a coherent formulation of materialism consistent with certain obvious facts by itself blocks a significant class of objections. One might count selecting option (3) of II.1 under the heading 'formulating materialism'. A more important example of formulating materialism correctly is its account of the logical form of psychological statements, clarity about which stymies a variety of objections. I have already mentioned the argument that materialism must be false because yellow after-images are yellow and nothing in the brain is yellow. This prompts the materialist to argue that after-images are virtual, that statements about after-images ascribe the monadic predicate 'x has a yellow after-image' (or 'x is yellow after-imaging'). If this thesis is true, there need be nothing yellow when someone has a yellow after-image, and the cited objection fails. This thesis, crucial to the materialist, is the topic of the next section.

3. The Monadic Thesis, with Applications

The *monadic thesis* holds that $P(x)$ is the logical form of 'x is sensing a yellow after-image', 'x is in pain', 'x is in a foul mood', and the like. This sections defends the monadic thesis and deploys it against a number of objections to materialism. The discussion here is limited to non-intensional psychological ascriptions; I defer until V.4 any discussion of the logical form of ascriptions which take propositional or quasi-propositional objects (e.g. 'I hoped the King of Argentina would come'). This division of labour does not endorse any fundamental distinction between two types of psychological states. One

[8] And the capacities of computers; see VI.2.

[9] Thus B. Medlin: '[Its] economy is so great and the difficulties of the rival theories so overwhelming and well known, that in practice the job boils down very largely to the rebuttal of objections' ('Ryle and the Mechanical Hypothesis', in Presley, ed., *The Identity Theory of Mind*, p. 95).

can regard after-images and pains as the objects of seeing and being-in in just the way states of affairs are the objects of hoping and believing. I treat the latter separately because they are sometimes singled out as presenting special problems for materialism. Davidson, for example, uses Quine's indeterminacy of translation thesis to support the anomaly of propositional attitudes with respect to brain states.[10] Obviously, the indeterminacy of translation cannot be applied in this way to after-imaging. Certainly, both materialists and their critics treat the identification of sensations as a simpler problem than the identification of more complex, object-taking mental states, and it is convenient to follow them here. Since V.4 concludes that both kinds of ascription are monadic, the present account of ascriptions of pains and after-images can be applied to ascriptions of hope and belief.

A final detail: the materialist also holds the logical form of the ostensibly *tri*adic ascription 'x has a pain in his foot' to be *dy*adic; that of the ostensibly quadratic 'x has a pain between his y and his z' to be triadic, and so on. These reductions are all part of the monadic thesis.

The monadic thesis is essentially the view Quine urges in 'On Mental Entities'.[11] He argues that such entities as non-public objects of sense are holdovers from an outmoded empiricism which science does not need. There are more positive arguments than this for the monadic thesis. One inconclusive argument for it, however, should be set aside immediately—the fact that it follows from topic neutralism, the thesis that (e.g.) 'I am in pain' amounts to 'Something is happening like what happens when my body is damaged'. (A variant of this thesis is defended in sections 4 and 5.) Exchanging the latter for the former analytically eliminates the pain, for 'Something is happening ...' is committed only to persons, times, and states. But all this shows is that topic neutralism is committed to the monadic thesis. Surely, one needs independent grounds for supposing pains are virtual before accepting topic neutralism. Once such grounds are laid, one can go on to claim that identifying mental phenomena amounts to identifying such states as being-in-pain. But the result about logical form must come first. Indeed, one might accept topic

[10] 'Mental Entities', in L. Foster and J. Swanson, eds. *Experience and Theory* (U. of Massachusetts Press: 1970), pp. 79–101.

[11] *The Ways of Paradox*, 2nd ed. (Harvard U. Press, Cambridge, Mass.: 1976), p. 226.

neutralism and the identification of the pain-state with a brain state, and yet maintain that the pain itself is a non-physical particular. Such a position is untenable only if pains can be shown, on independent grounds, to be virtual.

The main argument for the monadic thesis is the familiar observation that there cannot conceivably be an unexperienced pain.[12] If pains (etc.) were entities, and the logical form of 'x is in pain' were $P(x,y)$, pains would have to be non-physical things, for there are surely no physical things whose *esse* is *percipi*. But this moves in the wrong direction. Given Hume's law that no two distinct things can be necessarily connected, not even a non-physical entity can logically require the awareness of it. Whatever x is, x is one thing and the awareness of x another; so the existence of x cannot entail awareness of x. The plea that pains are non-physical and hence very mysterious will not circumvent Hume's law. That *esse* is *percipi* for pains shows, not that pains are unusual entities, but that pains are not entities at all:[13] a pain must be collapsed into the awareness of it.

The existence or possibility of unconscious ('unfelt') pain does not show the connection between pains and awareness of them to be merely contingent. All the phenomenon of unconscious pain shows is that one may *be in pain* without being aware that one is in pain. It does not follow that there can be *pains* that no one is aware of. Unconscious pains, if there are such things, do not threaten the monadic thesis, and indeed ascriptions of unconscious pain presumably have the same *logical form* as standard pain ascriptions.

It is sometimes claimed that x cannot feel y's pain. Philosophers dispute about the truth or significance of this claim: it seems to me best taken as reinforcement for the *esse* is *percipi* argument. If x were to experience y's pain, x's experience would be a different one from y's. If, furthermore, the numerical difference in their experiences entails a difference in the pain felt, x's pain is not an existence distinct from (what we ordinarily call) x's awareness of his pain. If x was aware of his pain as he is of a car, it could only be contingent

[12] Cf. T. Nagel, 'Physicalism', in Rosenthal, ed., *Materialism and the Mind-Body Problem*, pp. 96–111.

[13] D. Pears, for example, is unclear on this (see his *Wittgenstein* (Viking, N.Y.: 1970), chapter VIII). He rebukes the view that sensations could, like physical objects, be misidentified, for 'treating sensations as more like physical objects than they actually are'. But he never decides whether this shows sensations to be *non*-physical objects, or simply not objects at all.

that his pain was or could not be an object of public scrutiny. That x is aware of a car cannot *entail* that no one else is aware of it.

This argument is only reinforcing because the entailment from difference of experience to difference of object might be questioned. Perhaps someone else *could* experience my pain; or it could be *stipulated* that certain situations count as 'two experiences of the same pain' (e.g. if we both felt a twinge in the same arm when it was pinched). Both suggestions are fraught with difficulties,[14] but these difficulties need not detain us. For even if y could experience x's pain, it would only follow that x's pain is logically independent of x's awareness of it; it would not follow that x's pain could exist altogether unexperienced. Hume's law would still dictate the elimination of pain in favour of the state of being in pain.

The present account is committed to saying that the necessity of 'no pain without awareness of it' is a product of the linguistic fact that talk about a pain is a way of talking about the awareness. But doesn't this put the cart before the horse? Perhaps the fact that pains cannot exist unsensed is a synthetic necessary truth revealed to intuition through familiarity with pain. It sometimes seems to be a *fact* that there is a little glowing something inside us which simply cannot exist without our being aware of it. Isn't it question-begging to say on the basis of Hume's law that this *cannot happen*, that it is an illusion generated by a misunderstood linguistic convention? Surely our belief that pains cannot exist unsensed comes from our encounters with *pain*. True, we might not call anything a 'pain' unless it were like this glowing something in that its existence entailed awareness; in that sense 'no pain without awareness' might be a convention. But the existence of the glowing somethings which give the core use of 'pain' would not be a convention. Just asserting that 'no pain without awareness' is a disguised tautology accomplishes nothing without a convincing display of the tautology it disguises.

The problem lies in expanding '*esse* is *percipi* for pain' as 'pain p cannot exist without awareness *of* p'. This formulation, by specifying the awareness p requires in terms of p itself, suggests that p is independently specifiable and hence that the truth it formulates is

[14] Concerning the second: would the stipulation that any misfit be called a 'square circle' show that there could be square circles? The strategy of stipulation leads to the absurd conclusion that any logical incoherence can be trivially rectified. (Also see V.2.)

synthetic. This formulation is in any case objectionable because it generates an infinite regress: if p requires awareness of p, p requires awareness of (awareness of p), ... *ad infinitum*. So we must drop the assumption that p is the object of the awareness with which p is necessarily connected. This done, '*esse* is *percipi* for pain' means simply 'there cannot be pain without awareness'. The impossibility of pain without awareness can now be explained by saying that *the pain is the awareness*. More fully: the awareness p cannot exist without is the *awareness of something unpleasant*; and this is so because 'x is in pain' is another way of saying 'x is aware of something unpleasant'. The object of the 'accompanying' awareness is a bodily part, or external object or event. 'There cannot be a pain unless $(\exists x)$ (someone is aware of x & x is unpleasant)' is the definitional truth we need, and 'no awareness without awareness' is the tautology '*esse* is *percipi* for pain' disguises. True, 'awareness of pain' also has a non-tautological use, one that plays an important role in the discussion of privacy in V.1. But the sense of 'awareness of pain' at issue here is the one in which it is logically impossible for a pain to exist without awareness of pain. In that sense, the 'of' is the 'of' of constitution, the 'of' in 'a meal of roast beef and potatoes'. 'Awareness of pain' can also mean 'being aware that one is in pain'. In this sense one can be aware of one's pain as an object. But that is not the sense at issue here.

There are many ways of being aware of one's foot (say) that do not make for pain; hence 'x is in pain' must be construed as $(\exists y)$ (x is aware of y & y is unpleasant). It is pointless to complain that this expression circularly reintroduces the psychological notion of unpleasantness as a property of the object of awareness. The monadic thesis is not out to eliminate pain, only to circumscribe the logical form of sentences mentioning it. It is not a thesis about what painfulness or unpleasantness are, just about what it is that is painful or unpleasant. By explicating 'x has a pain in his foot' as 'x's foot is hurting him', the materialist does not avoid the notion of hurtfulness; but he does bring into relief what he wants to claim is physical: the state of being bothered by one's foot.

The monadic thesis has no trouble expressing or accounting for the fact that pains are located. Suppose I have a pain in my foot. Since it is my foot that I am aware of, it is no wonder that a description of my mental state refers to my foot. 'My foot' answers 'Where is your pain?' because it answers 'what is bothering you?' The monadic thesis renders 'Why do we locate some pains in the foot?' as the innocuous question 'Why does one's foot sometimes hurt one?' The answer to that is that we sometimes step on nails. The question 'Why do we locate pains in the foot' may be intended phenomenologically: 'Why does it sometimes feel as if my foot is hurting me? Why is the pain felt as being in *my foot*?' (There may be the accompanying suggestion that the monadic thesis leaves these phenomena inexplicable.) But answering these questions is as unproblematic as answering: 'Why does it sometimes feel as if my foot is in water? Why does it sometimes feel as if it is *my foot* that is wet?' The answer to the latter is that sometimes my foot *is* in water. Similarly, the answer to the former is that sometimes my foot *does* hurt me. A final question that the monadic thesis seems to leave begging is, 'Why do we think of pains as *things in* parts of the body?' But this is just a special case of the problem of why, in general, pains are reified beyond their status as virtual. Perhaps no one knows the answer to this: but so long as the monadic thesis can make good sense of legitimate talk of the location of pains—talk not already hostage to false metaphysics—this is not a matter the monadic thesis is required to explain.

The monadic thesis guides materialism around other standard objections. PL relativized to states requires that, given materialism, every property of mental states must be possessed by the appropriate physical states, and vice versa. Many writers cite properties that are said to apply to mental states but not to the appropriate physical states. The monadic thesis diagnoses these objections as mistakes about what the cited properties actually apply to. Consider again the location of pain. My backache is in my back, but the materialist identifies it with a brain state. How can something in my *back* be a state of my *brain*?[15] But what the materialist identifies as a brain state is not the pain, but my awareness of my back. If there were such a thing as the pain, it would be in my back and nothing elsewhere could be identical to it; but my *awareness* of my back need not be in my back, and can be identified with something situated elsewhere.

Or consider this well-known passage from Cornman:

> [W]e can talk about intense, unbearable, nagging, or throbbing pains. And yellow, dim, fading or circular after-images. . . . On the other hand

[15] Thus A. Collins, 'The Objects of Perceptual Consciousness in Philosophical Thought', *Social Research*, xl. 1 (Spring 1973), 166.

> we can also discuss publicly observable, spatially located, swift, irreversible physical processes. Thus if the Identity Theory is correct, it seems that we should sometimes be able to say truthfully that physical processes such as brain processes are dim or fading or nagging or false. . . . However, there surely is some doubt about whether these expressions can be truthfully used.[16]

Cornman assumes that 'is fading' is predicated of after-images, and that it is after-images the materialist says are brain states (or processes). But there is in fact no such thing as the after-image to be fading. One has after-images, and it is the state of having after-images which the materialist takes to be a brain state (or process). The state is not fading, nor need what it is identical with be fading either.

Cornman and Lehrer argue elsewhere[17] that if one's backache is identified with the firing of neural fibres, one must say (absurdly) that one's neural fibres ache. K. Campbell[18] gives this argument an extra twist: even if backaches are neural processes, achiness is a *phenomenal* property of backache-neural processes. Backaches may be physical, but the status of the backache-property achiness remains a problem for the materialist. Both arguments rest on the false assumptions (which are really two facets of a single mistake about logical form) that (i) what the materialist thinks is physical is the backache, and (ii) backaches are what have the property of achiness. What aches when one has a backache is one's back. The materialist knows this full well; what he says is the firing of neural fibres is the state of having an aching back. He is not committed to saying that neural fibres ache.

Campbell's twist recalls the double-aspect theory. It is hard to be sure about just what are the private aspect properties that advocates of the double-aspect theory like Bernstein suppose mental states to have, but certainly 'hurting intensely' or 'appearing hurtfully' is such a property of pain. If so, mental states do not have the properties ascribed to them by the double-aspect theory. What hurts a man with a backache is his back; if you will, his back 'appears hurtfully' to him. These are not properties of his awareness of his back. The double-aspect theorist might reply that the state of being aware of

[16] 'The Identity of Mind and Body', in Rosenthal, ed., *Materialism and the Mind-Body Problem*, p. 77.

[17] *Philosophical Problems and Arguments*, pp. 308–9.

[18] *Body and Mind*, pp. 104 ff.

one's back has private-aspect properties (although it is now not easy to see what they could be). Thus T. Nagel asks, rhetorically: 'Does it make sense . . . to ask what my experiences are *really* like, as opposed to how they appear to me?' and he remarks, in the same context, 'It is difficult to understand what could be meant by the *objective* character of an experience, apart from the particular point of view from which its subject apprehends it'.[19] This idea, that our ordinary relation to our mental states is to be aware of them or 'apprehend' them, rests on misreading the 'of' of identity in, say, 'awareness of pain'. If *A* has a backache, *A* is not, usually, *aware of* his awareness of his back, and it is pointless to ask how his awareness of his back appears to him. The appearance properties of his backache cannot be found in his awareness of his back hurting him, for there usually is no such awareness. True, one cannot be in pain without being aware. Misreading the 'of' here as the object-taking 'of' suggests that one cannot be in pain without being aware of being in pain. This step taken, it is then natural to ask how being in pain appears, and to posit special private-aspect properties for being in pain. Granted, one will take note of such facts as that one is in pain in moments of introspective self-consciousness. But these are special cases that do not justify bestowing private aspects on *all* cases of awareness. (I return in V.1 to awareness of one's awareness, and whether it presents any obstacles to materialism.)

Materialists themselves sometimes forget that the proper subjects of psychological ascription are persons, not mental entities, and concede more than they have to. Thus Smart:

> So I must agree that if sensations are brain processes and sensations are nostalgic, then some brain processes are nostalgic. This sounds an odd thing to say, but oddness is not the same as falsity. . . . Paul Feyerabend may be right in his contention that common sense is invincibly dualistic, and that common sense introspective reports are couched in the framework of a dualistic conceptual scheme [which resists locutions that may have to be countenanced].[20]

Such contortions are unnecessary. To say that I am having a nostalgic sensation is to say that *I* am being nostalgic. It is not to ascribe a property to the sensation. What nostalgia is identified with need not

[19] 'What it is Like to be a Bat', pp. 443, 448.

[20] 'Comments on the Papers', in Presley, ed., *The Identity Theory of Mind*, pp. 87, 91. Also see J. Schaffer, 'Could Mental States be Brain Processes?' *Journal of Philosophy*, lviii. 26 (Dec. 1961), 816 ff. In V.1 I look more closely at the thesis that languages can have biases.

be nostalgic. Error may be encouraged by the grammatical similarity between 'sensation of nostalgia' and 'sensation of being watched'. Being watched is one thing, the sensation of being watched another. But the sensation of nostalgia is nostalgia itself.

A group of objections to materialism that reverse the direction of those just canvassed begins with the remark that materialism entails that mental states have all the properties of brain states. It is then claimed that among the properties of brain states are spatial properties that cannot be assigned to mental states. It is said, for example, that thoughts have no spatial location; since brain processes do, the two cannot be identical. And, again, some materialists have taken the bait and suggested that a new linguistic rule might be introduced to the effect that 'a mental state is located in that place where its corresponding [brain state] is located' (Schaffer, loc. cit.). Such manœuvres are again unnecessary, and the objection is fallacious. Processes have no spatial location; so thoughts need have none even if they are brain processes. Objects are what have spatial location. It is nerve cells, not brain processes or states, that have locations. A process *can* be assigned the location of its constituents, but this is an extension of the word 'location' as it is used when denied application to thoughts, One *need* not ascribe location to either a brain process or the mental process it is identified with. The idea that materialism must ascribe location to mental states may be due to the error, by now familiar, of supposing that it is the identity of mental entities like sensations that it is in question. Entities like nerve cells are located, and mental *entities* would have to be identified with physical entities. But the materialist is not staking a claim about mental entities at all.

Similar remarks apply to motion. Cornman says that materialism entails 'mental phenomena are swift'.[21] B. Blanshard puts the difficulty more fully:

> [T]he experience of pain . . . is self-evidently *not* the same as a physical movement of any kind. That their identification is a confusion can be shown in various ways. First their properties are different: if a pain were any kind of physical motion, we could ask what its direction and velocity were, whereas it makes no sense to talk of the direction or velocity of a toothache.[22]

[21] In Rosenthal, ed., *Materialism and the Mind-Body Problem*, p. 77.

[22] 'The Problem of Consciousness', *Philosophy and Phenomenological Research*, xxvii. 3 (Mar. 1967), 318–19.

Blanshard is erroneously ascribing to motion a property that applies to objects. Motions do not literally have direction or velocity, although this way of speaking can be given a derivative sense: it is objects that move with one or another velocity in or one another direction. Particles, not motions, move swiftly. So the claim that having a toothache is a motion of particles does not entail that having a toothache moves. It is the particles whose motion the toothache is that move.

These reflections also assist the materialist past the objection that sensations are phenomenologically uniform—how then can they be millions of spinning electrons?[23] But a process itself can easily exhibit a uniformity and stability its constituents lack.

4. Topic Neutralism, 1

The monadic thesis should be supplemented by an explanation of the predicates occurring within monadic psychological ascriptions. The difference between the two pain-ascriptions 'x has a P-pain' and 'x has a Q-pain' must, presumably, correspond to different properties of the states of awareness in whose favour the P-pain and the Q-pain are analytically eliminated (and ultimately to differences in the brain-states these awarenesses are identified with). The monadic thesis has an easy time with some ascriptions. Parsing 'I have a pain in my foot' as 'my foot hurts' preserves and explains the reference to the foot. 'Nostalgic' in 'A is having a nostalgic sensation' is explained as applying to A himself. This suggests the general strategy of finding something that P characterizes literally when providing the semantics for ascriptions of P-ish sensations. (The materialist is not obligated to explain how P came to be misplaced.) The 'yellow' in 'I am having a yellow after-image' is trickier, since I am not yellow. Here the pressure is greatest to reintroduce after-images or the property of phenomenal yellowness. The pressure is not merely linguistic. There is something phenomenologically yellowish about a yellow after-image. Some philosophers express this by talk of 'being appeared to yellowly',[24] and the difference between 'yellowly' and 'greenly' cries out for explanation.

The standard materialist response to this problem is topic neutralism, the thesis, roughly, that 'I sense a yellow after-image'

[23] Cf. W. Sellars, 'Philosophy and the Scientific Image of Man', in *Science, Perception and Reality* (Routledge & Kegan Paul, London: 1963), p. 35.

[24] R. Chisholm, *Perceiving* (Cornell U. Press, Ithaca: 1957).

amounts to 'It is as if I were seeing something yellow'. The yellowness in the description of the after-image is explained as inherited from the yellowness of perceived yellow objects. Pressure to adopt topic neutralism is also exerted by Wittgenstein's obscure but suggestive argument against the possibility of a 'private language'. If, as has been thought, Wittgenstein has shown the idea of 'mental states' to be ill-formed, materialism becomes a thesis without a subject-matter. Topic neutralism, which urges a public translation for talk of private states, offers hope of reconciling the reality of private states with what is legitimate in Wittgenstein's animadversions against them.

More fully, topic neutralism is that the claim that

(a) I am having a yellow after-image

and

(b) I have a sharp pain in my hand

stand in a relation *R* to

(a′) Something is going on like what goes on when I see a lemon

and

(b′) Something is going on like what goes on when my hand is jabbed by a pin.

Proponents of topic neutralism standardly interpret *R* as synonymy, or analytic equivalence, but we will see in section 5 that so interpreting *R* renders topic neutralism implausible. I will then suggest a weaker interpretation of *R* that suits the materialist's purposes. Leaving *R* unspecified for now, let us say that a′ = *R*(a) and b′ = *R*(b). All the topic neutralist needs for now is that, if $x = R(y)$, y 'says no more' than x, and all occurrences of y are replaceable by x However, I will, for expository convenience, sometimes refer to the 'topic neutral analysis' of psychological statements

This promissory note to one side, the thrust of topic neutralism is clear. Monadic psychological ascriptions are explained by (their bearing *R* to) descriptions of events in the public world. What a man is aware of when he notices that he is in pain is (ιx) (x happens when e), where e is a public event. This may, for all this, be a non-physical private event, but that is not required by how we describe it. 'I am in pain' is neutral as to the kind of event being in pain is, since it is (R^{-1} of) a description using only physicalistic expressions.

R(b) leaves the ultimate satisfaction condition for '*x* is in pain' an open question for empirical science to answer. The materialist of course expects, because of the plausibility arguments of section 1, that science will determine that it is a brain process.

Commonsense reflection on how children learn to use 'pain' (our stalking-horse for psychological ascriptions generally) supports topic neutralism. A child first encounters 'pain' when his parents notice that he is aware of some bodily damage. He impales himself on a splinter and his mother commiserates, 'Oh, how that must hurt.' A didactic parent might injure him and announce, '*That* is being in pain.' A child learns pain in terms of events involving injury to his body; this suggests that, at least initially, the referential force of 'pain' is closely tied with that of 'what goes on when [public event]'. The child eventually notices that what goes on when he impales himself on a splinter may happen in the absence of splinters, and that this, too, is called 'being in pain' by his linguistic community.[25]

An event of a certain description may cue *A* to say 'I am in pain' even if *A* does not use this description as his reason, ground, or criterion for saying 'I am in pain', and even if *A* does not realize that his cue fits this description. 'Pain', when used by *A*, can refer to what goes on when ... without *A*'s realizing that this is what he is referring to. He is trained to say or assent to 'I am in pain' when a certain event occurs. It may require an outsider to discover what description an event must fit to elicit this response from *A*.

Since language teacher *B* has no direct control over internal events, how can *B* know that what language learner *A* finds similar to what goes on when he, *A*, is jabbed by a pin, is what *B* finds similar to what goes on when he, *B*, is jabbed by a pin? If *B* has to trust that *A*'s sense of similarity is sufficiently like his own, hasn't the present account foundered on a version of the problem of other minds? No, because all language-learning and conditioning, even those aspects of them having nothing to do with inner states, presuppose this pre-established harmony. Mathematics would be impossible if

[25] This is substantially Skinner's picture: '[Introspective] terms are established as part of a repetoire when the individual is behaving publicly. Private stimuli, generated in addition to public manifestations, then gain the necessary degree of control. Later when these private stimuli occur alone, the individual may respond to them. "I was on the point of going home" may be regarded as the equivalent of "I observed events in myself which characteristically precede or accompany my going home." [Apparently anticipating the requirement of topic neutrality, Skinner adds:] What these events are, such an explanation does not say.' *Science and Human Behavior* (Macmillan, N.Y.: 1953), p. 262.

children had no innate tendency to apply mathematical rules the same way in new circumstances.[26] If people did not tend to agree about what familiar objects a new object is similar to, language would be impossible.[27] Language is possible because evolution has shaped us to agree about what is similar to what. *B*'s assumption that *A* spontaneously generalizes his, *A*'s, conditioning stimuli as *B* does is a special case of an assumption that must be made, not only by any teacher of a word, but by any account of human linguistic competence. It is no objection to topic neutralism that topic neutralism must make it.

The remarks of the last few pages rest heavily on a stimulus-response model of learning 'pain'. Hasn't it been *proved* that the stimulus-response model cannot explain language acquisition? Hardly. There are some arguments purporting to prove that there can be no stimulus-response explanation for the acquisition of the *syntax* of natural languages; these arguments are examined in VI.4. Such arguments do not even address the acquisition of semantical abilities, and do not have the least tendency to show that terms and predicates cannot be taught through a programme of conditioning.

A number of contemporary positions are versions of topic neutralism, understood sufficiently broadly. D. Lewis, for example, holds that *R* ('I have a headache') is 'I am in whatever state has the causes and effects ascribed to headaches in the commonsense "theory" linking headaches to other physical and psychological states'.[28] Lewis, like Smart, takes *R* to be synonymy. This 'causal role' account agrees with the topic neutral claim that talk of headaches is talk about *whatever* comes sufficiently close to playing a certain causal role describable in physicalistic language, and bears physicalistically or topic-neutrally describable relations to other physicalistically or topic-neutrally describable states. This account is sometimes considered a 'functional state' approach (Rosenthal so lists it in the table of contents of his anthology), but such a classification is

[26] Cf. L. Wittgenstein, *Remarks on the Foundations of Mathematics*, trans. G. Anscombe, eds. G. H. von Wright, R. Rhees, G. Anscombe (Blackwell, Oxford: 1956); A. Heyting, *Intuitionism*, 3rd ed. (North-Holland, Amsterdam: 1971).

[27] Cf. Quine, 'Natural Kinds', in *Ontological Relativity* (Columbia U.P., N.Y.: 1969).

[28] 'An Argument for the Identity Thesis', in Rosenthal, ed., *Materialism and the Mind–Body Problem*, pp. 162–71.

misleading. Even if Lewis's claim is understood as 'headaches are whatever has the functional role psychological theory assigns headaches', the functional role intended is an interpreted causal role. As we will see in section 6, the functional state theory of Fodor and Putnam conceives a 'functional role' to be specified by a set of uninterpreted relations. The only difference between the Lewis and Smart approaches is in the degree of complexity of their topic neutral descriptions of mental states. Smart, at least in his earlier publications,[29] takes *R* ('talk of pain') to be talk of whatever it is that results from one typical cause of pain. For Lewis, pains can be individuated only by their place in a network of causal relations. This difference is much less than that between Lewis's view and the view that pains are individuated by their place in a network of abstract relations. Confusion is abetted by the fact that the functional state theory *is* a version of topic neutralism: it takes *R* ('I have a headache') to be 'I have whatever has the role assigned to headaches in abstract headache theory'. It agrees with Lewis that psychological states are individuated by their role in a network.

There is, furthermore, an obvious common link between the views of both Lewis and Smart and the Ramseyan account of theoretical terms. For the Ramseyan, the meaning of a theoretical term t of a theory $T(t)$ is given by the role of t in $T(t)$. 'Electron', for example, means 'whatever it is, if anything, that bears all the relations to observable phenomena and other posits that electron theory says electrons do'. The Ramseyan takes 'electron' to mean '$(\iota x)T(x)$', and, word magic aside, the statement that electrons exist to mean '$(\exists x)T(x)$'. Similarly, for both Lewis and Smart *R* ('being in pain') is '$(\iota x)T'(x)$', where T' is a more (Lewis) or less (Smart) elaborate account of the causal role being in pain plays. To say that there are pains is to say $(\exists x)T'(x)$.[30]

It is time to return to the problem that motivated topic neutralism: its account of what is yellow in yellow after-images. To begin with, one can distinguish two cases in which something is going on like what goes on when I see a lemon. One is when I *am* seeing a lemon.

[29] See n. 30 below.

[30] Lewis advocates a Ramseyan approach to theories in 'How to Define Theoretical Terms', *Journal of Philosophy*, lxvii. 13 (July 1970), 427–46. Smart's recent version of topic neutralism, 'Reports of Immediate Experience', *Synthese*, xxii. 3/4 (May 1971), 346–59 is close to Lewis's Ramseyan version. Smart is hard on Ramsey sentences in *Between Science and Philosophy* (Random House, N.Y.: 1968), 145–7, but only in so far as they are thought to aid instrumentalism.

In that case, what I am aware of is a lemon, which is yellow. But (a′) may also hold when I am not seeing a lemon. In that case, I am not seeing anything, although I may think I am seeing a lemon. What I am reporting when I say (a′) is that it is as if I were seeing a yellow lemon. The yellow thing involved in having a yellow after-image is the lemon; 'yellow' appears in (a) because what is going on when (a) holds goes on when a yellow object is seen. There is no need to postulate a yellow interior object of awareness or a phenomenal yellowness to explain the 'yellow' in (a).[31] In fact, topic neutralism is a linguistic explication of the Kantian thesis that outer experience is primary and a necessary condition for inner experience.

The relation of topic neutralism to the privacy of experience has occasioned much confusion. It has been claimed that topic neutralism cannot explain, or is incompatible with, the privileged access we have to our own mental states. The issue of privacy is complex, and will be treatedly separately in V.1. It is easier to correct the converse misunderstanding that topic neutralism is incompatible with our sensing public objects, permitting only internal states to be objects of immediate experience. Thus P. Herbst writes: 'Smart . . . refers to the object of immediate awareness as something which goes on in one. . . . This puts Smart in the same camp as Berkeley. . . . Smart has to hold that we experience experiences'.[32] It has even been suggested that topic neutralism leads to solipsism.[33] This misunderstanding can be cleared up with the reflection that two different awarenesses are involved in judgements like (a) and *R*(a). There is, first, my awareness of the lemon. Now in order to judge that something is going on like what goes on when I am aware of a lemon, I have, on occasion, to be aware of this first awareness; so there is, second, my awareness of my awareness of a lemon.[34] It is not clear that I cannot have both kinds of awareness, namely awarenesses of

[31] Cf. U. T. Place's discussion of the 'phenomenological fallacy' in 'Is Consciousness a Brain Process?' in *The Philosophy of Mind*, ed. V. Chappel (Prentice-Hall, N.J.: 1962), pp. 101–9.

[32] Presley, ed., *The Identity Theory of Mind*, p. 53.

[33] '[The topic neutral] program certainly does face the question that *if* the immediate object of my awareness in perception is always [*sic*] an inner activity, then what justifies my claims about any other things . . . ?' (Collins, 'Objects of Perceptual Consciousness', pp. 164–5).

[34] 'To be aware of the sensation of blue is *not* to be aware of a mental image. . . . It is to be aware of an awareness of blue'; G. E. Moore, 'The Refutation of Idealism', in M. Weitz, ed., *Twentieth Century Philosophy: The Analytic Tradition* (Free Press, N.Y.: 1961), p. 30.

lemons and awarenesses of those first awarenesses. Herbst fosters confusion and begs questions when he refers to '*the* object of immediate awareness', as if a man can be aware of only one kind of thing, as if the issue of what things a man could be aware of comes down to choosing between lemons and awarenesses of lemons. But nothing in fact or logic requires this. Let it be granted that any single awareness can have only one immediate object: if *a* is an awareness, the immediate object of *a* can be at most one of {a lemon, an awareness of a lemon}. This does not show that if the object of *a* is a lemon, there cannot be *another* awareness *a'* whose object is *a* itself. It is the latter sort of awareness one has when one notices that one is noticing a lemon, or one notices that it is now just as it was when one noticed a lemon. The existence of such reflexive mental states is compatible with the existence of outwardly directed states. It is salutary to fix on ordinary examples. We have all ridden buses, and when one rides a bus the object of immediate awareness is the bus and its lurching ride. But it is just in virtue of having ridden buses and having paid attention to their ride that we all know what it is like to ride a bus. The fact that if somebody tampered with our brains, we could tell when he induced in us the experience of riding a bus, does not mean that no one has ever been immediately aware of a bus ride.

I remarked that Herbst's point seems plausible if one conflates the awarenesses *a* and *a'*. An ambiguity in 'awareness' facilitates this conflation. The paradigm of one sense of 'awareness' is the awareness one has of a lemon before one's eyes: this is the kind of awareness *a* is—direct conscious encounter. On the other hand, 'awareness' may mean simply 'being apprised of'. Thus we say 'I became aware that others depended on me [or: of the emptiness of my life]'. *a'* exemplifies this latter sort of awareness. Assuming that the awareness of being aware of a lemon is an awareness of the *former* sort leads one to think that there is only one awareness involved, because the awareness of the lemon is of the former sort. One will then regard the lemon and the lemon awareness as incompatible candidates for the title 'object of awareness'.

There is no difficulty in holding that both *a* and *a'* are brain states. The materialist holds that noticing a lemon is a brain state, in some causal relation to a lemon. One sometimes notices that one is noticing a lemon or in a state like that of noticing a lemon. This is a more sophisticated noticing, and for the materialist, just a more sophisticated brain state: causally related to the first brain state. This topic is treated more fully in V.1.

I said something earlier about the acquisition of the first-person psychological vocabulary, and I will return to this topic in section 5. Certain points bear stressing here. There is no mystery about how I can learn to use such expressions as 'something is going on like what goes on when I see a lemon'. All I have to do is remember having seen a lemon. It is no more puzzling that I can get to know about and be trained to identify events involving myself than that I can get to know about and be trained to identify anything else. But the double aspect theorist might claim that the distinction I have made between an awareness of a lemon and an awareness of that awareness places a point of leverage at his disposal. I am admitting, even insisting, that people are sometimes aware of their mental states. Perhaps how these second-order awarenesses appear to their owners differs from how these awarenesses appear to outsiders. Even if seeing a lemon is a brain state, there is surely a difference between my view of my lemon-seeing experience and your view of it. True—but this does not show that the difference cannot be explained physicalistically. There is certainly a physical difference between us: I am hooked up to the nervous system in the lemon-seeing state. Prospects for such an explanation brighten with the reflection that the difference is not that my lemon-seeing experience looks yellow to me but not to you. We have long since disqualified all such 'standard' phenomenal properties as applying to lemon-seeings. But how then does one know, persists the double aspect theorist, when to call an internal state 'a lemon-seeing state'? There must be *some* descriptive property which justifies our use of the referring phrase, and perhaps this property is phenomenal. This worry is related to the view that referring terms must be logically linked with descriptions. I have begun chipping away at this by stressing that one can be trained to use a referring expression—such as 'what goes on when I see a lemon'—even if one does not notice the property which distinguishes its referent. I may use such an expression without using any descriptive backing. All that is needed, I think, to dislodge the double aspect theory altogether is a general account of the use of referring expressions which dispenses with the idea that they are disguised descriptions, and which applies to psychological language. I discuss such an account in section 5. If successful, it shows that our ability to refer to our awarenesses gives the double aspect theorist no reason to postulate phenomenal properties to explain how we do it.

Before turning to these topics, however, I want to show how the topic neutral analysis of perceptual reports treats the most recalcitrant intuition of phenomenalism, and provides a more adequate (and traditional) dissolution of phenomenalism than is customary in the post-Austinian literature. This success further confirms topic neutralism itself, and completes an argument promised on p. 67.

There is an empirical fact that will not go away however much one deplores the obscurities of sense-data discourse; it is this empirical fact phenomenalists take to show that all we really perceive are the contents of private sense fields. Consider the following arrangement. I first look at a bent stick. It is surely empirically possible that I then be brought face to face with a straight stick so placed (in a laboratory, say) that it looks *exactly* like the bent stick. I view a scene which, while not containing a bent stick, reflects light so that the same pattern of radiation strikes my eyes as struck my eyes when I saw the bent stick. Austin remarks[35] that a straight stick in water doesn't really look very much like a bent stick, but these two cases sidestep that complaint. Now, the fact that the phenomenalist seizes is that something about my experience is *exactly the same* in the two cases. It must be granted, I think, that this is so. It is this fact the phenomenalist is relying one when he introduces the generic word 'perception' for all perceptual consciousness, and when he speaks of both the cases described above as 'bent-stick-seeing experiences'. It is this fact the phenomenalist takes to show that, as he puts it, there is no intrinsic difference between veridical and non-veridical perception. (Suppose a brain scanner records the state of my brain when I see a barn. Here is the phenomenalist's fact *sans* illusion: if that information is used to reproduce that state in me when I am in a laboratory, I will (probably) lapse into the same conscious state I was in when I saw the barn. It is this state the phenomenalist calls a 'barn-seeing experience'.)

The realist must not simply deny this locution makes sense, as Austin does when he tasks the phenomenalist (in the person of Ayer) for not explaining what 'perception' means when he uses it to cover both veridical and non-veridical perception.[36] The phenomenalist can give the explanation I have just offered. The realist must give

[35] *Sense and Sensibilia*, ed. G. Warnock (O.U.P., Oxford: 1964), p. 29.
[36] Ibid., p. 47.

a satisfactory account on his own terms of this locution and its relation to the phenomenalist's prized fact. The clue is that the phenomenalist's 'perception' is a natural candidate for topic neutral analysis. What the phenomenalist intends to designate by it is whatever it is about me that is invariant in the two cases outlined. He nominalizes the fact that something is invariant by describing it as 'what is the same in the two cases'. This description is topic neutral, fitting the pattern given on p. 102. ('What went on both when I saw the barn and in the laboratory' is similarly topic neutral.) And what it is a topic neutral description *of* is a state of a percipient.

The realist uses this clue to argue as follows. The phenomenalist may be right that something about a fraudulent-stick perceiver is exactly the same as something about a bent-stick-perceiver. The transition to sense-data and private sense fields comes when the phenomenalist expresses this fact by saying that what the perceiver *perceived* both times is the same. Once this is granted, PL entails that the perceiver did not perceive a bent stick during the so-called veridical perception. But the phenomenalist is not entitled to this crucial step. He may be correct in saying that the *state* of the perceiver is the same in both cases; but it does not follow that *what* the perceiver *sees* in both cases is the same. 'A sees x' expresses a dyadic relation between perceiver A and object x, and it is a *non sequitur* to conclude that two things in the same state, perceptual or any other, bear the same relations to the same things. The phenomenalist's inference is as fallacious as concluding that two things in the same state must be *above* the same things. The phenomenalist is not entitled to a thesis about the objects of perception, even if he is entitled to one about the states of perceivers. He has, in traditional terminology, confused act and object; the 'act' being whatever is the same for veridical and non-veridical perceivers, the object being what they perceive.[37] A man may at time t see a bent stick and, at time $t' \neq t$, be in precisely the same state and see nothing at all. The phenomenalist might reply that a description of a state as a *perceptual* state must include reference to the object of perception. If he does, he has himself recast the empirical fact to be that my *states of consciousness* are the same in the two cases before us. Given

[37] See Moore. Russell blatantly confuses act and object in his 'Reply to Nagel': 'My seeing is certainly an event in me, though Mr Nagel is deeply shocked when I say that what I see is in me' (*The Philosophy of Bertrand Russell*, ed. P. Schillp (Harper & Row, N.Y.: 1944), p. 704).

the phenomenalist his (new) usage, it is an act/object confusion to infer that two identical states of consciousness are the same *perceptual* states.

When the smoke has cleared from this skirmish, the realist has gained ground. There was always something disingenuous about his protest that he did not know what the phenomenalist was talking about when the phenomenalist said that veridical and non-veridical perceptions have something in common. The realist can now accept what the phenomenalist has to say. The fact that the phenomenalist's 'perceptions' describe states blocks the inference to a community of objects of perception. Since these descriptions are topic neutral, conceding them to the phenomenalist does not *ipso facto* give him anything private or phenomenal. The realist can absorb everything the phenomenalist has a right to claim.

Construing 'what is the same ...' as a topic neutral description of a state allows the realist to concede the logical possibility that we are all in perceptual states appropriate to the perception of objects even though no one has ever seen anything. The realist claims: (x) $(x$ is seen $\supset x$ exists independently of minds). The realist's assimilation of legitimate phenomenalist talk has not compromised this, since the phenomenalist's point turned out not to concern what is seen. But his claim does not commit the realist to the conclusion that we ever do see anything. Why should he want to concede this? It may seem odd that realism should stand to win yet more ground from phenomenalism by being consistent with the non-existence of the external world, but this is the logic of the situation. The existence of a world beyond our perceptual states cannot be read off from these states themselves. It is logically possible for perceptions to exist without their objects. For various reasons, this fact is often thought to be especially consilient with phenomenalism.[38] But it now appears that realism is equally consilient with this fact. The realist can agree with the phenomenalist that you cannot read off from perceptual states whether they have any objects (all the while insisting that if they do, these objects are inhabitants of a public world). This agreement is now possible because the realist has an account of perceptual states that does not make commitments about the nature or reality of their objects. This is what the topic neutral analysis of perceptual states provides.

It is natural to object that R ('I am having a barn-seeing

[38] See e.g. A. Danto, *What Philosophy Is* (Harper & Row, N.Y.: 1968).

experience'), its topic neutral explication, has the seeing of barns, and thus barns, built into it: for it is 'what goes on when I *see a barn*'. This analysis apparently implies that successful use of a perception-description requires that I did see a barn, and hence that the construal of 'perception' I am giving the realist entails the existence of the external world. Didn't I say on p. 106 that topic neutralism is Kantianism writ linguistically? This may be so if *R* is synonymy, but not if, as I argue in the section 5, *R* is reference-fixing. The reference of a term can be fixed by a non-referring description.[39] The reference of 'bent stick perception' can be fixed by 'what goes on when I see a bent stick' even if I have never seen a bent stick, even if there are no bent sticks to be seen. In Kantian terms, the topic neutral thesis agrees that the *concept* of the inner presupposes the *concept* of the outer; but this by itself is no 'refutation of idealism'.

J. Hinton[40] argues, against this defence of 'experiences', that purported reports of the common element in actually seeing a barn and being so illuded turn out to be just the disjunction itself, 'Either [*A*] I am seeing a barn or [*B*] I am so illuded.' ($A \vee B$, for example, is entailed by both *A* and *B*.) Hinton rejects the suggestion that we might discover the common element is a brain state, that it is a brain state that is denoted by experience reports, on the grounds that this discovery presupposes there is a non-trivial element common to *A* and *B* of the sort that $A \vee B$ is not. The 'defender of experiences' takes the barn-seeing experience to be what tempts a man to believe in each case that he is seeing a barn (Hinton, p. 79), so he must regard what happens physiologically in the two cases as collateral information. 'The defender of experiences does not agree . . . that asking whether the perceiving is identical with some physiological event [and] . . . whether the being illuded is identical with some physiological event . . . are . . . more precise ways of putting the question' (ibid.).

If I grasp Hinton's argument, it works only against experiences conceived as items which are discriminated by phenomenal properties, and may then be discovered to be brain states. But I have argued that this is not the right way to think of experiences, the defender of experiences notwithstanding. 'What goes on when I see

[39] See Kripke, 'Naming and Necessity', in Harman and Davidson, eds., *Semantics of Natural Language*, Lectures I and II.

[40] *Experiences* (O.U.P., Oxford: 1973), esp. pp. 60–102, 124 ff.

a barn' denotes something its user has been trained to describe in those words in two cases: when he sees a barn and when he is illuded. The denotatum may turn out to be a brain state. Why should the brain state not count as what is going in the two cases, if indeed there is one brain state present in both cases? Why should we have to establish that 'I am having a barn-seeing experience' 'is not a mere vague or generalized report of what happened, before we can pose . . .whether the event which it explicitly reports is really one and the same as the event explicitly reported by some designated physiological statement' (Hinton, p. 71)? I can only make sense of Hinton's claim if he thinks that, to be worthy of the name, an experiential element common to *A* and *B* must be some item whose phenomenal properties are noticed and used as grounds for the felt similarity of *A* and *B*. But the materialist as I interpret him wants to jettison such objects as badly as Hinton does. For him, when one gives an introspective report, what is discriminably present is a brain state. And we have seen how far he can go with the phenomenalist if he takes the latter's talk of experiences to be topic neutral descriptions—of these brain states.

5. *Topic Neutralism, 2: Reference Fixing*

Topic neutralists originally interpreted *R* as synonymy; the resulting thesis has been roundly and accurately criticized. It is intuitively clear that 'pain' does not *mean* 'what happens when I cut my finger', nor 'what has most of the causes and effects ascribed to pain in pain-theory', nor 'what satisfies the role given pain in uninterpreted pain-theory'.[41] If *R* were analytic synonymy, it would be true by definition that cutting your hand hurts, whereas it is surely an empirical fact that cutting your hand hurts. The contingency of the link between pain and laceration is patent.

The 'analytic' topic neutralist might deny that he is committed to this implication. 'On my view also [he might reply] cuts cause pain, and the relation between them, being causal, is of course contingent. What I say *is* true by definition is that pain is whatever it is that is, contingently, caused by cuts. If *x* is the result of laceration, the connection between laceration and *x* is contingent. What is analytic

[41] Cf. T. Nagel, 'What is it Like to be a Bat?' and Kripke, 'Naming and Necessity'; also K. Campbell's 'imitation man' in *Body and Mind.* For the rest of this section I use 'pain' instead of 'being in pain' to hold down verbiage; see p. 117 below.

is that pain is whatever that x happens to be.'[42] This defence has equally counterintuitive implications, which are brought out by a Kripkean modal argument (see Kripke, 'Naming and Necessity'). If 'pain' means 'what happens when I cut my hand' it is a necessary truth that whatever happens when I cut my hand is pain. But this is surely wrong: had my neural wiring been different, hand-cutting would have tickled. It is logically possible that cuts have caused tickles even with the neural wiring I actually have. It is only a contingent truth that pains, not tickles, play the causal role they do. According to 'analytic' topic neutralism, *whatever* would have been (e.g.) the result of cutting my hand would have been *pain*. If tomorrow tickles begin to cause, and result from what, up to now, pains have caused and resulted from, *tickles will become pains*. True, we might come to *call* tickles 'pains', but we would surely be using 'pain' in a new way. Tickles could not possibly be what we now call 'pain'. Tickles could not be pains. Analytic topic neutralism rings false from even a linguistic perspective. I know what I call 'pain' by immediate acquaintance. *That state* (whatever it turns out to be) is pain. Were some other state to cause what *that* state causes, that other state would not be pain; to call it 'pain' would be to change the use of 'pain'.

The oddness of analytic topic neutralism shows up well against the background of the problem of evil. Why did God create pain? The theist explains: to warn us when our bodies are malfunctioning and to direct attention to the malfunctioning part. (The theist has not explained why God does not immediately correct the malfunctions or why he lets bodies go wrong in the first place, but that is irrelevant here.) Granted the need for an early warning system, replies the atheist, why did it have to be *pain*? Couldn't God have made self-monitoring more enjoyable? If analytic topic neutralism were correct the theist would have a decisive rejoinder: since 'pain' *means* 'that state which signals trouble and causes immediate spontaneous attention to the troubled part', *whatever* device God had chosen to do what pain does would have been pain. It was logically impossible for God to provide us with a painless early warning system, and the atheist is complaining about a logical necessity. Intuitively, however, the atheist's complaint makes perfect

[42] See J. Fodor and C. Chihara, 'Operationalism and Ordinary Language', in G. Pitcher, ed., *Wittgenstein* (Anchor, N.Y.: 1966) for a view like this. 'Cuts cause pain' is supposed, on this account, to straddle the analytic-synthetic line.

sense: there could have been some device other than pain to direct attention to injuries.[43] It is absurd to say that, had God implanted closed circuit TV monitors, monitoring closed circuit television would have been experiencing pain.

A Kripkean argument like that against Lewis-type analytic topic neutralism, incidentally, calls into question the underlying general Ramseyan account of theoretical terms (section 4). Surely protons rather than electrons could have accounted for the phenomena electrons in fact account for. Electron theory might not have been true of electrons. Electrons might not have had the causal powers they in fact have. But if 'electron' *meant* $(\iota x)T(x), T(x)$ as in section 4, these would be contradictions in terms. This is not to say that the Ramseyan account, which makes 'electrons satisfy electron theory' analytic, robs the existential statement $(\exists x)T(x)$ of empirical content; it does not. It is to say that since $(\exists x)T(x)$ could have been true even if electrons did not satisfy $T(x)$, 'electron' cannot mean '$(\iota x)T(x)$'. (Looking ahead, a Kripkean reinterpretation of 'electron' seems in order. It may be that 'electron' is a connotationless name whose reference is accidentally fixed by '$(\iota x)T(x)$'.)

It is tempting to retain what is wrong with analytic topic neutralism and jettison what is right. The first temptation is to agree that 'pain' is synonymous with some expression of English, that it has a connotation. The second temptation is to fault analytic topic neutralism on choosing, for the predicates that analyse 'pain', those describing the public occasions of pain. Anyone who yields to these temptations will suppose that 'pain' *is* definable in terms of some immediate phenomenal properties that mark pain off from other mental states. But this is to ignore our previous failure to find such properties, or even to find something for them to be properties of. If there are any immediate phenomenal properties, they are too recondite to be what one normally thinks of as defining properties of 'pain', although they might be defining properties of a neologizing sense of 'pain'.

It seems that the real source of the troubles of analytical topic neutralism is the assumption that 'pain' has some descriptive meaning. The evidence suggests that 'pain', rather, is a connotationless name whose referential use involves the public occasions of pain. It is this that analytic topic neutralists perceived, and the feature of topic neutralism that deserves to be retained. In this section I

[43] See pt. XI of Hume's *Dialogues*.

develop these claims in terms of Kripke's account of the relation between names and descriptions associated with them.[44] It offers a natural account of the use of 'pain', and suggests an interpretation of R that guides topic neutralism around the criticisms lately surveyed.

Kripke distinguishes *rigid* from *non-rigid* designation. A rigid designator 'r' designates the same object in all possible worlds, while a non-rigid or *accidental* designator 'd' does not. Eschewing[45] literal talk of possible worlds, 'r' is rigid if $\Box(r = r)$, and 'd' is accidental if $-\Box(d = d)$. Inspection shows that 'Clark Kent', 'Superman', 'electrical discharge', 'lightning', and 'brain state #37' are rigid, and that 'the mild-mannered reporter', 'the man of steel', 'what disturbs electroscopes', and 'the flashes in the sky' are accidental. The discussion of pp. 113–4 above is another way of saying that 'pain' is rigid. Many philosophers contest this distinction. It is objected, for example, that 'Ken Stabler' might have been the name of Joe Namath. True, but this shows only that 'Ken Stabler' *could have* rigidly designated Joe Namath, not that 'Ken Stabler' *does not* rigidly designate Ken Stabler. Another version of this objection is that since in other possible worlds Joe Namath is called 'Ken Stabler', 'Ken Stabler' does not designate the same entity in every possible world. But to say that 'Ken Stabler' is a rigid designator is to say that *we* use the expression 'Ken Stabler' of *our* language to designate the same thing in every possible world. 'Ken Stabler' is what *we* use to designate Ken Stabler when talking of a world whose denizens call him something else, or call someone else 'Ken Stabler'. After all, it is *we* who are saying 'In world w they call Ken Stabler some strange name and call Joe Namath "Ken Stabler" '. There is, finally, the objection that I can easily derigidify 'Ken Stabler' by naming my typewriter 'Ken Stabler'. But if so baptizing my typewriter derigidifies 'Ken Stabler', it also refutes the identity Ken Stabler = Ken Stabler—since the first Ken Stabler can be said to have a ribbon while the second one does not. We make some provision for univocality in the case of such identities, and we may suppose such a provision in force here (cf. remarking, upon being introduced to someone named 'Robert Redford', 'Not *the* Robert Redford?').

Rigid designators are closely connected with certain non-rigid

[44] 'Naming and Necessity.'
[45] With Kripke: ibid., fnn. 13–25.

designators, as, for example, 'Clark Kent' is connected with 'the mild-mannered reporter'. Frege and Russell took the connection to be synonymy, but a Kripkean modal argument shows this to be an error. If 'Clark Kent' meant 'the mild-mannered reporter', then 'Clark Kent is mild-mannered' would be analytic and hence necessarily true, whereas in fact an unhappy boyhood might have left Clark Kent irascible. The fact is that the characteristic of the referent of a word by which we learn it to be that word's referent is frequently a contingent characteristic of the referent. Kripke uses this fact to explain the relation of a rigid designator to its associated non-rigid one. You ask me who Clark Kent is and I tell you 'the mild-mannered reporter'; that is how you know whom I am designating by 'Clark Kent'. Similarly, if Clark Kent had happened to be a nameless mild-mannered reporter, we could have first baptized him by saying 'Let "Clark Kent" designate the mild-mannered reporter'. In Kripke's words, 'the mild-mannered reporter' *fixes the reference* of 'Clark Kent' without being part of its analysis. In general, accidental designators fix the (rigid) reference of the rigid designators with which they are associated.

This account works as well for monadic predicates. Thus, for Kripke, 'wavelength of cadmium light' non-synonymously fixes the reference of 'meter', even though 'metre' is an inseparable part of the monadic predicate 'is a metre long'. Also, 'tawny striped feline' fixes the reference of the natural-kind word 'tiger', even though both 'is a tawny striped feline' and 'is a tiger' are predicates. In my language, 'is a tawny striped feline' fixes the property 'is a tiger' expresses; the property that *in fact* all those tawny striped felines have. Therefore, to facilitate exposition, I will sometimes speak of 'pain' and its reference, rather than of the state expressed by 'being in pain'. When necessary, the monadic thesis can be re-invoked.

When *R* on p. 102 above is interpreted as 'fixes the reference of', topic neutralism becomes the thesis that the reference of psychological expressions like 'being in pain' are accidentally fixed by topic neutral descriptions of the form 'what happens when [public event]'. I will call such descriptions, used this way, 'neutral in the modified sense', or simply 'neutral'. Similarly, I will call the new form of topic neutralism 'modified topic neutralism'. There is no need to choose here between the Smart and Lewis versions of modified topic neutralism. Whether the reference of the typical psychological term is fixed by a network of laws or a single causal regularity is an interesting independent question. My own view is that Smart's early account is closer to the truth, and its simplicity makes it convenient to use. On either view, modified topic neutralism gives the materialist a way of referring to inner states that eschews phenomenal properties and ties talk of inner states to talk of public phenomena.

Modified topic neutralism avoids the implausible consequences of its analytic cognate. It allows the fact that lacerations cause pain to be contingent, just as it is a contingency that Clark Kent is mild-mannered. According to modified topic neutralism, had (what we now refer to as) tickles been the result of laceration, 'the result of laceration' would have accidentally fixed 'pain' to refer to tickles. Modified topic neutralism agrees with common sense that, no matter what, tickles could not have been pains—at most we might have called tickles by the name we now reserve for pain. The modified thesis is also compatible with the logical possibility of Campbell's imitation man and R. Kirk's zombies,[46] who are insentient but behave as we do. Behaviour which in us is caused by pain is not caused by pain in them. The modified thesis inherits, from Kripke's general account of reference fixing, the allowance that the descriptions in terms of which we learn to refer to pain might not have been true of pain.

An objection to the analytic thesis which carries over to the modified thesis is that no neutral description is even extensionally equivalent to 'pain'.[47] Damaged skin is neither necessary nor sufficient for pain felt where the skin is damaged. Not only do neutral descriptions fail as analyses, they are insufficiently discriminating even to fix the reference of psychological terms.

This objection is short-sighted. A man may indeed have pains in his hand unlike those associated with lacerated skin. But how *are* such pains described, if not as the sort of pain that comes from a pinch, or from gripping a tennis racket too long? These are all neutral descriptions, and reflection on how we communicate our pains to others provides endless examples of the aptness of such descriptions for fine discrimination. If anything, the variety of descriptions available in the public neutral vocabulary far outruns such a phenomenological vocabulary as we may have. At the more sophisticated reaches of psychological description we are forced to

[46] 'Sentience and Behaviour'.

[47] Cornman seems to make this point in an involved passage in Rosenthal, ed., *Materialism and the Mind-Body Problem*, p. 76.

rely on neutral descriptions to identify mental states. How else would one describe the pain of a merchant whose ship has foundered, if not in those words? If there is a problem about the adequacy of neutral descriptions at all, it is only with 'raw' experiences like searing physical pain, and how their subjects identify them.

The claim that neutral descriptions *always* originally fix the reference of sensation words follows from two lemmas: (a) if rigid reference to sensations is secured by description at all, it is fixed by neutral description even for the subject of the sensation, since the only *facts* he knows about pains are circumstantial. This lemma, in fact, is an adaptation of the heuristic language-learning argument of pp. 103–4 to the modified thesis. Lemma (b) runs: Wittgenstein's private language argument, correctly understood, shows that rigid reference to sensations must be fixed by description. Before arguing for these lemmas, however, I must address an obscurity in the present topic. Does 'the fixing of "pain" ' mean the fixing of 'pain' for each individual, or the once-for-all introduction of 'pain' into language? Is the meaning of the question 'How is "pain" fixed?' entirely clear? A possible suggestion is that this is just an instance of a cluster of problems attending the general notion of reference-fixing, and the materialist need only await whatever solutions are adopted in the general case. This is not altogether satisfactory, however, because of the ubiquity and antiquity of 'pain'. 'Lightning' and 'water' were presumably introduced at recognizable moments, and for them the question 'How was their reference fixed at the right historical moment?' is well posed. It is not clear that the same can be said for 'pain'.

The following idealization may be helpful. Suppose *A* has never experienced pain or anything remotely like it. In his 'original position' he is shielded by a 'veil of ignorance' from pain. He then experiences pain for the first time, and wants rigidly to designate it. How does he go about doing this? I suggest that answering the question 'How would *A* introduce a rigid designator for pain the first time he experienced it?' is a reasonable first approximation to answering 'How is the reference of "pain" fixed?' In what follows, then, I will understand questions about fixing the reference of pain as questions about how someone in the 'original position' could, would, or would have to fix the reference of 'pain'. Now for the lemmas.

(a) It is axiomatic that describing *x* is a matter of ascribing to *x* predicates that x satisfies. It is a matter, tautologically enough, of knowledge by description and not acquaintance. Thus, no matter how intimate is *A*'s awareness of x, *A* cannot describe x unless he is able to say something true about it. Forgetting the original position for a moment, consider the matter of describing a pain from both the external and internal perspectives: the descriptions others could apply to *A*'s pain and the description *A* himself could apply. Suppose *A* burns his hand at 3.00. Taking the external perspective first, it is clear that all anyone other than *A* knows about *A*'s pain can be expressed in a public vocabulary: it is what happened at 3.00, it is what happened when *A*'s hand slipped, and so on. Thus, if others than *A* are to fix the reference of '*A*'s pain' by description (and surely this is the only way they can fix it), they will have to resort to neutral descriptions. Others are shut off from *the experience itself* and must resort to the vagaries of circumstance to generate true descriptions.

But *A* is directly acquainted with his pain, or his being in pain, and surely, one supposes, *he* needs no such props to describe it. Some philosophers try to restore the symmetry between the external and internal perspectives by dismissing as illusory the idea that *A* is specially directly acquainted with his pain. These philosophers are denying the obvious (see V.1). A more plausible approach is to take to heart the idea that being able to describe something requires that one knows at least one predicate it satisfies, and to reflect that *A*'s immediate acquaintance with his pain does not guarantee that *A* knows any *descriptions* of his pain other than those others know. Granted, *A* is immediately conscious of his pain; he *has* it; he intuits its essence. But what does *A* know about his pain? It is here that the temptation to invoke phenomenal properties is most powerful. Sometimes one even wants *ineffable* phenomenal properties.[48] But there don't seem to be any phenomenal properties to do the job. Hurtfulness, we saw at length, is not a property of being in pain. Nor could those predicates that do describe the state of pain—'shooting', 'pulsing', and the like—be phenomenal reference-fixing descriptions for *A* in the original position. For someone who had not experienced pain before such descriptions would be covert

[48] 'I would think that fear isn't just a belief that something is dangerous and a corresponding tendency to avoid it. There's something more, but what is that?' Saul Kripke, quoted in the *New York Times*, 14 Aug. 1977. The materialist, of course, agrees that there is more.

comparisons with something public. 'The pulsing phenomenon', for example, would amount to 'what is going on with me and has the rhythmic properties of my pulse'. To describe a pain as shooting would be to compare it with the moving gash in a sheet of paper being ripped. These descriptions in their primitive use derive from public affairs, with similarity rather than co-occurrence or causal connection being the principle of derivation. For *A* they express contingent properties of pain, and his use of them to fix reference is consistent with the claim of lemma (a).

What *A* does know about his pain is that it happened when his hand slipped, it happened at 3.00, and so on. It seems reasonable to conclude that if this is the first time *A* has experienced pain, these sorts of properties are all he knows about it. So if *A* fixes the reference of 'pain' to this new phenomenon even for himself by description, he has to do it by the same neutral descriptions that others use.

(b) The argument for (a) may be held otiose on the grounds that the immediacy of pain obviates the need for fixing 'pain' by description. Perhaps we simply *notice pain*, and decide to call it something—or, in terms of our idealization, this is how someone in the original position would do it. Let us call this the *direct picture* of fixing 'pain'. Wittgenstein's private language argument (PLA) holds, against the direct picture, that 'an "inner process" stands in need of outward criteria'.[49] PLA does show, I think, that the direct picture is wrong, but it has to be reformulated along the Kripkean lines we've been pursuing if its resources are to be tapped. As commonly understood, PLA and its official demonstrandum are wildly implausible. It becomes more plausible when its demonstrandum is taken to be that the reference of sensation words must be fixed by descriptions couched in public terms. So transposed, PLA provides reason for rejecting the direct picture.

The most curious aspect of section 580 of the *Investigations* is its apparent violation of Hume's law. In this it resembles analytical behaviourism, and this is why Wittgenstein's defenders have so much difficulty with the charge that he is a behaviourist. Suppose the criterion for 'pain' is toe-clutching—or, to accommodate the context-sensitivity of 'pain', that one criterion for 'pain' is toe-clutching immediately after toe-stubbing. Wittgenstein's elusive notion of criterion seems to require at least that if '*X*' is a criterion for '*Y*', '$X \supset Y$' holds in virtue of 'logical grammar'. But then

[49] *Philosophical Investigations*, sec. 580.

Wittgenstein is saying that it is not a contingent truth, but a matter of 'logical grammar', that if you clutch your toe you are in pain—or, more elaborately but no less paradoxically, it is logically necessary that if you clutch your toe just after stubbing it, you are in pain. But surely being in pain and toe-clutching (or post-stub toe-clutching) are two different things and by Hume's law cannot be necessarily connected. The collision of PLA with Hume's law is what is responsible for the astonishing intellectual vertigo PLA can induce. The plausibility of Wittgenstein's rejection of an incommunicable subject matter just compounds the confusion. Much of the literature surrounding PLA is the effort of philosophers impressed by the rejection of logical privacy, yet loyal to Hume's law, to get used to the idea that pain isn't a 'distinct existence' from context-bound caprioling.

PLA can banish private names without violating Hume's law if reformulated as the claim that the reference of even a designator for a private state or object must be fixed by a description couched in wholly public terms. Section 580 should read 580_K: an inner process (no scare-quotes) stands in need of an outward reference-fixing. The whole point of modified topic neutralism is the compatibility of 580_K with Hume's law. It remains a contingency that when you clutch your toe after stubbing it your toe hurts, even if the linguistic community uses your carryings-on to teach children 'pain'. Wittgenstein went wrong as did Russell in the general theory of names: having noticed that at one point the only description we have of our pain is, say, 'what you get when you put your hand on the stove', he concluded that 'pain' *means* 'what you get ...' This diagnosis applies to all 'criteriological' approaches to mental phenomena, such as Strawson's.[50]

Just as the conclusion of PLA becomes more plausible when reinterpreted to be about reference fixing, so does its principal argument.[51] The *nervus probandi* of PLA[52] is the claim that no sense attaches to the distinction between correct and incorrect reapplication for private names. Since the criterion for reapplying 'pain' construed privately would be 'it seems like pain again', either (i) the distinction between 'pain' applying and 'pain' merely *seeming*

[50] *Individuals*, chap. III.

[51] In 'Kripke's Argument against the Identity Thesis', I discuss Wittgenstein's subsidiary teachability argument in a Kripkean setting.

[52] *Investigations*, secs. 243–310.

to apply collapses, or (ii) since 'seems like pain again' must have 'seems to seem like pain' again as *its* criterion, a regress is generated which blocks the application of 'pain' altogether. Now it is generally conceded that *if* the direct picture entails that no distinction can be drawn between correct and incorrect applications of 'pain', the direct picture entails, absurdly, that 'pain' is meaningless. Many philosophers, however, reject the antecedent of this conditional on the grounds that all PLA shows is that the privacy of pain makes it impossible to *tell* when 'pain' reapplies correctly. Unless PLA relies on some objectionable form of verificationism, it does not show that the correct/incorrect distinction cannot be drawn for private names.[53]

This impasse can be broken if 'private name' is reconstrued to mean 'a name whose reference is fixed neither by ostension nor by a designator whose constituent predicates apply to publicly observable objects, "pain" being an example'. Then Wittgenstein's point is that the direct picture of how *A* fixes the reference of "pain"—by noticing pain and calling it 'pain'—is in fact an account according to which *A* refers to pain by making essential use of a *description*: 'what I initially referred to as "pain" '. Wittgenstein is right. For consider: on every occasion after the initial encounter with pain, when *A* asks himself whether some new occurrence is pain, he is asking, on the direct picture, 'Is it like what I referred to as "pain" at the first encounter?' He must ask himself whether what he is now experiencing is like what he originally called 'pain'. But what is wrong with that? We can no longer fault it for generating a regress, since 'It seems to me that I am in pain' is no longer the criterion for 'I am in pain'. But now the referential force of 'pain', how *A* refers to his pain, has been presupposed, rather than explained, by the direct picture. To adapt a phrase of Kripke's, 'the question of reference is thrown back on the question of reference'.[54] This circumstance finds the direct picture in violation of a condition (C) Kripke places on accounts of reference:

> For any successful theory, the account must not be circular. The properties which are used [to determine the referent of a word] must not themselves involve the notion of reference in a way that it is ultimately impossible to eliminate.[55]

[53] See e. g. J. J. Thompson, 'Private Languages', in S. Hampshire, ed., *Philosophy of Mind* (Harper & Row, N.Y.: 1966), p. 137.

[54] 'Naming and Necessity,' p. 283.

[55] Ibid.

(C) is obviously correct, perhaps analytically so. I take it that (C) can be specified for particular words and for particular classes of words: the properties used by a successful theory of how a particular word (or class of words) refers must not make uneliminable use of the notion of that word's reference (or reference by any word in the class). Even '*This* is pain' sins against (C)-specific; for the explanation of what *A* is referring to by 'pain' must be 'what *A* originally referred to as "this" '. And we would still be without an account of how 'pain' refers.[56]

(C) tells us that a *theory* of reference cannot be circular, but, it might be objected, the revamped PLA shows only that *A* has to use a description involving 'reference' if he fixes 'pain' non-descriptively, not that the *theory* that *A* can so fix the reference of 'pain' viciously involves the notion of reference. But it does. The direct picture explains what 'pain' refers to as 'what *A* referred to by "pain" [or "this"]', and that directly violates (C). In any case the line between *A*'s falling back on reference and a theory about *A* falling back on reference is hazy. Consider the theory that a good tennis player is one who believes he can beat most other good tennis players (confidence is the name of the game). This theory does not, strictly speaking, use 'good tennis player' to explain what a good tennis player is; it only uses the idea of someone thinking something about good tennis players to explain what a good tennis player is. Yet it would hardly help anyone who did not already know what a good tennis player is. So this theory of tennis excellence rates as circular. In just this way a theory is circular if it explains the reference of a word in terms of what a user of that word thought he was referring to by it.

The referential force of 'pain' cannot be explained by supposing that each of us attends to his pains and says 'this is what I will henceforth call "pain" '. If we are to do more with pain than *be in pain*—if we are to refer to this state—it must be through identifying it by a description which makes no use of the idea of referring to it. There is much merit in Wittgenstein's leading principle that the naming of external objects and their states cannot just be transposed without further ado to the internal scene. However intuitively

[56] K. Donnellan lays down a similar requirement to block question-begging explanations of reference, in 'Proper Names and Identifying Descriptions', Harman and Davidson, eds., *Semantics of Natural Language*, p. 365. The paragraph from p. 365, line 22 to p. 366, line 5 is a scholium on the impossibility of private names, and an explanation of *Investigations*, sec. 263.

appealing is the idea that we can name pain by *looking within*, introspection is altogether dissimilar from visual observation. Procedures for naming items discriminated in one's visual field—and discriminated in the visual fields of others—may not work for naming phenomena when the discrimination is introspective.[57]

The reader is invited to reflect a final time on the close connection between the double aspect theory and the description theory of names. 'Pain' is the name of an inner state. If a name is synonymous with a definite description whose satisfaction is the criterion for the application of the name, pain must satisfy a unique description employed by the user of 'pain'. A natural candidate for such a description is: 'that state which presents such-and-such an appearance'. This is how one might come to suppose that being in pain has appearance properties, a mistake reinforced by the ambiguity of 'awareness of' in 'awareness of pain'. But we now see that pain need have no special criterial property at all to explain the success we have in using 'pain'. We can drop the question of what appearance properties users of 'pain' must notice. An explanation of the use of 'pain' as prompted by internal cues can no longer be accused of missing the phenomenal element.

Appendix: An Improvement in a Principle

In 'Kripke's Argument against the Identity Thesis' I made a mistake in characterizing one aspect of Kripke's view of reference.[58] This mistake might appear to neutralize my reply therein to Kripke's argument against materialism, since my reply was directed against a position Kripke never literally maintained. This is a misapprehension. This appendix corrects the mistake and the misapprehension.

If 'r' and 'r'' are rigid designators, $r = r'$ entails $\Box(r = r')$. Since all objects can be rigidly designated, all identities are necessary. This confronts Kripke with the question: why do some identities *appear* to be contingent? If $r = r'$, how is it that we can imagine $r \neq r'$? Kripke's answer is this. Suppose the accidental designator 'd' has

[57] To their credit, private names have turned out not to involve any circularity or indeterminacy in the notion of 'similarity' for private states. Once names for private states are properly introduced, there is nothing problematic in the idea that two private states are similar or dissimilar. Malcolm, Geach, and others have been over-hasty in rejecting the analogical solution to the problem of other minds on the basis of a supposed indeterminacy here.

[58] Pointed out to me by M. Slote and P. Teller in correspondence, and G. Sher in conversation.

actually fixed 'r' on r, and $r = r'$. One can be said to imagine that $r \neq r'$ if one is imagining 'd' to have fixed 'r' rigidly on some other thing $r'' \neq r$. One is not really imagining r not to be r', but some other thing r'' not to be r'. (One may *think* one is imagining r not to be r'.) Let us say that one is then *K-imagining* $r \neq r'$. The K-imaginability of $r \neq r'$ is thus compatible with r being r' in all possible worlds, for what one is imagining is not that r is not r', but that the *sentence* '$r = r'$' is false. Non-standard semantics is not at issue. In imagining '$r = r'$' to be false in such a way as *not* to be imagining $r \neq r'$, one is, per the usual referential semantics, imagining that what 'r' refers to is not what 'r'' refers to. But one is now imagining that 'r' refers to something other than r'—one is imagining a possible world in which the reference of 'r' has been accidentally fixed on a different object r'' than the one r' it has actually been fixed on. So the referential truth-condition for what one is imagining is $r'' \neq r'$.

K-imaginability can be generalized. Suppose 'd' has accidentally fixed the reference of 'r' rigidly on r, and $\Box P(r)$. One can K-imagine $-P(r)$, and perhaps *think* one is imagining a situation in which r is not P, iff one is actually imagining that 'd' had fixed the reference of 'r' on some $r'' \neq r$, and $-P(r'')$. The first kind of K-imagining is an instance of the second, and arises when '$P(x)$' is specified as '$x = r'$'. In my article I attributed to Kripke the principle KP: a necessary condition for $r = r'$ and for it to be K-imaginable that $r \neq r'$ is that both 'r' and 'r'' be fixed by accidental designators 'd' and 'd'' such that $-\Box(d = d')$. This was needlessly strong. Looking to the general case, I should have used KP′: a necessary condition for $P(r)$ to be necessary while $-P(r)$ is K-imaginable is that 'r' be fixed by an accidental designator 'd' such that $-\Box P(d)$.

This bears on the issue I took with Kripke in the following way. Kripke says that, since 'pain' is not fixed accidentally, 'pain p is brain state b' cannot, contrary to what the materialist holds, even *appear* contingent (be K-imagined to be false). I formulated this as the claim that '$p = b$' violates KP, and used lemmas (a) and (b) to show that '$p = b$' is, *contra* Kripke, consistent with KP. But Kripke's challenge is more accurately rendered as: materialism is wrong because $P(p)$ = 'pain p is a physical phenomenon' violates KP′ (since 'pain' is not fixed accidentally). But lemmas (a) and (b), which entail that 'pain' is fixed accidentally, also entail that, *contra* Kripke, $P(p)$ is consistent with KP′. In fact, making it KP′ that materialism must satisfy strengthens my argument. If '$p = b$' is to satisfy KP, it must also be shown that brain-state designators are fixed accidentally; this may not be so, and my treatment of the topic in my article was altogether too perfunctory. But the question of how brain-state designators are fixed is quite irrelevant to whether $P(p)$ satisfies KP′.

6. *Functionalism and Anomalous Monism*

This discussion of topic neutralism has touched in passing on the so-called 'functionalist' theory, treating it as an abstract version of Lewis' analytic topic neutralism. Like the latter, the view that mental states are specified by their role in a network of uninterpreted relations can be modified along Kripkean lines. Let us assume this done, and read it henceforth as a thesis about the reference-fixing rather than the analysis of psychological terms. Functionalism requires special attention, however, because its proponents suggest that it is an *alternative* to materialism, and their arguments for saying that functionalism might be true while materialism is false survives its Kripkean transposition.

Numerous obscurities surround functionalism, and its name appears to have gained a wider currency than any clear understanding of the thesis itself. It is sometimes not even clear what kind of 'theory' functionalism is; I side firmly with Place[59] in taking it as a thesis about the semantics of psychological language. Putnam himself often describes functionalism as the empirical theory that psychological states happen to be whatever play certain functional roles. But this formulation seems to leave functionalism open to the objection that scotched analytic topic neutralism—that it implies, implausibly, that if tickles had caused what pains now cause, tickles would have been pains. A more plausible statement of this approach to functionalism is: psychological states are whatever happen in fact to play certain functional roles. But this thesis is indistinguishable from the claim introduced in the previous paragraph, that mental states are denoted by designators whose reference is *accidentally fixed* by functional-role descriptions. But we still need a better account of 'function'.

The word 'function' appears to offer a clue. As used by biologists, to say that a state or structure *s* of an organism has a function is to say that *s* conduces to the well-being of the organism, and that

[59] 'Comments', in Capitan and Merrill, eds., *Art, Mind and Religion*, p. 64.

this fact in turn explains the existence or persistence of *s*.[60] To say that *s* has a function, on this analysis, is to say that *s* has a special kind of causal role. If 'function' is understood this way functionalism is the view that psychological state names refer to states of organisms which benefit organisms, and whose existence or persistence is explained (via Darwinian evolution) by this service. However, functionalists do not firmly tie the characterization of psychological states to any service they render organisms,[61] nor, so far as I can tell, do they think the use of functional language entails any view about how these states came to be or why they persist. Moreover, construing 'function' this way would collapse functionalism into a special form of Lewis's theory. It seems safe to conclude, then, that functionalists do not use 'function' as biologists do when they talk of the 'function' of peristalsis.

Sometimes functionalists seem to identify 'function' with 'role assigned by a theory'. A psychological state, on this view, is any state of the organism which plays a systematic causal role in the organism's life, it being the job of specific psychological theories to specify the role. Any such theory, to be called 'psychological', must contain descriptions of the behaviour of organsims. (If each empirical theory yields a different 'implicit definition' for psychological terms, how can they be about the same thing? The answer, I take it, is that there is no clear line between change of belief and change of meaning.) This is a natural way to interpret Putnam's description of his view, that psychological terms are part of a theory, and psychological terms are what, if anything, make the theory true. It also makes natural Putnam's view that to believe in other minds is to hold a certain *theory* about why other people behave as they do.[62] But if so, 'functionalism' threatens again to become another word for Lewis's causal role account, the sense of difference attributable to the functionalist's emphasis on *theory*. This emphasis does not mean that functionalists are offering a theory of the mind,

[60] See L. Wright, 'Functions', *Philosophical Review*, lxxxii (Apr. 1973); 139–68; M. Levin, 'On the Ascription of Functions to Objects', *Philosophy of the Social Sciences*, vi.3 (Sept. 1976), 227–34.

[61] Putnam occasionally notes the usefulness of psychological states, but he makes no systematic effort to exploit this idea. He talks merely of 'functional organization'; see 'The Mental Life of Some Machines', in H. Cartaneda, ed., *Intentionality, Minds and Perception* (Wayne State U.P., Detroit: 1966).

[62] 'Other Minds', in R. Rudner and I. Scheffler, ed., *Logic and Art* (Bobbs-Merrill, Indianapolis: 1972).

as opposed to a theory of 'the mind'; it just means that their theory makes essential reference to empirical theories.

The most reasonable interpretation of functionalism as a distinctive position on the mind–body problem is that psychological theories are not theories about the causal role played by psychological states, but are *uninterpreted* theories. The roles assigned to psychological states in psychological theories are given by special uninterpreted relations. In Putnam's version, psychological-functional states are *logical* states, the states described by *abstract* Turing programs (for details, see VI.1). The relations between entries on the machine table are purely algebraic, and their intended interpretation need not be causal. Like any formal system, an abstract Turing program can be realized in a variety of heterogeneous ways, and any realization of the right sort of Turing program is a realization of a system of psychological states. On this view it is as absurd to ask what psychological states *are* as it is to ask what the states described by a Turing program are, or what the additive operation of uninterpreted group theory is. This reading of Putnam is supported by his well-known argument that if a small region of someone's brain were replaced by circuitry that did the same job as the lobotomized grey matter, he would probably continue to be in the same mental state. Thus, his mental state cannot be identical to any brain state; rather, his mental state must be *anything* that 'does the job' done by the excised portion of the brain. Similarly, it is often argued that animals have pains, etc., even though the particulars of their wiring differ from ours. It must then be the 'functional role' a particular bit of wiring plays that makes its activity pain, rather than the intrinsic nature of the wiring or its activities.

Attention to the term 'valve lifter' clarifies the thrust of functionalism.[63] To call something a 'valve lifter' is to describe what it does, what role it plays in a system it is a part of. One and the same object can either be or fail to be a valve lifter, depending on its place in various mechanical arrangements. Conversely, physically dissimilar objects can both be valve lifters. Camshafts are valve lifters in automobiles, a muscle is a valve lifter in the human heart. 'Being a valve lifter' is a functional state a thing satisfies not because of what it is, but what it does.

This example brings out another important link between functional-

[63] The example is J. Fodor's; see his *Psychological Explanation* (Random House, N.Y.: 1968).

ism and the axiomatic account of abstract theories. An object x can be a valve lifter only if there are other things y, z, ... *simultaneously* playing certain other functional roles. x can be a valve lifter only if some y is a valve; and y can be a valve only if it controls the flow of a fluid z (z may be a liquid, a current, or information), and so on. The application of a functional description typically requires the simultaneous application of an n-tuple of functional descriptions. Similarly, the interpretation of an axiomatic primitive in a model requires the simultaneous interpretation of all the other primitives of the axiomatic theory; an object cannot be 0 unless, so interpreted, the Peano axioms come out true; i.e. unless 'successor' and 'number' are also simultaneously satisfactorily interpreted. On this score functionalism coheres well with the so-called 'interdependence of the mental', the fact that psychological descriptions come in bunches. We can ascribe a belief to a man only if we know his desires, and we can ascribe a desire to him only if we know his beliefs. If he ignores a refrigerator, this might be because {he is hungry, he believes there is no food in the refrigerator}, or because {he believes there is food in the refrigerator, he is not hungry}. His behaviour supports the attribution of either pair.[64] To ask if A is in mental state m is to ask if m is a member of an n-fold set of psychological states $\{m_1,..,m_n\}$ such that the simultaneous ascription of all the m_i is (best) supported by A's behaviour. So the description of a man's state of mind is very like the simultaneous interpretation of all the primitives of an axiomatic theory. Its easy assimilation of the interdependence of the mental is a point in favour of functionalism.

This interpretation of functionalism is most faithful to writers like Harman:

> A functional account says how the functioning of a [reasoning] process can *be* a process of reasoning by virtue of the way it functions. That is, a functional account says how the functioning of such a process allows it to be correlated with the reasoning, taken to be an abstract inference, which the process instantiates. To be more precise, the relevant correlation is a mapping F from mental or neurophysiological processes to the abstract structures of inference. If x is a process in the domain of F, then $F(x)$ is the (abstract) reasoning that x instantiates. Such a mapping F is a *reasoning instantiator*.[65]

[64] See Davidson, 'Psychology as Philosophy', in J. Glover, ed., *The Philosophy of Mind* (O.U.P., Oxford: 1976).

[65] G. Harman, *Thought* (Princeton U.P.: 1972), pp. 49 f.

We can generalize Harman's function to that of a *psychology instantiator*, which maps processes to the abstract structures of an overall psychological theory. If F is a psychology instantiator, and D, a set of brain processes, is the domain of F, then $F(x)$ is the (abstract) psychological state x instantiates. More fully: suppose $T(p_1,...p_n)$ is psychology (or some specific psychological theory), construed as a set of sentences containing uninterpreted primitives $p_1,...,p_n$ and constants that describe the behaviour of organisms. Even if T describes an abstract Turing machine, it must also specify how machine states tie in to incoming energy and the physical movements of its container. Let D be a domain and F a function from D to $\{p_1,...,p_n\}$. If $\langle x_1,...,x_n \rangle \varepsilon D^n$, and $T(F(x_1),...,F(x_n))$ holds, F is a psychology instantiator.[66]

Functionalists like Putnam and Fodor oppose their view to materialism. As I understand them, they dismiss 'what are mental states?' as a pseudo-question, just as 'what is a valve lifter?' and 'what is machine state S_i?', taken as requests for *physical* characterizations of valve lifters and S_i, are pseudo-questions. Since mental states, valve lifters, and S_i are functionally identified, they are not extensionally equivalent to any physical properties or projectible disjunctions thereof. Models for psychological theories need have nothing more in common beyond *being* models of the theory, just as two Boolean algebras may have nothing in common beyond being models of the axioms of Boolean algebra, and what that entails. Indeed, 'psychology' might be realized in a non-physical domain.

Before considering whether this consequence of functionalism is really incompatible with materialism, some demurrers about functionalism itself are in order. Consider its account of consciousness. On the face of it, it makes no sense at all to hold that consciousness is an *uninterpreted* state. It is quite as impossible for me to be in a state referred to by an uninterpreted expression as it is for me to perform an uninterpreted operation on two numbers or two physical objects. 'Consciousness', 'pain', and the like do not seem to refer to multiply interpretable slots; they refer to definite phenomena. Consciousness cannot be what has the properties ascribed to it in the abstract theory, for these are not definite properties at all.

[66] This account seems faithful to Harman's intentions in 'Knowledge, Reasons, and Causes', *Journal of Philosophy*, lxvii. 21 (Nov. 1970), 849–50.

In any case, the contrast between abstractly defined roles and the states that satisfy them, as opposed to concrete roles satisfied by states with specific causal properties, is not entirely clear. While the role *R* itself may not be causally described, any state *S* that plays (interpreted) role *R* in system X, can only play *R* because of *S*'s specific causal properties. If a certain circuit in a computer has the function of adding 2, this is not a role specified in terms of the causal properties of circuits; but it is the causal properties of the circuit that accounts for its ability to behave in such a way that, in the computer of which it is a part, it does something intepretable as 'adding 2'. So—is what makes the circuit a 2-adder its causal properties, or the role it plays (the fact that it is part of a system which satisfies an abstract description of an adding machine)? Since it plays this latter role because of the former, we should give the former as our answer. True, we sometimes explain the behaviour of our circuit by saying 'it's a 2-adder' rather than by citing its causal properties;[67] but this sort of explanation works because we are presupposing that it is part of a system which satisfies a certain abstract description—and it satisfies this abstract description because of its specific causal properties. These points apply, of course, *mutatis mutandis*, to consciousness. In conjunction with the fact that consciousness cannot literally be said to be an *abstract* state, it is not clear that we have been offered a new angle on the nature of consciousness at all.

Sometimes, to be sure, functionalists speak as if, given that '*P*(*x*)' is a functionally defined psychological predicate, '*P*(*x*)' does not imply '*x* is sentient'. For Putnam, as I understand him, to say

[67] '[T]he behavior of, say, a computing machine is not explained by the physics and chemistry of the computing machine. It is explained by the machine's *program*. Of course, that program is realized in a particular physics and chemistry, and could, perhaps, be deduced from that physics and chemistry . . . [but] the latter prediction may be highly unexplanatory. Understanding why the machine, say, computes the decimal expansion of π, may require reference to the abstract properties of the machine . . . Although our psychological properties have their realization in our biological make up, psychology has . . . an *autonomous* explanatory function.' Thus Putnam, in *Philosophical Papers*, ii (C.U.P., Cambridge: 1975), pp. xi–xii. He elaborates this view on pp. 295–9 of the same volume. It is this idea that the acausal functional explanation is *autonomous* that I think is precisely wrong. (See p. 83 above.) I am of course prepared to grant that, pragmatically, one can sometimes more easily grasp and predict a system's behaviour using non-causal categories. I would enter similar reservations about the identification of mental states with states of information-processing that Sayre has proposed in *Consciousness* and *Cybernetics and the Philosophy of Mind* (Humanities, Atlantic Highlands, N.J.: 1976).

that a computer wants to win a game of chess is *just* to say that it is in an internal state which makes it behave in certain ways, *without* the implication that the computer is conscious.[68] If this is how functionalists intend their theory, it simply fails to address the mind–body problem. So the functionalist must intend his theory to be about the psychological vocabulary allowed its normal freight of implications about consciousness, and indeed about consciousness itself. At this point, however, the points raised on p. 132 suggest that we are back to a special case of the causal role theory.[69]

Let us suppose, however, that functionalism can be made coherent enough to assert: psychological terms have a physically heterogeneous denotations; models for psychology have nothing in common beyond satisfying psychology. Materialism is entirely consistent with this assertion. To see this, we must distinguish between type–type and particular–particular identities for mental states. Let M be a type of mental state—being in pain, say—and let $M(s)$ mean that particular mental state s is of type M. Similarly, let $P(s)$ mean that particular state s is an instance of the physical state-type P. Let M and P be as in II.1. Now 'nomic monism' is the claim that every mental state type is identical to some physical state type:

$$(1)\ (M)(M \varepsilon \mathrm{M} \supset (\exists P)(P \varepsilon \mathrm{P} \ \&\ (s)(M(s) \supset (\exists s')(P(s') \ \&\ s = s')))).$$

We are granting that functionalism has refuted (1) (if we exclude unprojectible disjunctions of singular physical event descriptions as types). It remains open to the materialist to argue that, while (1) is false, every instance of any psychological state is identical to some instance of *some* brain state-type or other. This 'particular–particular' identity thesis is

$$(2)\ (M)(M \varepsilon \mathrm{M} \supset (s)(M(s) \supset (\exists P)(P \varepsilon \mathrm{P} \ \&\ (\exists s')(P(s') \ \&\ s = s')))).$$

To deny (2) because (1) is false is to commit a familiar quantifier shift fallacy. Even if no laws connect mental states to brain states, every mental state might still be a brain state. In terms of psychology instantiators, materialists under pressure from functionalists would claim that every domain of any psychology instantiator is a set of physical processes: more precisely,

[68] Cf. e.g. 'Minds and Machines', in S. Hook, ed. *Dimensions of Mind* (Collier, N.Y.: 1961).

[69] N. Block and J. Fodor offer a related criticism in 'What Psychological States are Not', *Philosophical Review*, lxxxi (Apr. 1972), p. 173.

$(F)(F$ is a psychology instantiator $\supset (y)((i)(i \leqslant n \ \& \ y = F^{-1}(p_i)) \supset y$ is physical)).

To see why this really is a version of materialism, consider valve lifters again. A *hydraulics instantiator* is any mapping G which correlates a particular structure to the abstract structure of hydraulics, whose primitives are $h_1,...h_m$, h_i being 'valve lifter'. Materialism about valve lifters is the claim that if G is a hydraulics instantiator, $(G^{-1}(h_1,...,h_m))_i$ is a material object. Perhaps the inverse images of the various hydraulics instantiators have nothing physical in common, nothing in common beyond realizing hydraulics; perhaps the valve lifters of this world have nothing in common beyond being mapped to h_i by some hydraulics instantiator. For all that, every valve lifter might be a material object. As long as all realizations of psychological processes are physical processes, it is quibbling to deny that materialism is true; just as it would be quibbling to deny that, if materialism about valve lifters were true, valve lifters are all material objects.[70]

Willingness to settle for particular–particular identities frees the materialist from two other worries. One, not directly bearing on the philosophy of mind but liable to cause thoroughgoing materialism trouble in the long run, is the relation of action to behaviour. Arguments abound to show that action-descriptions are context-dependent: the same physical movement can be a different action (or no action at all) in a different context; and physical movements of unlimited heterogeneity can be actions of the same sort if they occur in suitable contexts. How then can an action be a bodily movement, or a bodily movement caused by a brain event? But again, all the contextualist argument shows is that no *type* of action is identical to any *type* of bodily movement; it does not refute the claim that every particular action is some bodily movement or other. To think it does it to commit the $(x)(\exists y)/(\exists y)(x)$ switch.

The other worry is Davidson's 'anomalous monism', to be discussed more fully in chapter VI. Davidson claims[71] that there can be no laws connecting brain states with propositional attitudes,

[70] A tack not unlike this one is taken by W. Lycan in 'Mental States and Putnam's Functionalist Hypothesis' (*Australasian Journal of Philosophy* lii. 1 [May 1974], 48–62). However, as I understand him, Lycan wants to preserve type–type identities.

[71] 'Mental Events', in Foster and Swanson, ed s., *Experience and Theory*; and 'Psychology as Philosophy', in J. Glover, ed., *The Philosophy of Mind.*

which are individuated by their propositional content. His main support for this seems to be Quine's thesis of the indeterminacy of translation, which implies that ascriptions of propositional attitudes are relative to schemes of translation, which may be inequivalent while faithful to all possible data.[72] Now the materialist might well ask why this does not show particular propositional attitudes to be fictions, and the ascription of them to be semi-conventional, not even pretending to individuate mental states. If they do not, the materialist can hardly be faulted for not producing laws connecting brain states with non-entities. If, however, Davidson wants to maintain that there is a truth about ascribing propositional attitudes—although inaccessible—the materialist can say that, for all Davidson has shown, each particular propositional attitude might be a brain state. Davidson even seems willing to grant this. Why isn't this materialism? Having settled for a very fine-grained materialism, we might look again at the two arguments on p. 129. Is it really so plausible to say that an organism with different wiring could have an experience *exactly* like mine? I think not. The experience of a sparrow with a broken wing is probably *like* the one I had when I broke my ankle, but not as like it as your pain would be if you broke your ankle. Rather than being counterintuitive, this consequence of materialism seems the simple truth. Why then do we call the bird's state 'pain'? Here functionalism is of real help. The sparrow's mental state does play a role in determining the bird's behaviour quite like that played by my mental state. Moreover—presumably—what it's like to be the bird is rather similar to what it's like to be me. So there is a family resemblance between the two mental states which justifies and explains the interspecific application of the single term 'pain'.

I suspect that functionalists have supposed their theory to be an alternative to materialism because of the surprisingly extensive use of functional descriptions in science. Most physics textbooks, for example, describe Hertz's discovery of electromagnetic waves by saying that he made a spark jump between the heads of a condenser in a sphere. 'Condenser' is a functional description; a condenser is something that stores electricity and releases it all at once. We are not given a physical description of Hertz's apparatus; we are told

[72] See Quine's 'Ontological Relativity'; for an example of indeterminacy without the inscrutability of reference, see my 'Forcing and the Indeterminacy of Translation', *Erkenntnis*, 1979.

that there was something which *does* a certain thing, and the story can be understood even if one does not know what, physically, the condenser was. It may be circumstances like this that suggest that 'functional' marks a *kind* of description. This would be a mistake; Hertz did not store electricity in an abstract functional role or in something that can store electricity *because* it satisfies a certain abstract description of a role. Physicists avail themselves of functional descriptions when, for example, some experimental design utilizes a part of physics that is simply taken for granted. Textbook authors just assume the reader knows enough about electricity that they don't have to go into condensers. Similarly, mathematicians feel free to instruct their readers to 'take the first derivative' without bothering to define the differential operator in δ–ε terms.

V

Materialism, 2

I HAVE so far deferred discussion of two of the most serious problems for materialism: the apparent incorrigibility of our knowledge of our own mental states—the privacy of experience—and the intensionality of propositional attitudes. Section 1 of this chapter presents a materialist account of privacy. Sections 2 and 3 consider views of Rorty which spring from the problem of privacy and lead to more general issues in philosophy of mind and philosophy of language. Section 4 argues that the phenomenon of intensionality offers no insuperable problems for materialism.

1. Privacy and Incorrigibility

The immediate access we have to at least a great many of our own mental states presents the most intuitively forceful objection to materialism. If I am in pain I don't *find out* or gather evidence that I am in pain. I cannot be *wrong* in thinking that I am in pain. I am immediately aware that I am in pain; I am the 'final authority' on whether I am in pain. (If this is held not to be true of pain, it is true of it seeming to me as if I am in pain.) On the other hand, it is suggested, I could not have such knowledge of any physical state of affairs.[1]

The materialist should concede that there is an issue about privacy. I am closer to my own mental states than anyone else is, and my knowledge of them at least appears to differ from any knowledge I could have of any other subject-matter and from what anyone else's knowledge of those states could be. Materialism must accommodate these facts. Ryle dismisses the phenomena of privacy and privileged access as a grammatical mistake, the inflation of a truism. 'Only I can have my pains', he says, belongs in the same logical area as 'Only I can catch my catches'.[2] This is correct, but

[1] See K. Baier, 'Smart on Sensations', *Australasian Journal of Philosophy*, xl. 1 (May 1962), 57–68.

[2] *Concept of Mind*, p. 239.

entirely beside the point. Consider my physique, something only I can have. True, no one holds that I have privileged epistemological access to my physique, or worries about a consequent problem of other physiques, even though my physique is just as 'logically private', as 'logically unshareable', as my experiences are. This is echoed in Wittgenstein's remark: 'I cannot be said to learn of [my sensations]. I *have* them'.[3] But what all this overlooks is that the rest of the world can *see* my physique, and can see that I have the physique I have. But not only am I the only person who has, I am the only person who can witness (in a sense that needs explaining) that I have, the experiences I have. Even though only I can have my physique, my physique is no mystery to you; but my experiences *are* a mystery to you. This is the privacy intuition, and the Rylean analogy fails to address it. (I will return to why Wittgenstein thought that 'I have my sensations' is all there is to be said about privacy.)

Another quick way with the privacy problem is appeal to the opacity of 'A is aware of x'. The fact that I am aware that I am in pain and not aware that I am in brain state b no more shows that pain is not b, than my being aware of being in New York and my not being aware of being in Bagdad on the Hudson shows that New York $\neq$ Bagdad on the Hudson.[4] If my being in pain $= b$, awareness of my being in pain *is* awareness of b, whether I know it or not. This is something the proponent of privacy will grant; what he wants to know is how I could have the immediate access to my brain states that I have to my experiences, whatever the description, if any, I am aware of them under. Whatever being in pain is, I cannot be wrong in thinking I am in pain—and how could this be true of a brain-state even if it is not required that I identify it *as* a brain state? Notice that the materialist cannot explain how I can be aware of my pain without being aware of b by saying that pain is how b appears to the brain whose state it is. That is the double aspect theory.

The privacy objection runs 'you can't be wrong about your mental states while you can be wrong about your brain states'; so doesn't it run afoul of Wittgenstein's plausible aphorism 'where you can't be wrong you can't be right'? Perhaps not. Wittgenstein's conclusion that since you can't be wrong about your mental states it is senseless to claim to know that you are in pain is certainly counterintuitive

[3] *Investigations*, sec. 246.
[4] Harman, *Thought*, p. 37.

enough to prompt rejection of the aphorism. Anyway, the 'can't' of the aphorism is obviously susceptible of numerous interpretations. Perhaps those senses in which we 'can't be wrong' about our mental states are not ones to which the aphorism applies. The next order of business, then, is to distinguish the various senses of 'you can't be wrong', and see which ones describe our relation to our mental states.

Before turning to this, however, a preliminary point should be noted. The privacy objection runs that I can know that I am in pain without consulting any sort of evidence, while if you want to know what it is like to be me you must ask. Yet you have as much access to my nervous system as I do; so what I know about when I know I am in pain is not my nervous system. But this argument uses a false premise. I do have a relation to my nervous system that you don't, that of being *hooked up* to it. Perhaps this patent physical asymmetry between my relation to my nervous system and your relation to it, in conjunction with a proper understanding of the 'can' in question, explains in physicalistic terms how I can know without inference what is going on with me. At any rate this physical asymmetry blocks the argument that immediate access must be physicalistically inexplicable because there is *no* physical differentia of systems exhibiting privileged access. One aim of a materialist account of immediacy, then, is to show that it is a phenomenon potentially explicable by the physical relation of my nervous system to its various subsystems.

When philosophers discuss privileged access, they seem to have three things, not always distinguished, in mind: directness, infallibility, and incorrigibility. These three notions in turn may be entangled with questions about the causal conditions of belief and knowledge.

Let us say that A is *directly aware* that p if A does not *conclude* that p; otherwise, A is indirectly aware that p. (We can explain 'A is directly aware of object x' as 'A is directly aware that x is present'.) A is directly aware that p when there is no way A got to know that p, where 'a way of getting to know' is any inferential process A performs that results in belief, or any evidence from which A draws conclusions. A can be directly aware that p even if there are causes for A's belief that p. A mark of direct awareness is that, if A is asked 'How did you know?' or 'why do you believe?' he will only be able to shrug his shoulders.

What action theorists call basic action—action not done via the doing of some other action—is an analogue of direct awarness. An action *a* can be basic even if the doing of *a* was caused; *a* is basic so long as no other action of the same agent was among its causes. The awareness is basic because *A* does not use anything in the causal chain resulting in his belief as a basis for concluding *p*. The causal chain explains how *A* knows *p*, but not how *A* got to know *p*. This compatibility between directness and causation means there can be physical models for direct awareness (see fig. 1 below). Note also that *A*'s direct awareness of *p* says nothing about the epistemic status of *p* or *A*'s warrant in believing it. You can non-inferentially believe a falsehood (although we are reserving 'direct awarness' for non-inferential belief in a truth); and you can be directly aware of a proposition which is in no way self-evident.

Our awareness of our mental states is direct. Baier and others are right when they point out that I do not *find out* that I am in pain. It is part of what distinguishes introspective knowledge. It is this fact that may have led some philosophers to deny that we have knowledge of our mental states. Consider the following plausible principle: if *A* knows *p*, there is a way *A* got to know *p*. This principle is in fact ambiguous. It might mean that there is always 'a way *A* got to know *p*' in the sense explained on p. 139. So understood it is false. Or, it might mean that there is always a causal explanation for *A*'s coming to know *p*. So understood the principle is true, but it has, so understood, no bearing on introspective knowledge, since directness is compatible with causation. My knowledge that I am in pain may be both direct and the result of a causal process. Sceptics about introspective knowledge may have confused the irrelevant true form of the principle with the relevant, false, form. Similarly, privacy objectors who notice that introspective knowledge is direct and that knowledge of one's nervous system would involve causal processes may have concluded that introspection is not knowledge of the nervous system by missing the compatibility of directness and causation.

Another feature of introspective knowledge is that it can't be wrong; since directness is irrelevant to warrant, directness can't be the whole story about introspection. It may be thought that introspection is infallible, where a belief that *p* is *infallible* if '*A* believes *p*' entails *p*. Hume's law, that no two distinct existences are logically connected, entails that there is no infallible knowledge. *A*'s belief that p is one thing and p is another; it is always logically possible for A to believe that p while p is false. Privileged access, therefore, cannot be explicated as infallibility.[5] (*A fortiori*, any argument against materialism that premises the infallibility of introspection is unsound.)

Before defending this rejection of infallibility in more detail, let me push on to a weaker epistemic notion that might take up the slack left by directness. Let us say that A knows p *incorrigibly* if it is causally impossible for A to be wrong about p if A believes p. 'A believes p' and certain laws of nature entail p; that is why we are never wrong. Some of our knowledge of our internal states is incorrigible. If it *feels as if* running will hurt my knee, it generally turns out that running does cause my knee to hurt. If it feels as if my thumb is behind my back, my thumb never fails to be behind my back. Of course there is no logical necessity here, and the causal paths in question can be interfered with so that it feels to me as if my thumb is behind my back, while in fact my thumb is in front of me. But in standard circumstances there are causal processes which as a matter of fact always eventuate in true belief.

The materialist construes privileged access as the two-fold fact that one's knowledge of one's inner states is direct and incorrigible. Suppose I feel a pain in my leg. This, says the materialist, is a brain state. I (that is, my entire nervous system) am so constructed that whenever I am in this state, it is possible for me to become directly aware of this state. This direct awareness is another brain state. The belief that I am in this first state is always right. No one else can have incorrigible knowledge of my states since the causal route between my awareness of my leg and my awareness of this awareness is more direct and reliable than the causal route between my awareness of my leg and any other nervous system's awareness of my awareness of my leg. In particular, any other route must go through my behaviour.

It is a contingent fact that we know incorrigibly what we are directly aware of. Perhaps the only things we know incorrigibly are those we know directly. One can imagine worlds in which incorrigibility was detached from directness, worlds so constructed that looking something up in an Almanac was causally certain to result in true belief. There might be worlds in which one formed non-

[5] See D. Armstrong, *A Materialist Theory of the Mind* (Routledge & Kegan Paul; New York: 1968), chap. 6 for similar reflections.

inferential opinions which were usually wrong. (One would learn to distrust this spontaneous tendency to believe.) We might have been directly and incorrigibly aware of what in this world we are indirectly and corrigibly aware of. Suppose someone 'just knew' what was happening on Arcturus. When you ask him how he knows, he asks you how you know where your thumb is. Evidently the limits of the self are set by the limits of direct, incorrigible knowledge and basic action. If our hypothetical subject could also act basically with Arcturus as we act basically with our thumbs, Arcturus would be *his* in just the way my thumb is *mine*. It also seems—and this may reflect deep facts about the causal structure of the world—that we have direct incorrigible knowledge of whatever we can act basically with. It might prove interesting to ask what would become of the concept of the self if there were a split between knowledge and power here.

There are natural objections to the foregoing account of privileged access. When I have a pain in my leg, it is logically necessary that I am *aware* of this: pains must be conscious. It is inconceivable that one have a conscious (as opposed to 'unconscious') pain and not be aware of it. The mistake here is carelessness about what one is aware of when one is in pain. I argued in IV.3 that pain *is* an awareness—of one's leg, say. It is the fact that pain is an awareness that suggests that it is logically impossible to be in pain without being aware you are in pain. But this latter awareness, that you are in pain, is not the same awareness as the one logically guaranteed by your being in pain (the pain itself). The latter awareness is the awareness that you are aware of your leg. It is logically necessary that you are aware if you are aware of your leg, but not logically necessary that you note that you are aware. If, however, you do take note, the notes will be incorrigible.

'Awareness of pain' is ambiguous. If you say 'I am aware of a pain in my leg' you are not claiming to be aware of pain. In this sense of 'aware of pain', awareness of pain entails pain because the 'of' is the 'of' of identity. If the 'of' in 'awareness of pain' is the 'of' in 'the pen of my aunt', pain does not entail awareness of pain. Awareness of pain appears infallible when these two 'ofs' are run together.[6] Take this parallel case. I hold object *o* up to mirror *m*: *m* reflects *o*, and I refer to 'the image of the reflection of *o* by *m*'. Since a reflection *is* an image, it is logically necessary that when there

[6] See Hinton's discussion of 'torture' in *Experiences*, pt. I.

is a reflection there is an image of the reflection. But suppose there is another mirror *m′* reflecting *o* being reflected by *m*. We might also call what *m′* shows 'an image of the reflection of *o* by *m*'. This second 'image of' does not use the 'of' of identity, and it is in this sense merely contingent that there is both a reflection and an image of the reflection. Conflating the two senses of 'image of' might suggest that reflections are logically peculiar, logically connected to images they are distinct from.

The intuition that knowledge of one's sensations is infallible dies hard. Perhaps it is merely causally necessary that when I believe I am in pain I am in pain. But surely if it feels to me as if I am in pain, I cannot be wrong about that. It is logically impossible for me to be wrong about its feeling as if I were in pain. This argument plays upon the ambiguity of 'feel' noted in IV.4. If 'feel' means 'am under the impression', there is no reason to think that '*A* feels he is in pain' entails '*A* is in pain'. The 'can't be wrong' here must be incorrigibility. However, the word 'feel' also has a sense in which 'feeling of pain' is synonymous with 'pain'. In that sense, to say that one has the feeling that one is in pain, or 'feels as if he is in pain', means feeling as one feels when one is in pain; i.e. *being in pain*. In this sense it is indeed logically impossible to feel that one is in pain without being in pain; but only because when one is in pain, one is in pain. In that sense, 'feeling that one is in pain' is not a state distinct from actually being in pain, so the entailment holds without yielding a case of infallibility. Here is a seductive chain of equivalences: I believe I am in pain ≡ It feels to me as if I am in pain ≡ It feels to me as it feels when I am in pain ≡ I am in pain. The move from the second to the third sentence makes the pun on 'feeling'. I suspect Wittgenstein dismissed talk of knowledge of one's sensations as empty in part because he understood 'feeling that one is in pain' in the second sense, and noticed the triviality of inferring from it that one is in pain.

By invoking two distinct awarenesses in introspection—awareness of one's leg and awareness of one's awareness of one's leg—the materialist avoids certain incoherences any doctrine of privileged access is allegedly heir to. Ryle says the very idea of introspective certainty requires, absurdly, that mental states be 'self-intimating'.[7] But no mental state is required here to be self-intimating in any objectionable way. When I am introspectively aware that my leg

[7] *Concept of Mind*, pp. 158 ff.

hurts, the second awareness is the object of the first just as a wall might be the object of a first-order awareness. Nor is the second-order awareness expected to be like the first awareness. My awareness that I am in pain is as much like *being apprised* that I am in pain as it is like the awareness I have of my leg, being special only in being direct and incorrigible. Nor need my awareness of my leg be *self-revealing*; it 'reveals itself' to my introspective consciousness, but in no more problematic way than my shirt 'reveals itself' when I look at it. This account, finally, makes the Humean argument against infallibility natural and even obvious. Just as it is logically possible for me to have a shirt on and not be aware of it, it is logically possible for me to be aware of my leg and not be aware of *that*.[8]

One can construct a physical system to react to its internal states in a way no other system reacts to the internal states of the given system. Such a system is a physical model for direct and incorrigible awareness, and shows that physicalism is compatible with privileged access. Such a 'consistency proof' does not require, or pretend to show, that the physical system described, or any physical system, is introspectively aware of itself; only that every plausible description anyone has been willing to offer of introspection can be satisfied by a physical system. Consider the configuration marked *C* in fig. 1. Lights b_1 and b_2 are wired in parallel to a device *R* which closes

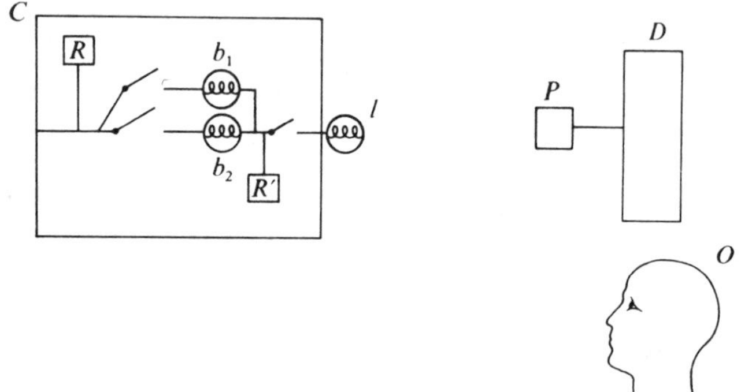

Fig. 1

[8] This account of introspection is suggested by Quine's and Skinner's. Quine understands consciousness to be 'a faculty of responding to our own responses' ('On Mental Entities', p. 227), and Skinner calls introspective reports verbal responses to our discriminative responses (*Science and Human Behavior*, pp. 275–6). Recall that Skinner calls perceiving a 'response'.

one circuit at a time. The internal states of *C* are $\{b_1$ is on, b_2 is on$\}$. *C* is sealed, so it is impossible to tell from outside which b_i is on or to establish any electrical path from the b_i to a terminal outside *C*. The resistance of b_1's filament is greater than that of b_2's, so b_1 passes a current of lower amperage into light *l* on *C*'s outer surface; *l* glows more brightly when b_2 is on than when b_1 is. (Let us call these two states of *l* 'b_1-illumination' and 'b_2-illumination'.) Thus *l* reacts *immediately* to *C*'s internal state and is, as things are, the only thing that does so. Moreover, given the laws of electrical conduction, *l* reacts 'incorrigibly' to *C*'s internal state: it is causally impossible for *l* to give off b_2-illumination when b_1 is on. The analogy between *l*'s response to the b_i and introspection can be extended by adding a device *R′* which determines whether the link between the b_i and *l* is closed. We do not always introspect, and *C* need not automatically monitor its inner states.

Contrast *l*'s relation to *C*'s internal states with that of a human observer *O* or a photoelectric cell *P* poised opposite *C*. Let *O* know about the internal construction of *C* and let *P* be connected to a program *D* which determines, in an obvious way, which b_i is on from the light hitting *P*. The routine *D* executes to display the internal state of *C* (a routine which uses the same information *O* uses to infer *C*'s internal state from *l*'s brightness) is how *D* 'knows' *C*'s internal state. The reasoning *O* runs through is how *O* knows *C*'s internal state. Neither *O* nor *P* know directly what is going on in *C*. Moreover, things may go wrong inside *D* or *O*, or the space between them and *C*, which leads them to err about *C*'s internal state. The contrast between *C*'s reaction to *C*'s inner states and those of *D* and *O* to *C*'s inner states is just that between a man's knowledge of his inner states and the knowledge anyone else has of them. *C* could even be trained to respond to its inner state. Originally some external cause *E* triggers *R* to close the b_1 circuit. So originally *l* goes on when *E* impinges on *C*. Eventually *C* 'learns' to respond to b_1's being on even in the absence of *E*. *C* needn't know anything about its internal state learn to react to it. For *C*, b_1 being on is simply 'what goes on when *E* is present'.

The direct/indirect distinction comes out, under this analogy, as a matter of black and white: for *O* and *D* there is a way to get to know what state *C* is in, while for *C* there is not. But incorrigibility appears as a matter of degree. As long as copper conducts electricity and coefficients of resistance stay what they are, *l* will emit

b_i-illumination precisely when b_i is on. But if D is well made and P is pressed close to l, D will also, as a matter of causal necessity, display 'b_i is on' precisely when b_i is on. This is as it should be. Ryle has emphasized that I may have a clearer idea of what is on your mind than you do. Quine suggests replacing the iron curtain between public and private with a smoke screen. Certainly the *subject-matter* of beliefs about inner states have turned out to be pedestrianly empirical—whether, for example, you are now in the state you were in when you last saw a lemon. It in no way differs from the question of whether you are wearing what you wore when you last saw a lemon. The difference lies only in directness, and incorrigibility construed as a matter of degree which peaks for one's own case.

When a system like a man or C is monitoring itself, *who* or *what* is doing the monitoring? It is sometimes supposed that *this* will elude the materialist's net, and that it might present an insuperable problem for *any* theory of the self.[9] What is doing the monitoring could not itself be monitored during the monitoring. Even if the monitor could monitor itself *qua* monitored, it could not monitor itself *qua* monitoring. Kant called this ultimate center of consciousness the 'transcendental ego', and combined the best of Hume and Descartes by denying that it was either observable or physical. But Kant did not take this to mean that the transcendental ego is a *non*-observable (non-physical) object. He took it to mean that 'the concept of the "I think" which accompanies all judgement' is not the concept of an *object* at all.

There is no need to acquiesce in Kant's opaque dissolution of the problem of the elusive ego. The materialist can take 'the "I think" which accompanies all judgement' as topic neutrally denoting whatever monitors self-monitoring systems, and say that it is the system itself. 'x is monitoring x' is how we describe a whole human nervous system, where the property of being self-monitoring may well be reducible to the execution of various sub-routines by various parts of a self-monitoring system.[10] Further reflection on Fig. 1

[9] Cf. T. Nagel, in Rosenthal, ed., *Materialism and the Mind-Body Problem*, pp. 109–10; also see K. Gunderson, 'Asymmetries and Mind–Body Perplexities', in Rosenthal.

[10] 'Being self-monitoring' would be, in Dennett's language, a predicate at the 'personal' level of description; see D. Dennett, *Content and Consciousness* (Humanities, N.Y.: 1969). This is of course compatible with the property it expresses being reducible to sub-personal properties.

makes this suggestion attractive. What is monitoring C? Not just l, for it is l's hook-up with the b_i, R, and R' which makes l's behaviour a response to C's internal states. Not C, since it is the part l of C which is doing the monitoring. Rather than monger any more mystery, it seems best to say that 'C is a self-monitoring system' is a shorthand description of the whole configuration C and the various facts just recited. One might choose to count C as the whole apparatus minus l, and then say that it is the system $\{C, l\}$ which is monitoring the state of C. This threatens to generate a regress, since we still have no system monitoring *itself*. But if we do make this verbal decision, why not make another one and say that the system being monitored by the system $\{C, l\}$ is not C but $\{C, l\}$?

C of course cannot also monitor the process by which C monitors its internal state. C cannot keep an eye on l's behaviour. The only thing that could do that would be a super-system C' which contained C as a proper part. C' might for example be the system $\{C, P, D\}$, with P monitoring the monitor l. C' is also monitoring itself, and part of itself is a self-monitoring subsystem. That *this* regress is in the offing should be no surprise, nor any reason for abandoning C as a physical model for introspection. It may not be strictly true that the nervous system is incapable of monitoring the process by which it monitors itself. The nervous system *may* have a direct and incorrigible relation to its own lower-level monitorings—this would correspond to direct awareness of our awareness of our inner states. Surely, however, there is some n such that nth-order introspection is humanly impossible. We can trace the sequence of physical systems C, C', C'',... until we find the appropriate physical model for our knowledge of our internal states. More sophisticated knowledge than that of the processes by which the nervous system directly and incorrigibly responds to its responses to its responses... would be a corrigible and indirect part of physiology and control theory.

The self seems elusive because 'what is introspecting my internal states?' is so posed as to expect as an answer something other than the self whose internal states are being monitored. But what besides system S could be such that its *self*-monitoring monitored the states of system S? The problem of the self remains of a piece with the problem of substance (III.5).

2. *Rorty's Replacement Thesis*

Some materialists take the physicalistic explicability of privacy to require a more radical devaluation of privileged access than that recommended here. In addition to denying that introspection is infallible, they deny that it is or ought to be even especially incorrigible. This prompts them to recommend a change in our view of first-person introspective reports: we should allow them to be overridable by external evidence. This recommendation, in turn, is sometimes accompanied by the recommendation that the introspective language of ordinary English be replaced by a physicalistic language. Thus R. Rorty suggests that if science discovers that being in pain is brain state *b*, we should train children to say 'I'm in brain state *b*' rather than 'I'm in pain' when reporting their inner states. This would eliminate the unwanted dualistic implications of ordinary language.[11]

The following model may clarify Rorty's position. Consider a man whose hand is sealed in a box which also contains an aggressive shrew. He knows without inference that something is going on in the box, while others must observe his behaviour to determine what is going on in the box. The man has 'privileged access' to the shrew. At the same time his beliefs are obviously corrigible—his belief that the shrew is biting him could be overridden by X-rays. As I understand Rorty, he is suggesting that this ought to be adopted as the correct model for introspection. Reports about our inner states are the logical analogues of the man's reports about the shrew, and are similarly corrigible. The meaning-rules which govern 'pain', and which *now* forbid pain reports to be overridden by external observation, should be changed to permit this. Children would be taught to say 'pain' when *b* is going on, since science will have discovered that *b* is what was going on when we used ' "pain" in the old rough-and-ready way" '.[12] If an EEG showed that brain process *b′* was going on, a subject would no more hesitate to retract the claim that he was in pain that our original subject would hesitate to retract claims about the shrew falsified by X-rays.

I discuss in the next section Rorty's broad claim that languages can have built-in theoretical biases. Here I will consider the more standard criticism that Rorty's thesis simply avoids the issue, either by changing the subject of the current mind–body problem, or

[11] 'Mind–Body Identity, Privacy and Categories', in Rosenthal.
[12] Ibid.

because the current mind–body problem re-emerges in Rorty's own terms. I think these criticisms are correct; and I will end this section with a discussion of how the dispute between Rorty and his critics looks to modified topic neutralism.

Rorty, along with other contemporary 'revisionary' metaphysicians, holds that such are the possibilities of conceptual growth that even a *meaningless* sentence can become meaingful. Words could acquire new criteria of application. Rorty cites the familiar example of 'metre': 'A metre is (now, but was not always) what matches the Standard Metre'.[13] Similarly, even if our criteria for 'sensation' *now* involve the final authority of the subject, we might find it convenient to introduce new criteria that permit this authority to be overridden. Against this, other philosophers have claimed that what Rorty is really talking about is a change of subject.[14] Consider this new criterion for 'trout': a trout is any group of printed pages enclosed by covers. It used to be meaningless to say that a trout has a happy ending, but now it is meaningful. If conceptual growth requires it, we can expand the scope of icthyology in this way. But surely I am just changing the subject away from trouts; Rorty's problem is to distinguish his manœuvre from this one. Consider again the example of the metre. It is literally contradictory to describe the change Rorty mentions as showing that there was a time when a metre was not coincident with standard s, but is now coincident with s. This entails that two things could be a metre long but differ in length. It entails that an object can be less than a metre long at t and exactly a metre long at t', $t' \neq t$, without changing its length. Surely the correct description of 'changes in the metre' is that the *word* 'metre' at one time denoted one length and at another time denoted another length.

Some extensions of words are, to be sure, 'natural', and sometimes sentences can become meaningful without involving any intuitive meaning-change. If it is stipulated that 'the temperature of a team's team spirit' is the average body temperature of all the team members at half-time, one can meaningfully say 'The team spirit had a temperature of 99°' and still, intuitively, be talking about what one is talking about when one says 'Team spirit is essential for victory'. Such extensions appeal to the innate sense of analogy at work in all language learning. What Rorty needs to show—and what looks

[13] Ibid., p. 193.
[14] See e.g. N. Malcolm, *Problems of Mind* (Harper, N.Y.: 1972), p. 72.

very unlikely—is that the stipulations he envisages are more like this one than the one about 'trout'.

The other side of this coin is that instituting physiological first-person introspective reports would give them a use they do not have in their present third-person employment, indeed the very use current introspective reports have. (Cornman and Bernstein stress this.) The mind–body problem resurfaces in Rorty's physiological Utopia as that of the denotation of these erstwhile purely physiological reports in their new usage. It is, of course, open to Rorty to insist that it has the same function, and it is hard to see how to adjudicate the issue. But even if we give this issue to Rorty, it is hard to see how his thesis can handle the statement 'It seems to me as if I am in *b*', which will become the general form of introspective reports in a language stripped of sensation words. Thinking back to the Rorty model for introspection, we glided past what is probably the most natural objection to it: while the man's beliefs about what the shrew is doing are corrigible, he can't be wrong in the same way about what it *feels as if* the shrew is doing. Knowledge of this sort is the proper isomorph in the present model to introspective knowledge, and Rorty's thesis leaves quite unaddressed the issue of what to do with it.

The dispute between Rorty and his critics takes on a different cast to the modified topic neutralist. If 'being in pain' is the name of an inner state, there is nothing unfeasible or even interesting in Rorty's suggestion. We are free to choose any expression we please as a new name for that inner state, and train members of the next generation to use it when they are in pain. One could of course select the name of the brain-process being in pain is (if it turns out to be a brain process)—it being pointless to dispute about the *right* name for something. If pain were a brain state, only the existence of a meaning postulate connecting pain with something nonphysical could justify saying that pain has been eliminated rather than identified. But modified topic neutralism recognizes no such postulate. Meaning postulates spell out the connotations of expressions, and 'pain' is a connotationless name. Rorty has often motivated his 'eliminative' materialism with the argument that 'We cannot define "mental" as something that might turn out to be either mental or physical'.[15] True: *if* 'pain' had a meaning, its definition would

[15] 'Incorrigibility as the Mark of the Mental', *Journal of Philosophy*, lxvii. 12 (June 1970), 402.

presumably imply 'is something non-physical'. But modified topic neutralism sees the mental/physical contrast as a theory about the mental, not a condition built into the meaning of psychological terms.

Modified topic neutralism finds linguistic conservativism correct but beside the point, establishing as little as Rorty's programme would change. As long as introspective language is a matter of naming psychological states it hardly matters what language we use, and Malcolm, Cornman, and Bernstein have fallen into the same trap of thinking that some names are better than others. Rorty himself sometimes comes close to recognizing this:

> [L]et us imagine two sets of people, one raised to speak conventional English and the other raised to use only neurological reports. . . . Are these two groups experiencing the same things when they are simultaneously manipulated in various ways? Intuition perhaps suggests that they are. But what is this same thing, the intensity of the pain or the X-character of the brain process? . . . Either answer would do equally well. . . . If both sets of sentences are playing the same reporting role, then either 'entails what is stated' by the other. . . .[16]

This reference to the 'X-character of the brain process' versus 'the intensity of the pain' suggests a final, more substantial difference (or sense of difference) between Rorty and his critics. If you hold that ordinary introspective reports are defined via the phenomenal appearance properties of mental states, one will find a genuine gap between Rorty terms and ordinary ones. Ordinary ones will express these appearance properties while even the extended physicalistic language Rorty envisages will be innocent of them. So the real disagreement between Rorty and his critics is the existence of phenomenal appearance properties, which the objective vocabulary of physiology does not recognize, or allegedly lets in surreptitiously when given a new use. Here I think Rorty is right, and I will not rehearse the arguments against the double aspect theory.

The last few pages have suppressed the issue that prompted the replacement thesis: can introspective reports be overridden? If the question is whether scientific developments could lead us to override the infallibility of introspective reports, the answer is that we do not *now* have, or credit ourselves with having, infallible access to our mental states. This holds independently of Rorty's replacement thesis. We do have incorrigible access, and will continue to have it

[16] 'In Defense of Eliminative Materialism', in Rosenthal, p. 228.

even in Rorty's physiological Utopia. Even if a man's judgement that he is in brain state *b* is corrigible, he can't be mistaken if he believes that it is with him as if he were in brain state *b*, just as the shrew-box subject cannot be wrong in thinking that it is with him as if what is going on in the box now is like what went on just before. We need posit no phenomenal properties to explain this, and the impossibilities are merely causal.

3. Language and Conceptual Frameworks

Rorty's argument appeals to the idea that a language may contain prejudices or commitments so basic that the only way to avoid them is to shift to another language. In particular—and this is an impression many writers share—it is claimed that ordinary language has built-in Cartesian prejudices.[17] The general claim is interesting in its own right, and has attracted wide attention.[18] It is worth discussing here; if the general case fails, so in particular does Rorty's.

Languages have no prejudices. It is people who have prejudices and make prejudicial statements. Language is just a system of concepts—i.e. predicates—in which *anything* can be said. If a particular language L lacks a predicate P, P can always be added to L. If L were truly biassed against P its extension $L+P$ would be ill-formed or inconsistent. But a *language* cannot entail a contradiction; only contradictory sets of sentences can.

Before turning to the Sapir–Whorf hypothesis and expanding on this suggestion, a clarification of the replacement thesis shows how misleading it is to describe a scientific elimination as the elimination of a *word*. Take the discovery that the things thought to satisfy the meaning-postulate for 'witch' in fact do not. This did not eliminate 'witch' from English; 'witch' is still in dictionaries. What has been eliminated—from the corpus of sentences most English-speakers regard as true—is the sentence 'There are witches'. Even if Rorty were right both about materialism and the meaning of 'sensation', what would literally have been eliminated is the sentence 'There are sensations', from any true theory of the world. 'Sensation' itself would neither be nor deserve to be banished from English. The

[17] Cf. P. Feyerabend, 'Materialism and the Mind–Body Problem', in D. J. O'Connor, *Modern Materialism* (Harcourt, Brace & World, N.Y.: 1969), pp. 82–98.

[18] The *locus classicus* for the 'Sapir–Whorf' hypothesis is B. Whorf, 'A Linguistic Consideration of Thinking in Primitive Communities', in *Language Thought and Reality*, ed. J. Carroll (M.I.T., Cambridge, Mass.: 1956).

elimination Rorty has in mind involves the retention of 'sensation' and the adoption of the sentence 'There are no sensations'.

The Sapir–Whorf hypothesis has to be approached from a number of different directions, since a number of grounds are commonly cited for the claim that languages can harbour theses. Consider again the matter of witches. Granted, trivially, we can assert the sentence 'There are witches' in English; perhaps the availability of the predicate 'x is a witch' invites us to. But, There are witches' is a mistaken belief that admits of formulation in English, not a claim that the mere use of English commits one to. That English is not committed to 'There is a witch' is shown by the simple fact that its denial, 'There are no witches', is also a sentence of English. Containing a word is a far cry from containing the existential thesis that the word applies. Nor is the invitation to subscribe to the thesis very pressing. English contains 'round square', but practically every English speaker knows there are no round squares.

Another argument for a strong version of the Sapir–Whorf hypothesis is that different languages correspond to, or are, different ways of partitioning the world. Eskimos notoriously have seventeen words for snow, while we have only one. Another way of putting this is that Eskimos have different words for different kinds of snow, and we do not. But all this shows is that Eskimos make finer discriminations about snow than we do, which is only natural given their way of life. They need to know what kind of snow snowed (will the seals come out in it?) and we don't. The big point is that we are not *wrong* when we say 'it snowed'. It did snow: snow is crystallized water, and that's what came down. We didn't say what kind of snow snowed, and an Eskimo might. But this does not mean we were wrong. Since what the Eskimo says entails what we say, he can hardly be right while we are wrong. The Eskimo spoke more precisely, but we can easily replicate the Eskimo's distinction in English. Suppose 'flurg' refers to heavy snowball-packing snow, and 'blurg' refers to light fine snow. There, we've done it; translated 'flurg' as 'heavy snowball-packing snow' and 'blurg' as 'light fine snow'. (It is absurd to inject the possibility that we can make no sense of the Eskimo's use of 'flurg' and 'blurg'. If we cannot, what makes us say he is using them to refer to two different kinds of snow?) True, there are no word–word translations between natural languages: a single word in one language may be mapped to a long story in another. But it is pointless to require expressively equivalent languages to be word-for-word intertranslatable. French is translatable into English even though the English 'not' goes into the more verbose 'ne . . . pas' construction of French. Similar remarks apply even to preservation of grammatical category under translation. Suppose locution l of language L belongs to grammatical category G. There is no reason that its translate l' of L' should also belong to G. This is not always realized. Whorf says that the Hopi do not have the Western notion of time because they do not tense their verbs. This is a *non sequitur* because the Hopi do in fact make the usual temporal distinctions, only with nouns rather than verbs. Their past tense for (their translate of) 'John is tall' is (their translate of) 'John is tall yesterday'. That we express with particles what they express with words does not show that English and Hopi temporal notions are mutually unconstruable, or that Hopi induces a different perception of time.[19]

But what if, so far as we can tell, 'blurg' and 'flurg' pick out the *same* kind of snow? Sometimes the Eskimo calls the same sample 'flurg', at other times 'blurg', and when we ask him the difference between flurg and blurg he shrugs his shoulders. Does this mean that he sees the world differently than we do, making distinctions we can't pick up? Not at all. The facts cited dictate the unexciting conclusion that 'flurg' and 'blurg' are *synonyms*. It would be absurd for an Eskimo philologist to decide that Americans have an inscrutible conceptual framework because they call indistinguishable items both 'bachelor' and 'unmarried man'. It is equally absurd to argue that co-reference shows the Eskimo framework ineffable relative to ours.

Suppose, in the synonymy case, the Eskimo reports that a disposition to call a sample of snow 'flurg' or 'blurg' corresponds to different states of mind. This by itself does not overthrow the synonymy interpretation. After all, 'rare steak' and 'burned piece of cow' are roughly synonymous, and certainly coextensive, but the attitudes accompanying them differ. One phrase puts steak in a good light, the other puts steak in a bad light. We can accord attitudinal differences to the Eskimo and thereby keep his words intelligible.

Some writers object to use of the synonymy concept in formulating

[19] The evidence is inconclusive on whether speakers of languages in which nouns rather than particles mark temporal distinctions are less punctual, guilt-ridden, or prudent. But anyway these are not cognitive differences, and there is surely the question of what is causing what here.

translational hypotheses. Yet this restriction renders the Eskimo's anomalous verbal behaviour even easier to construe: we must now say that he believes that all flurg is blurg and all blurg is flurg. 'Flurg' may even be for him a theoretical term, where he believes blurg is a reliable sign of flurg. This again is no basis for denying that Eskimo talk is entirely construable in English. We need only ask him about his snow theory. Any in-principle objection to finding out that he believes blurg to be a sign of flurg works as well against finding out that an English speaker takes a shrill whistle to be a sign of hysteresis, and using this to explain why he refers to the sound emanating from a speaker now as 'that shrill whistle', now as 'hysteresis'. The Eskimo's belief structure may be so unusual that we never do penetrate it. But so might the beliefs of the English speaker. So the language he speaks cannot be what accounts for the inscrutability of a speaker's theory.

A final consideration to support the Whorf–Sapir–Rorty view is the fact that the ostensibly observational terms of a language may be theory-laden; and one cannot avoid the theory without repudiating the terms. Thus 'sunrise' is not just a description of what we see in the morning: it is a description of what we see in the morning according to the geocentric cosmology. Saying the sun rose commits you to geocentrism. One fact which evidently fails to impress advocates of this argument is that English speakers who habitually use 'sunrise' will, if asked, deny that the sun moves. 'Commitment' is being used here in a sense so weak that a speaker can be committed to something he explicitly rejects. Why the fuss about being committed to dualism in a way that leaves us free to reject it? But the trouble with this final argument is deeper: it overlooks the fact that an expression can be detached from the theory that coined it. A heliocentrist can use 'sunrise' to refer to what the geocentrist falsely believed was the sun moving, and explain his use of 'sunrise' as 'what geocentrists were referring to by "sunrise" '. It is common practice to use a description without endorsing the theory that led to its introduction. I can use 'what you refer to as my "obstreperous behaviour" ' to refer to something I did without seconding your evaluation of it. Even expressions derived from causal hypotheses can be thus detached. If *X* was believed to be caused by *Y* and commonly called 'the result of *Y*', a sceptic about the causal hypothesis can continue to refer to *X* as 'the result of *Y*' with the understanding that he means 'what is falsely believed to be the result of *Y*'. If this seems too cumbersome an account of ordinary discourse, the complexity was occasioned in the first place by the thesis that referring expressions are wedded to theories.[20]

4. Intensionality

A wide variety of psychological states are *about* something, or have intensional objects. A number of philosophers take this to present a difficulty for physicalism: a thought cannot be a brain state (it is said) because the relation of a thought to its object differs from any relation a brain process can bear to anything.

> How, indeed, can any purely physical state of any purely physical object ever be a state that is *for* something, or *of* something, in the way that my desires and thoughts are such? And how, in particular, could a purely physical state be in this sense *for* or *of* something that is not real?[21]

This is the *intensionality argument*; the present section discusses and eventually rejects it. The intensionality argument seems to have intimidated materialists, who characteristically concentrate on mental states like sensations which ostensibly lack intensional objects. The intensionality argument cannot show that objectless mental states are not brain states. Materialism, however, is a general thesis about all mental states, and must come to terms with aboutness and intensionality.

The core of the intensionality argument is contained in the familiar observation that one never simply thinks or wishes; one thinks about or wishes for something. Even such states as free-floating anxiety are best understood as anxiety about everything, or about *something* bad to come.[22] The object of an object-taking mental state, furthermore, is essential to the state itself. It is inconceivable that a state have a different object than the one it does have. If I am hoping for a raise, that *same* hope could not have been for a sunny week-end. Not only would I be hoping for something else, it would be a different hope. My thought of Columbus is internally related to Columbus; change the object to Vespucci and you change the thought. And this yields the argument:

[20] For a further discussion of these topics, see my 'Vs. Ms.', in *Sex Equality*, ed. J. English (Prentice-Hall, N.J.: 1976), pp. 216–19; also my 'On Theory-Change and Meaning-Change', *Philosophy of Science*, forthcoming.

[21] R. Taylor, *Metaphysics*, 2nd ed. (Prentice-Hall, N.J.: 1974), p. 14.

[22] See A. Kenny, *Action, Emotion and Will* (Humanities, N.Y.: 1963), pp. 60 f.

> The problem for the brain state theorist becomes even more intractable in connection with some mental entities which are described with the aid of individual internal object clauses. . . . My suggestion is that if a farmer hopes for the death of his wife, there is no way of individuating either his hope nor any alleged experience of hoping, which does not mention [*sic*] *what is hoped for*. But, so the argument runs, this cannot be an external relation between his hope and the death of his wife, since his hope is compatible with his wife's survival, and also with her being dead already, or even with his not being married [?]. That it is for the death of his wife and nothing else that he hopes is therefore an internal property of the farmer's hope, and it is this property which it seems unintelligible to regard as a property of any brain state at all.[23]

My Columbus-thought is necessarily of Columbus, but what internal relation could brain state *b* have to Columbus? It is easy to imagine any physical relation between *b* and Columbus not holding while *b*'s self-identity is preserved. Had Columbus never existed my brain might well be in precisely the condition it is in when I think of Columbus, yet *b* would then have had *no* relation to Columbus. And what relation can *b* bear but physical ones? No relation *b* bears can simulate aboutness: so *b* is not an object-taking mental state.

Another facet of the intensionality objection is the absurdity of asking someone how he knows what the objects of his intensional states are. If there is a knock on the door at the moment the floor creaks, and you ask me which one is frightening me, I cannot be wrong when I say I am afraid of the knocking. I need not inspect my mental states to find out what their objects are, nor do I treat statements about what they are as revisable. Can materialism accommodate such knowledge, which *seems* more than incorrigible—infallible, in fact? (I will eventually argue that we have incorrigible access (only) to some aspects of our intensional states—the other aspects not being knowledge at all.)

Freud is sometimes thought to have challenged the absurdity of

[23] Herbst, 'A Critique of the Materialist Identity Theory', p. 63. Cp. A. Melden: 'nothing can be an act of volition that is not logically connected with that which is willed—the act of willing is intelligible only as the act of willing whatever it is that is willed' (*Free Action* (Humanities, N.Y.: 1962), p. 53). Melden is here preparing the way for a non-Humean account of the relation of intention to action. To use notation introduced below, his argument relies on the premise that an intention *i* and its content *C*(*i*) are related as logically independent events cannot be. This presupposes that there is a *dyadic relation* between *i* and *C*(*i*). An application of the conclusions of this section is that there is a dyadic relation only when *i* and *C*(*i*) bear to each other the relations which logically independent events bear to each other, and in that case, *i* is a candiate cause of *C*(*i*).

wondering if we are right about what the objects of our mental states are. A Freudian case would be this. I see a face on the wall which frightens me. Anyway I *think* it is the face that is frightening me, but a psychoanalyst discovers that the face reminds me of how my father looked many years ago just before beating me. So I am frightened not of the face, but of my father. The memory of my father (or my own patricidal rage) is so painful, however, that I 'transfer' the fear of my father to the face.

Such an account of my fear of the face is a misdescription of an important empirical discovery about the causes of psychological states. What the psychoanalyst has discovered—and what Freud proposed is there to be discovered—is *the cause of my fear of the face*. I am afraid of the face, instead of being amused by or indifferent to it, because it resembles something long ago associated with pain. The past experience may have been so unpleasant that it is now impossible for me to become aware of the cause of my present fright.[24] This discovery about causes, however interesting, is compatible with the face itself being what I am afraid of. Indeed, if a psychoanalyst cites the childhood episode as the (unrecoverable) case of my present fright, his causal account entails that it is the face that is the object of fright. For what he is explaining is why I am afraid of *the face*. To suppose his account shows that I am not afraid of the face would be for it to abandon the data it was contrived to explain. Even waiving this point, there is nothing in Freud's discoveries about the impact of childhood experiences on later life to call into question the idea that the objects of thinking are what, without benefit of instruction, they seem to be. Freud's claims, even if true, do not lessen the materialist's need to accommodate whatever is correct in the intensionalist objection.

[24] Specifying the relevant sense of 'impossible' is complicated by the fact that my 'un-Freudian' fear of snakes may have been caused by a long-forgotten perusal of a herpetology text. My reading of the text is the cause of my fear of snakes, as my father's beating (or my response) is the cause of my fear of the face. The difference is that if I endorse a fear as rational, I will cite the episodes causing it as justification of the fear itself. If I remember the text I will offer it as my reason for fear. If I could be convinced by other evidence than memory that the cause of my present fear was that text, I would not take this as a reason for revising my estimate of snakes or regarding my fear as irrational. The mark of the Freudian case is that not only is it causally impossible for me to remember the cause of my fear of the face, but even if I did I would not cite that cause as my reason for fearing the face. If I could be brought by other means to agree that my father's face was the cause, I would take this as a reason for adopting a new attitude toward my fear of the face.

It is worth remarking that behavioural learning theory, at least as popularly interpreted,[25] is not innocent of the mistake lately scouted. It is often supposed that a dog does not love his master, but loves the food he has come to associate with his master. But surely it is more plausible to say that the dog does love his master, his love for his master having been caused by the association of his master with an unconditioned reinforcer like food. Learning theory is best understood as explaining how attitudes become directed to the very objects they seem, to uninstructed common sense, to have.

The thesis that mental states are internally related to their objects collides with physicalism only under a sharper formulation. If m is a mental state, let $C(m)$ be its intensional object, or *content*: C (my thought of Columbus) = Columbus, and C (my hope that someone is coming to dinner) = someone's coming to dinner. If $n = C(m)$, let us say that m is *about* n, or $A(m,n)$. Nothing hinges, of course, on thus thinking of thoughts as (virtual) entities instead of analytically eliminating them in favour of talk of persons thinking. The intensionalist can make his claim just as easily if he agrees to take as basic the predicate 'x is thinking about y'. He will then argue that *I* can't be a physical thing, since nothing physical can sustain *this* relation to anything. (Similarly, my eventual suggestion that 'is about n' is a monadic predicate of thoughts becomes, under this more austere rendering, the suggestion that 'is thinking about y' be reconstrued as the monadic predicate 'is a y-thinker'.) $A(m,n)$ is said by the intensionalist to be non-physical in two respects. (1) Since $A(m,n) \supset \Box A(m,n)$, $A(m,n)$ violates PL at its second variable place. Columbus may be the best Genoan fisherman, but my thought of Columbus is not a thought about the best Genoan fisherman. (Failure of PL is necessary for a relation to be internal. Even if insufficient, it is a satisfactory approximation here.) (2) $A(m,n)$ does not entail $(\exists x)A(m,x)$. I can be thinking about the present King of France even if there is no present King of France.

I will not challenge the intensionalist premise that all physical relations obey PL and EG. What must be stressed is that the intensionalist argument is coherent only if formulated in terms of PL and EG. If aboutness is not a relation, it is of course not a relation that brain states cannot bear; it is also not a relation that mental states bear, and the intensionalist argument runs aground.

[25] See, e.g., G. Harman, *The Nature of Morality* (O.U.P., New York: 1977), p. 139; but also see pp. 149–50.

If it *is* a relation, the intensionalist must be claiming that it differs systematically from physical relations; and the sharpest systematic difference is failure of PL and EG.

So formulated, the intensionalist argument rests on a muddle which can be distangled in two stages. The first stage consists of showing that to the extent to which aboutness ostensibly violates PL and EG, it is not dyadic. When *C*(*m*) does not exist or sustain co-referential substitution, '*A*(*m*,*C*(*m*))' is the ascription of the monadic predicate 'is a *C*(*m*)-thought' to *m* (see IV.3). When aboutness is internal it is not a relation, hence not a relation which brain states do not bear. The second stage consists of understanding, unhindered by worries about extensionality, how a brain state can satisfy such unusual monadic predicates as 'is a Columbus-thought', which mental states do admittedly satisfy.

Such exertions may seem unnecessary. Some materialists meet the intensionality argument head-on by citing uncontroversially physical objects that exhibit aboutness. T. Nagel cites the example of a wooden sign which says 'Fishing is forbidden'.[26] But this tactic is vulnerable to the objection that the aboutness exhibited by physical objects depends on their employment by beings with minds: the aboutness of the sign depends on the fishing-thoughts of the men who designed it and of those who see it. Some philosophers might dismiss such a rejoinder as resting on a psychologistic view of meaning, and claim that even if the human race were annihilated the sign would continue to say something about fishing. The intensionalist could concede this, but add that 'the sign would continue to be about fishing' just means that the sign would in that case have the unmanifested dispositional property of being able to produce certain thoughts. The issue comes down to the analysis of 'The sign would say "Fishing is forbidden" even if nobody saw it', an issue as unclear as the issue it was invoked to resolve. The intensionalist's hand has lately been strengthened by Grice's reintroduction of a measure of psychologism into the theory of meaning.[27] Grice makes the existence of intensions on the part of the sign's creators necessary for the sign to have 'non-natural' meaning: a physically similar object which had come to be through natural processes would not have been about fishing. We are thus back to the two-stage strategy.

[26] In Rosenthal, ed., *Materialism and the Mind–Body Problem*, p. 107.

[27] 'Meaning', in Rosenberg and Travis, eds. *Readings in the Philosophy of Language*.

The first stage is to show that whatever supports the claim that some given mental state is internally related to its object also shows that the ascription of this mental state is monadic; and where aboutness is genuinely dyadic, it obeys PL and EG. To see that this is so, consider the aptest description of *m*, my hope that the King of France is coming to visit. There being no King of France, there would seem to be nothing my hope is related to. Since we are assuming that *m* is internally related to *C*(*m*), my mental state would be exactly what it is now if there were a French King, so even if there were a French King, my hope would not be a relation between *m* and him. To appreciate the force of this point, consider for a moment some entities proposed by philosophers to keep my hope dyadic—there must be such objects if calling my hope a relation is not to be evacuated of meaning, and by hypothesis the object is not the flesh-and-blood King. Some philosophers have posited special intensional objects which subsist but do not exist. Taking such an entity to be the object of *m* is mistaken in two ways. The obvious problem is the intrinsic strangeness of these entities. Much more damaging is the fact that such posits, even if accepted, do not supply *m* with an appropriate object. I do not hope that an intensional, subsistent, King of France will visit. I want the real thing, someone who can sign treaties. The subsistent King cannot sign treaties; he can only subsistently sign subsistent treaties. Had I wanted a subsistent King of France, I would not have wanted the King of France. The only candidate for *C*(*m*) is flesh-and-blood royalty; and if none exists, there is no thing that I want to come to call.

Another kind of entity which has been proposed as that to which a man (or a hope) bears the aboutness relation are propositions, sentences, or descriptions.[28] The idea is that my wanting even a non-existent apple is a matter of my bearing the want-true relation to the sentence 'I have an apple', or the want-satisfied relation to the description 'an apple of mine'. Now whatever the merits of such analyses, they do not render my desire for the non-existent apple dyadic. What they do is analyse '*x* wants *y*' in terms of a dyadic relation *other than wanting*; they *replace* wanting by wanting-true, wanting-satisfied, or the like. If I want to bite an apple, and this in turn means that I want-true the sentence 'I bit an apple', it does not follow that I want to bite the sentence 'I bit an apple'. Wanting a sentence to be true is not wanting the sentence. The fallacy here

[28] See A. Danto, *Analytical Philosophy of Action* (C.U.P., Cambridge: 1973).

would be that of analysing an (ostensibly) relational predicate '$R(x,y)$' as '$R'(z,w)$' and concluding from this that the relata of R are actually z and w.[29] Analysing wanting as a relation between a person and a representation does not justify a dyadic construal of wanting.

Similar remarks apply retrospectively to the subsistent-entity construal of desire. Suppose there *were* such entities, and my desire that the French King visit were analysable as a relation of some sort between me and the subsistent French King. The relation cannot be wanting (see above), so let it be notional wanting. For me to want the King of France to visit is for me to notionally-want the subsistent King of France to visit. This does not make my wanting the King to visit dyadic; it entails at most that notional wanting is dyadic. Indeed, it would seem that notional wanting satisfies PL and EG. If the subsistent King is the most prominent abstract entity, what I want to come to call is the most prominent abstract entity. Moreover, the very point of positing subsistents was that *there be* something I notionally want to visit. The same holds for wanting true: if sentence S = sentence S', and I want S true, I want S' true; and *if* wanting-true is dyadic, then *there is something* I want-true.

So: if $A(m,n)$ is relational at all, it is a relation between m and and $C(m)$. Since $C(m)$ sometimes does not exist, $A(m,n)$ is, despite appearances, not dyadic at all in those cases. (The argument for this has nowhere presupposed that all relations are extensional.)

The following alternative account of the connection between m and $C(m)$ suggests itself. $C(m)$ is not something to which m, independently identifiable, is related; in citing $C(m)$ one is saying which mental state m is, one is identifying m. This is the real force of the remark that the identity of a thought is given by its object. In saying that $C(m)$ = Vespucci, I am saying that m is a Vespucci-thought rather than a Columbus-thought. The logical form of 'm is a thought of Vespucci' is $V(m)$; or, in the more austere person version, the logical form of 'A is thinking about Vespucci' is $V(A)$. Similarly, 'My fear is fear that my car will break down' does not express a relation between my fear and an event; it ascribes an individuating monadic predicate to my fear.

Philosophers loyal to ordinary usage may insist that my thought

[29] See my 'Extensionality of Causation and Causal-Explanatory Contexts' for instances of this fallacy in discussions of identity and of causation.

is still *of* Vespucci. This is unobjectionable so long as it is conceded that, when the ontological chips are down, this locution goes monadic. Semantic notions, so often invoked here, are very misleading. Recall Herbst's claim (p. 157 above) that there is no way to individuate a hope without mentioning what is hoped for. This occurrence of 'mention' is dangerously ambiguous. If 'mention' has the extensional force it has when opposed to 'use'—when it is synonymous with 'reference to'—Herbst's claim is false.[30] If what is hoped for does not exist, it is impossible to mention it in the referential sense of 'mention', the sense which gives intensionalism bite. On the other hand, Herbst might mean only that to describe some mental states one must *use* referring expressions. Whatever the problems raised by the use of such expressions in describing mental states, it is compatible with the failure of the term used to mention anything, and even with failure of the term to occur purely designatively. The need to 'mention' $C(m)$ in this sense does not advance the intensionalist argument. Only if $C(m)$ must be mentioned in the semantical sense of 'mention' are intensional ascriptions dyadic, and potentially problematic for materialism. Clinging to the ordinary unanalysed expression 'hope for y' allows the intensionalist to play the referential sense of 'mention' off against the non-referential sense. When the need to 'mention y' in a description of hope for y is properly understood, it ceases to support the claim that my hope for y bears a special relation to a possible non-existent.

Sometimes it is indeed natural to construe $A(m,C(m))$—i.e. the relation between the m-thinker and $C(m)$—as dyadic. Suppose some apple p exists and I stand in a direct epistemic relation to it—I have seen p and thought a good deal about it (see II.4). It is clearly in order to say, when I want p or a bite of p, that my wanting is a relation between me and p, or that my want stands in a relation to p. It is of p that I want a bite. Paradigm cases of relational wanting occur when the object of the want is borne a direct epistemic relation. But such cases provide no support for the intensionalist. If my want for p is relational, it is relational because I am directly epistemically related to p. Thus EG holds, since p exists. It is superficially circular to argue that PL holds because the relation between me and p is directly epistemic, but the claim becomes more plausible when we look at concrete cases. Suppose I have seen p and thought a good

[30] See the discussion of identification in I.3.

deal about it. (Not all my beliefs about *p* have to be true.) You know that *p* is the reddest apple in town. What could be more natural than for you to say that I want the reddest apple in town? This would be an acceptable way of describing my want to someone else even if it overrides the descriptions I would be willing to give of *p*. My relation to *p* is so fixed that an objective observer can detach his description of what I want from my descriptions of it. And this is just to say that PL holds. To just the extent that your description of my want is tied to how I would describe my want, a correct description of my want becomes invariant to the existence or non-existence of *p*, and thereby ceases to be a relation between me and *p*. Where PL fails, I am in the state of wanting to relieve my state of being without something answering to a certain description. It is easy to extend the conventions (E) and (I) of III.4 by distinguishing dyadic talk of 'want of *p*' from monadic talk of '*p*-wanting'.

The present account allows a want of *p* to become a *p*-wanting without a change in internal state. Thus if at *t* I have want of *p* and unbeknownst to me *p* ceases to exist at $t' > t$, I become a *p*-wanter at t' without there being any change in my conscious state. This is no paradox because the change described is not a change of state. If my only grandchild dies unbeknownst to me, I cease being a grandfather without changing any monadic states. When a mental state *m* is related to its object, the relation is contingent. The *state* can persist unchanged if its object winks out of existence. Revision of the logical form of an intensional ascription is an editorial comment made from the outside. The analogy with 'know' is patent. There need be no change in my belief state for me to cease knowing an occasion-sentence '*p*': all that need happen is that '*p*' become false. Thus, even if all the relations between brain state *b* and *p* are contingent, *b* may still be the desire for *p*, *all* the relations between *p* and the desire for it being contingent.

A popular objection to the monadic construction of intensional ascriptions (the 'monadic thesis, extended') focuses on the referring terms used in the allegedly monadic predicates. The monadic thesis must regard the (non-designative) occurrence of these normally designative terms as a typographical accident. This entails, however, that there are as many primitive monadic psychological predicates as there are possible objects of psychological states. The cruces of the 'uneliminability objection' are that this would make language learning impossible, and would leave manifest logical relations between intensional states unexpressible.

Consider first the language-learning argument.[31] If '*A*' and '*B*' are non-synonymous, the monadic thesis must regard '— is an *A*-desirer' and '— is a *B*-desirer' as independent primitives. Even if '*A*' and '*B*' are logically equivalent, the two expressions may be primitive if the derivations of '*A*' and '*B*' from each other are difficult. Defining the two ascriptions from '— is a --- desirer' by recursion requires that '— is an --- desirer' contains two variables, which is just what the monadic thesis denies. Yet, the argument runs, a language with infinitely many primitive predicates could not be learned. Even a child who knew what it was to be an *A*-desirer, knew what *A* was, knew what *B* was, and had mastered recursive substitution, would need independent instruction to master what it is to be a *B*-desirer. To suppose otherwise would be to suppose that a child who understood 'rattle', 'rat', 'cat', and recursive substitution thereby understood 'cattle'. We would be attributing a use-mention confusion to the child. When, then, would the child find time to learn any more than finitely many intensional ascriptions? Since children obviously do learn the psychological expressions of natural languages, the monadic thesis is false.

My former student Mark Alley has explained why the monadic thesis has no such empirical consequence as the unlearnability of natural language. For why could a child *not* systematically confuse use and mention when acquiring language, especially when the typography and phonetics of intensional ascriptions invite him to do so?[32] Consider quotation, another referentially opaque construction that invites monadic treatment and lies vulnerable to the language-learning argument.[33] Indeed, Davidson even holds that we assert quoted sentences; if not, there would be infinitely many primitive predicates of the form '— is a "*P*"-sayer' for learners of natural languages to master, in defiance of the fact that children do learn '— is a "*P*"-sayer' for all values of '*P*'. Now the problem with the language-learning objection is not just that Davidson's alterna-

[31] Its *locus classicus* is D. Davidson, 'Theories of Meaning and Learnable Languages', in Y. Bar-Hillel, ed., *Logic, Methodology and Philosophy of Science* North-Holland, Amsterdam: 1972); also see Wittgenstein's *Blue Book* (Harper & Row, N.Y.: 1965), p. 21.

[32] Cp. Quine's conjecture that mastery of identity requires use-mention confusion: *The Roots of Reference* (Open Court, Ill.: 1974).

[33] Davidson, 'Theories of Meaning'.

tive approach to wanting and quoting leaves unexplained what one wants when what one wants does not exist, or how to quote someone we disagree with. The chief problem is that it misconceives what a theory of logical form is *for*. To say that a certain theory of logical form accuses children of committing errors in acquiring language is not to say that these errors are empirically detectable, as computational errors committed in the learning of arithmetic are, or that these errors should be (or are even capable of being) corrected. All parties to the debate agree about what *happens* during language learning—where substitutional operations are performed, for example. One party is proposing an account of the logical form of language, and an account of logical form addresses a different set of issues. According to the monadic theory of logical form, some of the substitutional steps taken are fallacious; it is not suggesting that these steps *do not occur*, or that children should stop taking them. The monadic thesis is a framework for analysis which passes unflattering judgement on some of what it analyses.

Tarski's definition of truth offers a precedent. According to Tarski, language *N* is inconsistent if it contains the predicate 'true in *N*'. A less alarming version of this result is that, if *S* is an English sentence, '*S* is true' is not a sentence of English, but of meta-English. Some critics balk at the idea that we contradict ourselves or switch languages every time we remark on the truth of an English sentence. But to balk here assumes that the inconsistency Tarski uncovered is accompanied by the usual signs of inconsistency (and perhaps the prospect of more satisfactory alternative procedures). In fact, however, the situation is just that Tarski's overall theory redescribes what happens during talk of truth. Tarski's theory reclassifies ordinary talk of truth as either inconsistent or not in the language it seems to be.

The error theories for intensional predicates, quotation and truth agree with our ordinary conception of what happens; they simply count it as erroneous. Contrast this with a 'normal' error theory. I find that a batter is striking out because he takes his eye off the ball. My diagnosis of his mistake involves a small, ruinous nuance unnoticed by the batter. It carries the clear implication that he will profit from changing his ways. Neither my error theory nor Tarski's says that something ruinous and unnoticed is going on, nor do they imply that we will speak more effectively if we change our ways.[34]

[34] Kripke has recently argued with great force that Tarski's theory is indeed counterintuitive: see his 'Outline of a Theory of Truth', *Journal of Philosophy*,

The objection from the suppression of logical relations does not even require so much homage as an error theory. The monadic analysis does not prevent the *contents* of intensional states from bearing their proper logical relations. Those relations that it does block it blocks properly, for they are not logical relations at all. Suppose I hope that John and Sam are both tall. The logical form of this description of my hope m is 'm is a John-and-Sam-are-tall hope', or $JS(m)$. If m' is the hope that John is tall, its logical form is $J(m')$. There might seem to be a connection between JS-thoughts and J-thoughts of the form $(\exists x)JS(x) \supset (\exists x)J(x)$. (In the person idiom: any John-and-Sam-are-tall hoper is a John-is-tall hoper.) This conditional is clearly invalid, but it is proper that the monadic thesis bar such inferences. There is indeed a deductive relation between 'John and Sam are tall' and 'John is tall', which considerations of logical form should capture. There is, however, only a causal relation between the existence of two hopes, one that John and Sam are tall, the other that John is tall. It is a contingency of human psychology that anyone who hopes for one will hope for the other, no more a matter of logic than the fact that anyone who has had dealings with dental drills becomes averse to them.

One source of confusion is the fact that we attend to the contents of beliefs, hopes and the like for purposes of evaluating them. We extract p from the ascription of p-belief (perhaps committing a use/mention fallacy in so doing) to assess p's logical connection with the extracted contents of other beliefs. But the theory which evaluates belief—logic—has no special connection with the theory of the *presence* of beliefs. That belief is not closed under entailment is demonstrated by the fact that there are people who believe a set of sentences that entails 'There are infinitely many primes', but who do not believe that there are infinitely many primes. The explanation of the extensive coincidence between the causal and logical orders of psychological states is just that among the beliefs most people have is belief in the laws of logic (and willingness to use modus ponens). No theory of the logical form of beliefs need explain, or even be compatible with, the fiction that belief is closed under entailment. Another source of confusion is our reluctance to attribute the belief that p but not the belief that q if p obviously entails q. In that case belief that q is a criterion for belief that p.

lxxii. 20 (Nov. 1975), 690–716. The unavailability of the Tarski precedent would not change my main point.

But if we won't *say* that A believes p unless A believes q, it is clear that we do not regard p-belief and q-belief as two independent states. So the fact that the ascription of p-belief entails the ascription of q-belief does not provide an example of a logical relation between the existence of two beliefs. Further proof of this is the evident conventionality of the decision as to how obvious the entailment from p to q must be for ascription of q-belief to be a criterion for ascription of p-belief.

This causal conception of belief is sometimes thought to collide with the two-fold fact that we form our beliefs on the basis of reasons, not causes, and that we drop beliefs we come to believe are not the result of reasoning. The facts are as claimed. It is necessarily true that we want our beliefs to be reasonable. But the reasonableness of a belief, its being formed 'for a reason', is compatible with its being caused. As I understand it, 'p is a reasonable belief' means 'the belief that p was caused by belief that q, where q entails or supports p'. (Similarly, 'A believes p with reason' means 'A's belief that p was caused by his believing some q which also supports p'.) What critics of such a conception stress is that what I *think about* when I am deciding whether to accept p is q; what I ask myself is whether q supports p sufficiently. (I might go on to question q as well.) Unless I regard q as supporting p I will not come to believe p; and if someone shows me that I was mistaken in thinking that q supports p, where q was my sole support for p, I will forthwith cease believing p. I think about q's *logical* bearing on p. Now this describes accurately enough what goes on when one adopts a belief, but it describes a *causal process*—thinking about q, asking myself if q supports p—that results in my believing p. Of course, *I* don't think about whether my belief that q causes my belief that p. I am too busy thinking about q and its relation to p. But this is entirely compatible with my thinking about q and about q's relation to p being causally efficacious events. So the fact that prospective believers worry about the evidential rather than causal pedigree of their beliefs leaves the causal conception of believing untouched.

Another common objection to a causal account of belief is an alleged incompatibility between my believing p and my believing that my belief was caused.[35] This incompatibility is non-existent. If I find out that the cause of my believing p was believing q, and I also

[35] Cf. R. Trigg, *Reason and Commitment* (C.U.P., Cambridge: 1973); and S. Hampshire, *Thought and Action* (Viking, N.Y.: 1960).

believe that *q* is good grounds for believing *p*, I will not revise my estimate of *p* at all. It is easy to reconcile one's belief that the stock marketed plummeted with one's belief that one's belief that the stock market plummeted was caused by Walter Cronkite saying so on TV. Whether acquaintance with the cause of a belief makes one abandon the belief itself depends on the cause.

The final move in this dialectic is to ask how, if I regard my beliefs as caused, I can know that the causes of my beliefs are causes that make my beliefs reasonable. They might not be. Is not my belief that the causes of my beliefs are reasonable just a further caused belief? This objection betrays a misconception about the aim of a theory of what reasonable belief, and knowledge, are. If the reasonableness of belief that *p*, or knowledge that *p*, is defined *by any condition D at all* one can always ask how a prospective *p*-believer or *p*-knower can know that *D* is satisfied. It is, thus, clear that the theory that a reasonable belief is a belief *caused* in a certain way fares no worse with respect to an incipient regress than *any* theory which says that a reasonable belief is a belief that is *D*, for some condition *D*. For we can equally well ask the latter how a *p*-believer can know, or reasonably believe, that his belief is *D*.

But even if one could *not* know or reasonably believe that one's belief that *p* is *D*,[36] it would not follow that one's belief that *p* is not reasonable. The most that would follow is that the reasonable *p*-believer could not know that his reasonable *p*-belief was reasonable. And this of course is compatible with his *p*-belief being reasonable.[37] A special case of this is that in which belief that *p* is reasonable because caused in the right way. That the *p*-believer does not know or reasonably believe that his belief that *p* is caused in the right way does not entail that his belief that *p* is unreasonable. Thus, the view that beliefs are caused no more leads to a sceptical regress than does any other theory of belief.

Indeed, there is no reason why, if beliefs are caused and reasonable beliefs are beliefs caused in the right way, we can't know or reasonably believe that we know (or reasonably believe) what we know (or reasonably believe). Grant that *A* reasonably believes *p* if his belief

[36] This does not follow, of course, just from the fact that knowing that *D* holds of *p* is independent of reasonably believing *p*, which requires only that *D* holds. I turn below to alleged difficulties in knowing or reasonably believing that *D* holds.

[37] It would *not* follow that he believed that his *p*-belief was unreasonable; that *would* be incompatible with reasonably believing *p*.

that p was caused by belief that q, and q supports p. To say that A reasonably believes *that* is just to say that A believes [A's belief that p was caused by belief that q, and q supports p], and this latter belief was caused by A's believing r, where r supports the bracketed sentence. This again applies a general remark about all analyses of reasonable belief. If A's belief that p is reasonable iff $D(A,p)$, then A's belief that [A's belief that p is reasonable] is reasonable iff $D(A,D(A,p))$. The reasonability theorist can always reapply his analysis to beliefs having embedded beliefs unless he has hamstrung himself with an analysis which permits only beliefs with no embedded beliefs to be reasonable—and no standard analysis does that.

What I called 'the final move' conflates the question 'How can I know p?' with the question 'How can I know that I know p?' Sceptical arguments of all stripes thrive on this conflation: they ask how we can be sure that some proffered analysis of knowledge or justification holds in any given case, and think they have raised the question of how we can be sure of anything.[38] But all they have raised is the question of how we can be sure we know anything. The impossibility of settling this latter doubt (if indeed it cannot be settled) is compatible with every man knowing many things. But further pursuit of scepticism is beyond present purposes, which was to show the compatibility of the monadic thesis with language learning and such logical and causal relations as hold between psychological states.

Once intensional ascriptions are taken as typically monadic, the intensionalist argument becomes oddly resistant to clear statement. The intensionalist gets his longest run by posing these two questions to physicalism: (1) How can physical objects or states satisfy predicates which contain non-designative occurrences of referring terms?, and (2) Is one's knowledge of the intensional objects of one's mental states compatible with these states being physical?

One kind of reply to these questions must be dismissed.[39] This reply takes the use of the intensional vocabulary for describing a system as a matter of the adoption of that vocabulary by an observer external to the system. On this view, we ascribe intensional predicates to systems when other kinds of description—mechanistic, say—

[38] Documenting this claim would obviously be a major undertaking.

[39] Cf. Putnam, 'Minds and Machines', in S. Hook, ed., *Dimensions of Mind* (N.Y.U.: 1960); 'The Mental Life of Some Machines'; and Dennett, *Content and Consciousness*.

become too cumbersome for prediction. Apart from whether this approach sheds sufficient light on what the intensionalist shift is a shift to, it conflates the question of the appropriateness of a certain as-if attitude toward systems which may not literally be in intensional states with the question of the nature of the states satisfied by systems actually in intensional states. A satisfactory answer to the first might leave the second unaddressed. The ease with which we predict the behaviour of a chess-playing computer by thinking of it as wanting and planning may indeed be evidence that the computer really wants and plans to win. But this sort of ascription of intensional states depends on prior understanding of literal instances of wanting and planning. Indeed, it sometimes appears that the ultimate aim of the as-if strategy is to assimilate the ascription of intensional states of human beings to the as-if attitude we occasionally take to feedback systems. Apart from undercutting itself, such a proposal flies in the face of the fact that whether I fear snakes does not depend on whether observers can predict my behaviour if they assume I am. To say I fear snakes is not to say something about the most convenient way to think of me, but something about the way I actually am.

Pictorial representation is a better clue to the logical features of predicates like 'is an *A*-thought'.[40] It is clear that there can be unicorn-pictures even in a unicornless world; that 'unicorn' is an uneliminable part of the predicate 'is a unicorn-picture'; and that a unicorn-picture is not a hippogryph-picture even though 'unicorn' and 'hippogryph' are extensionally equivalent. To understand how a picture can be an *A*-picture would help to understand how a thought can be an *A*-thought.

This precedent best applies to question (2) on p. 170. How does the creator of a picture *know* what the picture is about, that it is an *A*-picture? The question is best answered obliquely: this is not something he *knows* at all, but something he *stipulates*. It has the representational properties it has becomes he has decided that it has them. He knows what its representational properties are only in the strained sense in which a man can be said to know the upshot of his own stipulation. This is the thought to follow: many of the puzzling

[40] Cf. Danto, *Analytical Philosophy of Action;* 'Representation Properties and Mind–Body Identity', *Review of Metaphysics*, xxvi. 3 (July 1973), 401–11; Goodman, 'On Likeness of Meaning', in L. Linsky, ed., *Readings in Philosophy of Language* (U. of Ill., Urbana, Ill.: 1952); Wittgenstein's *Blue Book*, pp. 39 ff.

aspects of knowledge of the intensional objects of thought become comprehensible if thinking is taken on the model of stipulation. Since I cannot discuss here whether the view of representational painting I've conscripted takes sufficient account of the need for resemblance between representation and represented, I will sidestep the issue by speaking of story-telling. I will argue that knowing that one is thinking about *x* is like knowing that a story one is telling is about *x*. I raised earlier the prospect that knowledge of the contents of thoughts differs from knowledge of sensations. This is why. Our 'knowledge' of what we are thinking about seems infallible because it is not knowledge at all.

If I begin to tell a story by saying 'Once upon a time there was a princess . . .', it would be absurd to ask me 'How do you know it was a princess?' It is not that I know it was a princess; I have stipulated that I am talking about a princess. The authority I have over the content of my story is not the sort of epistemic authority I have over my sensations, or a personal expertise. It is a matter of the social authority by which I have the right to choose a topic of conversation. *Thinking* about Columbus is like telling a story in just this way. If I describe some hypothetical situation to you (or even to myself) by saying 'Suppose Columbus had drowned at sea . . .' you cannot ask me how I know it is *Columbus* I am supposing to have drowned at sea. The question is absurd, asked by another or myself, in just the way the parallel question about my narrative was. I was *stipulating* that it is *Columbus* whose nautical adventures are up for consideration.

My claim that I am talking about a princess, made right after saying 'Once upon a time there was a princess . . .', cannot be false. It is impossible for me to have said this and not have embarked on the story of a princess. But it does not follow that I *know* that my discourse *is* about a princess. Here the concept of making a mistake is inappropriate in the way some philosophers have thought it is for all avowals. There is no question of knowing the contents of one's own stipulations; there can be no discrepancy between the stipulation and its subject-matter because the stipulation creates the subject matter. This moral becomes especially clear on the sort of causal analysis of knowledge I endorsed earlier. Let us take, for simplicity's sake, the particular analysis which makes 'the truth-condition of *p* is part of the cause of *A*'s belief that *p*' necessary for '*A* knows that *p*'. This analysis, in conjunction with Hume's law, entails that the truth-condition of *p* be logically independent of *A*'s belief if *A* is to know *p*. The subject-matter of my narrative, however, is *given* by the narration, so even if my narration is construed as expressing a belief about is subject-matter, there is no truth-condition for this belief apart from the belief itself. There cannot then be the causal relation required for knowledge. The same applies to the utterance of a thought or the description of an imagined scene. I am supposing Columbus fell overboard. If so supposing (or knowing that I have so supposed) involves correctly identifying the figure falling overboard, where are the truth-conditions for my belief about the identity of this figure to cause this belief, apart from the episode of supposition itself? There are none. Mistake is also ruled out, for I can neither be wrong nor accidentally right in identifying what I am thinking about, where '*A* is accidentally right about *p*' means '*p* is true but *p*'s truth-condition does not cause *A*'s belief that *p* in the right way'.

This situation contrasts with our direct knowledge of objectless mental states like sensations. There is no way I get to know that I am sensing, but there still is something to know. My having a yellow after-image is one thing and my believing that I am having a yellow after-image is another. The first, I argued, causes the second, and that is how I come to know what sensation I am having. But if I picture Columbus falling overboard, I do not examine the picture and come to believe 'So it's *Columbus* I am supposing . . .'. Indeed, if this were what supposing was like, everything I have said about supposing Columbus to have fallen overboard would apply to the picture. If scrutiny of a mental picture resulted in a true belief about who I am supposing to have fallen overboard, there would be no such thing as being right about who I was *picturing* falling overboard. The answer to 'What makes the picture a picture of *Columbus*?' could only be that I *say* it is of Columbus. Why not save a step and use this answer for the question 'What makes my supposition a supposition about Columbus?'

I can of course hold ordinary beliefs about the subjects of earlier narratives and suppositions. I might tell a story about a prince and later believe that I had told a story about a princess. This is compatible with a stipulative account of narration. My belief and its subject matter are distinct when I am recalling the subject of a narrative I told the previous day. Similarly, if I think about Columbus at *t*, I may forget by *t'* who I was thinking about at *t*.

I can have ordinary beliefs and make ordinary mistakes about earlier intensional states. But my *narrative* is not a report on what my narrative is about, nor is my thinking a report about what I am thinking about.

There is another way I might be said to be mistaken in identifying what I am imagining. Suppose I say 'Suppose Columbus had been a neutrino . . .'. It is appropriate to object that, stipulation or no, I am not imagining *Columbus* to have been a neutrino, since Columbus *couldn't* have been a neutrino. Should I persist in claiming that I'm supposing Columbus to have been a neutrino, I might be accused of saying something false. The narrative analogy for this is the *reductio ad absurdum* proof. If I put a figure on the blackboard and call it an isosceles triangle with unequal base angles, I will eventually come around and say 'So our triangle was not isosceles after all'. Was I at first talking about an isosceles triangle with unequal angles? We could say that the issue of correctly identifying the object of a counter-identity supposition does not arise. We could say that I really *was* imagining that Columbus was a neutrino, or that an isosceles triangle was scalene, and that what I imagined turns out to be absurd, unrealizable. On the latter decision I really did imagine that an isosceles triangle was scalene and that Columbus was a neutrino. Still, what was I *imagining* when I imagined this? Perhaps I visualized a streaky emulsion plate on the bridge of the *Santa Maria*, and I said 'This is Columbus'. Is the difference between Columbus and a neutrino too great for this to be a successful act of dubbing? The pictorial analogy suggests not. Suppose I paint a series of picture that go from minutely naturalistic renderings of Columbus, to impressionistic, to abstract expressionistic, and finally to a naturalistic rendering of an emulsion plate—and I christen them all 'C. Columbus'. There seems no good reason to deny that they are all Columbus-pictures, some more accurate than others. Where would the line be drawn? If this is an acceptable account of the logic of painting, it is an acceptable account of imagining the impossible. But I don't insist on this, the issue being a side-issue.

The fact that I *stipulate* what I am imagining is apparently what lies behind Sartre's opaque claim that the imagination is absolutely free. Sartre is right if he means that when I am imagining Columbus what I say about him cannot be assessed for *appropriateness* or *accuracy* against any external standard or template, as can a description of

Columbus. Sartre is also right if he means that, since a necessary condition for adopting a project is an act of imagining how the world could be, adopting a project is similarly invulnerable to assessment against external standards. But these facts are compatible with the claim, which Sartre wants to deny on the basis of the freedom of the imagination, that an act of imagination and the subsequent adoption of a project are *caused.* Indeed, it does not even follow from Sartrean freedom of the imagination that my project-defining acts of imagination are insusceptible of moral criticism—assessment against a moral template—as Sartre holds. For while it is up to me how I imagine how things could be, it does not follow that it is up to me whether how I am imagining things to be is a good way for them to be. It is a confusion to suppose that my authority in deciding *what* to imagine extends to authority over the value of what I decide to imagine.

The analogies between thinking and narrating have been introduced to blunt the intensionality argument, not as a theory of what thinking is. But even thus regarded, the analogy covers only mental *acts.* Only acts can be likened to *acts* of stipulation. Perhaps thinking is like narrating up to the unintelligibility of 'How do you know what it is about?' But what of object-taking mental states like fear which happen to a man and whose intensional objects are not decided on? A further look at Sartre brings this problem into relief. Sartre's celebrated claim that we *decide* what emotions to have is the extension of the narrative model of intensionality to emotions. Sartre thinks that since we decide on the objects of thought, we must decide on the objects of fear and hope. To say that my current emotions are uncontrollable products of my past is, for Sartre, the hypocrisy of bad faith. Perhaps Sartre adopts this position because the unification it provides for explanations of *all* intensional states outweighs its oddness. But whatever its startling implications about the scope of human freedom, Sartre's position is just empirically false. When a piece of flesh nauseates me, I am nauseated by the flesh; I don't 'nauseate the flesh'. The reaction is involuntary. I seem to have the same sort of knowledge of what nauseates me that I had in the imagination case, yet I don't decide that it is the flesh that is nauseating me. This case resists assimilation to the narrative model. That it is the flesh that nauseates me is logically independent of my belief that it is the flesh that nauseates me.

This knowledge of the objects of involuntary intensional states is not an example of what Anscombe calls 'mental causation'.[41] Her idea is that, since it makes no sense to say 'I thought the flesh nauseated me, but it was really the story of the accident', my knowledge that *C*(*m*) is the cause of *m* does not, as do most singular causal judgements, rest on inductively established regularities. Ordinary causal judgements are as secure as the general laws they rest on; since judgements of mental causation are infallible (Anscombe seems to reason), they must be extraordinary causal judgements. The present issue, however, is not how 'mental causation' or knowledge of it is possible, or possible given materialism. Anscombe's argument moves from the infallibility of my knowledge of the content *C*(*m*) of *m* to infallible knowledge of the cause of *m*. Whatever the merits of this argument, it is the *former* that is offered as a puzzle for materialism. In any case 'mental causation' cannot be offered as a further puzzle for materialists, since there is, in reality, no such thing. Since *C*(*m*) often enough does not exist, it cannot be the cause of *m*. In such cases knowledge of what *C*(*m*) is cannot be knowledge of a special causal relation between *m* and *C*(*m*), since non-existents cause nothing.[42] Anscombe's argument evidently confuses the content of a mental state with its cause, and then confuses knowing (infallibly) what the content of a mental state is with an entirely fictitious infallible knowledge of its cause. 'Mental causation' is a misnomer for the fact, already before us, that one's knowledge of the object of one's intensional state is infallible.

Knowledge of the objects of involuntary intensional states is best assimilated to the direct, incorrigible knowledge we have of sensations. My fear of snakes is a state so causally related to me that I can know non-inferentially and with no chance of error that I am afraid of snakes. To take seriously the monadic thesis is to take seriously the idea that the *only* autobiographical fact there is for me to know is that I am afraid of snakes, that I am a snake-fearer. What a man knows immediately is not what the objects of his intensional states are, but what intensional states he is in. This is the right twist to give the point that an intensional state is internally related to its object. Knowing what intensional state I am in logically carries with it the use of the term that ostensibly mentions the object

[41] *Intention* (Cornell U.P., Ithaca: 1963), pp. 16–17.

[42] Cf. Danto, *Analytical Philosophy of Action*, pp. 156–8.

of the state. It is not as if I know I am afraid, and then raise the further question of what I am afraid of. Rather, I move from ignorance of my mental state to knowledge that I am afraid of snakes. Knowledge of the objects of intensional states seems like a separate piece of (infallible) knowledge because (e.g.) the word 'snake' can be detached from the description of the state. We erroneously suppose it represents something further to know about the state itself. That I can immediately answer the question 'What mental state are in you?' presents no difficulties by itself, since it can be treated the way we treated the parallel question about sensations. The problem of intensionality is that we can also immediately answer what seems to be the further question 'What is the object of the mental state you are in?' I suggest there is no such further question.

Another source of the appearance of a problem is the fact that I can report that I am afraid without reporting what I am afraid of; you can know I am afraid without knowing what I am afraid of; and I can describe my mental state as 'fear' without using 'snake'. These facts have limited implications. You can know that a body of discourse is narrative without knowing the subject of the narration; a sentence can be described as 'stipulative' without use of a description of what it stipulates. This does not show a logical gap between a narrative and its subject. In fact, 'fear' stands to 'snake-fear' as genus to species, determinable to determination. In saying that I am afraid without saying what I am afraid of I leave something out only in the sense in which I leave something out when I describe a colour as blue without adding the shade. I do not leave anything out as I do when I say that Jones was on top, and I don't say on top of what.

Here, at last, is where the notion of the unconscious may be helpful in explaining the felt difference between intensional states and sensations. Being a snake-fearer, even a fearer of *that* snake, is, like having a sensation, a state it is logically possible for me to be in without knowing it. But this also *actually happens* for intensional states. I may be disposed to undergo occurrent episodes of snake-fearing without knowing that I am so disposed, and I may (as Freud has it) be undergoing an episode of fear without knowing it. Subliminal perception seems to offer a partial parallel for sensations. But this difference, whatever its ramifications (it has some for the defence of compatibilism: see VII.3), does not assist the doctrine of intensional objects or the intensionality argument.

I have considered the logical form of intensional ascriptions and first-person knowledge of intensional states, while skirting question (1) of p. 170. The physicalist would prefer to defer this and other questions about the nature of intensional states until more is known about the physiological reality underlying them and the representation of targets in self-regulating mechanisms. But this leaves unmet a further line of resistance in the intensionalist argument. How are intensional predicates *possible*? Why are some states describable only through the use of referring terms in non-designative positions? There are doubtless real problems here, but the obscurity of intensional states must not be overplayed, lest they become stumbling blocks for any theory of the mind. We don't want to conclude that intensional states are impossible. Anyway, the bearing of the how-possible question on physicalism is limited. Most charitably construed, it elides into two others, often treated interchangeably: (3) What do ascriptions of intensional states *mean*? and (4) What kind of evidence does an observer use to ascribe such states?[43] The two are connected, since answering (4) may show something about (3), perhaps even that a correct answer to (3) will raise problems for materialism. But by itself (3) presses on materialism no harder than does the general how-possible question. Materialism has no special obligation to analyse '*A* is a snake-fearer' unless there is some independent reason for thinking it means something that can't hold of matter. There are, in fact, two interesting arguments to this effect, one concerning the evidence for ascribing intensional ascriptions, the other concerning the nature of physicalistic reduction.

To take the former, a certain force can be allowed the claim that on even a liberal conception of evidence, ascriptions of incompatible intensional predicates may, in a given situation, all be compatible with all the evidence. But what is 'all the evidence'? If it includes all true intensional ascriptions (whether or not they are physicalistically reducible), incompatible intensional ascriptions would obviously not be compatible with all the evidence. If it means 'evidence formulated by sentences using only predicates satisfying PL and EG', this again includes all intensional predicates, monadically construed. To get an issue joined, predicates that by presystematic lights ascribe intensional states must be explicitly excluded. Call the result of this exclusion 'extensional evidence': it includes all actual human

[43] An example of (1), (3) and (4) all being run together is G. Sher, 'Armstrong on Impossible Desires', *Philosophical Quarterly*, xxvii. 108 (July 1977), 227–35.

behaviour and dispositions thereto, and brain states under neurological descriptions. It is claimed that the ascription of incompatible intensional predicates may be compatible with all possible extensional evidence, and that this in turn shows the intensional to be irreducible to the extensional. The initial claim seems correct. Suppose I want to climb the highest mountain. I buy pitons and become excited as my charter flight approaches Nepal. But the plane crashes and I die without having assaulted any mountain at all. The totality of the evidence recited is compatible with my having wanted to climb the highest mountain and my having wanted to climb the second highest mountain. Even knowledge of what I would have done had my flight not crashed would not have helped, for I might have wanted to climb a 30,000-foot mountain and what I would have done is—gone home. Extensional evidence can identify the object $C(m)$ of a state m only if I stand in some extensional relation to $C(m)$, only if m is dyadic. If $C(m)$ does not exist, extensional evidence cannot entail that I am in a state whose object is $C(m)$—i.e. that I satisfy the monadic predicate 'is-a-$C(m)$-desirer'.

Before assessing the danger this underdetermination raises for physicalism, I want to get out of the way a bad argument against it: the argument that I can *report* what I wanted to climb. My verbal behaviour, in fact, has no privileged place in the range of extensional evidence. Determining what I want on the basis of what I say I want presupposes an interpretation of my saying. If, idiosyncratically, I use 'the highest mountain' to denote Annapurna, my assertions must be construed accordingly if my aspiration is to be recognized. Normally the interpretation of my words is unproblematic relative to the extensional evidence. There is usually an optimal translation *T* of an idiolect, and this supplies an optimal theory of the intensional states of its user. But if what a man wants comes out *very* peculiar under *T*, we rule out *T* on the basis of the improbability that anyone has the wants *T* imputes. At some point it is reasonable to say that a man only appears to have a desire, the assertion by which he publicized it having been mistranslated. Even if we can specify this point (and this may involve an element of convention), and even if in translating idiolects this point is never reached, its existence teaches a moral. Self-ascriptions of intensional states are not data, modulo translation, for the intensional states the utterer is in, because translation involves prior assumptions about the presence of intensional states. This 'indeterminacy of translation', which holds up to the totality of extensional evidence, blocks the use of a man's words as an entrée into his intensional states. His utterances are just part of the data we are trying to understand by, among other things, attributing intensional states to him.[44]

The materialist can allow that, in the indicated sense, intensional idioms are irreducible to extensional evidence, but not in a way that affects materialism. The unavailability of behavioural criteria for the ascription of intensional states raises a problem only for *analyses* of the form: 'A is an x-fearer' = df. 'A engages in behaviours $b_1,...,b_m$'. But not only is materialism under no obligation to proffer such analyses—it does not aim at analysing psychological predicates at all—but it rejects such analysis on independent grounds: the brain states with which it identifies intensional states are logically and evidentially independent of behaviour. And since the materialist thinks that descriptions of behaviour just fix the reference of intensional ascriptions, he can accept the result that 'A is an x-fearer' is not analysable as 'A is in an internal state which causes $b_1,...,b_m$'. However, the present underdetermination also implies that the materialist cannot even tell us which behaviours are used in fixing the reference of psychological ascriptions. True again, but surely the modified topic neutralist is not obligated to do *that* for specific psychological predicates. The present underdetermination raises an interesting problem for the materialist reduction of intensional states only if it implies that there could be no way that intensional ascriptions could become introduced in the way modified topic neutralism suggests they are. I try at the very end of this section to indicate how, in fact, intensional ascriptions could be learned even given the acknowledged irreducibility of the intensional to extensional evidence. If there is a general argument proceeding from this irreducibility to the unlearnability of the intensional vocabulary, I do not know it.

Still, it might be thought that the poor fit between intensional

[44] Quine notes the link between the intensionalist objection to materialism and the indeterminacy of translation: 'Evidently, then, the relativity to non-unique systems of analytical hypotheses invests not only translational synonymy but intentional notions generally. Brentano's thesis of the irreducibility of intentional idioms is of a piece with the thesis of indeterminacy' (*Word and Object*, p. 221). Quine strengthens his hand by limiting the extensional facts to stimulus meaning, but the indeterminacy considered here (which I take to be Davidson's, in his papers 'Mental Events' and 'Psychology as Philosophy'), withstands the addition of further 'fixed points in radical translation' to the extensional evidence.

language and the language of extensional evidence creates a presumption that no smooth reduction of the intensional to the physicalistic will be possible. This presumption can be blunted in several ways. It should be no surprise that the criteria for identifying mental states are independent of those for identifying physical states. Water had to be identified by non-chemical criteria before it could be discovered to be H_2O. If (unlike the water case) the evidential basis for ascribing mental states turns out to be weak in certain ways, this only means that we will never know precisely which mental states are which brain states. If a man is in brain state b, and the extensional evidence points equally to m and m' as his mental state, we will never know if $m = b$ or $m' = b$. But this is compatible with materialism.

Sometimes proponents of the irreducibility thesis argue in a different way: ascriptions of intensional states are interpretative comments on one's overall behaviour, and do not correspond to any distinguishable states of mind.[45] It is thus unreasonable to expect that intensional predicates express any distinguishable brain state. Whatever this is, it is no objection to materialism; if intensional states are not states at all, why should they be brain states?

There is a tendency to overestimate the point that intensional ascriptions are vague, context-bound, and fail to pick out a 'natural kind'. 'Bald' is inherently vague and context-bound, but nobody doubts that physicalism can give a complete account of the states of a man's head. This ties in with the more general point that one system of description may be reducible to another even if there is no point-for-point reduction of one description in the first to a single description in the second. Not every distinction men have made will be mirrored isomorphically by a distinction in a scientifically sophisticated system of description; but so long as a distinction is not wholly chimerical it will have a counterpart in the later scientific scheme.[46] The fourfold classification earth/air/fire/water can be matched by an extensionally equivalent fourfold classification in

[45] Quine (*Word and Object*, pp. 210 ff.) takes intentional idioms to be 'dramatic projections' of ourselves into the place of another—man or mouse—and he goes on to remark that intensional states disappear 'if we are limning the true and ultimate structure of reality'. Quine of course is a physicalist, but he prefers to eliminate intensional states rather than struggle with identifying them with brain states.

[46] K. Lehrer's remarks on 'materialism and belief' in *Knowledge* (O.U.P., Oxford: 1974), p. 244, get this point exactly wrong.

modern physics. The new partition is artificial and admits of no interesting laws because the original classification did not cut nature at the joints. Presumably the reduction of the intensional framework of descriptions to the physical will be of this non-isomorphic sort. Look at predicates as principles of collection based on similarity. The predicate 'red' groups together a class of things that men once found similar; this group is also regarded as significantly similar by physics. Other predicates—like 'moves quickly'—group together cases that kinematics would classify diversely. But kinematics can contrive a predicate which covers this group.[47] So too mental states which once struck us as similar enough to warrant being called 'fear of snakes' may not seem similar at the level of physics. But physics can, with its own resources, select the class that was once held to be a natural unity. To want anything stronger would be to put a demand on the reduction of frameworks that parallels the impossibly stringent demand on translation that each word of one language be mapped to a single word in the other.

These reflections have touched on the last residue of the intensionalist objection: what *is* an intensional state, what is the principle of similarity which governs the use of an intensional ascription? A story about how intensional predicates are learned addresses this last cluster of problems. Stories about how words are learned are not always a sure guide to meaning, but a myth here is instructive. Since fears-cum-their-objects are like sensations, we may presume that children learn intensional predicates as they learn sensation words (see IV.4). As there is, furthermore, no circularity in using fear of mice to explain how children learn '— is [am] afraid of mice', let us begin with a child who exhibits fear of mice. His mother sees the child jump whenever a mouse appears, and says 'You're afraid of mice' or, more likely, 'It's silly to be afraid of mice; they're harmless.' In this way the child discovers what to call what he is experiencing: it is called 'fear of mice'. This is not to say that he finds out what he is afraid of; just what people call the state he is in.

Mother, of course, may make inductive errors. It isn't mice that scare the child, but running things. If the child already knows what mice are, he may commit a useful use-mention confusion and tell his mother that it is not *mice*. (This may not be a confusion; he may have a direct epistemic relation to mice and running things, his intensional state being dyadic.) If the child is a true innocent,

[47] e.g. x moves quickly $\equiv$ the velocity of $x \geqslant x$'s length/sec.

unfamiliar with mice and 'mice', only further observation will tell his mother what agitates him. The child can help her by pointing to what mother knows are mice. A still mouse alarms him, a scurrying kitten does not. This is not a matter of the child discovering what he is afraid of, as Russell[48] once suggested. It is mother who is making inductive discoveries. What the child comes to be ever better informed about is the correct description of his fear, his experience. His mother misinformed him about what his experience is called through *her* initial inductive misidentification of his experience. This hurdle leaped, the child knows that what he experiences when he sees or thinks of mice is called 'mouse fear'. He also notices that he experiences what he spontaneously classifies as a similar experience when faced with dogs (see p. 000, fnn.). What to call this new distress? Well, it's just like what he has learned to call 'mouse fear' except that it involves dogs rather than mice. What is more natural for a semantic tyro than to commit a use-mention fallacy and report to his mother 'I am afraid of dogs'? Indeed, when mother taught him 'mouse fear' she might have encouraged this conflation in two ways. The less blatant is the realistic one I've been supposing: she uses 'mice' both referentially and non-referentially in the sentence she uses to instruct her child about what to call his experience. Or else, she might say 'It's silly to be afraid of mice; they're harmless.' Cross-reference is an open invitation to construe 'mice' in 'afraid of mice' referentially.

The child need never execute deliberate inductions. The whole process may be a matter of stimulus generalization mediated by awareness of nothing more than the stimulus (fear) being generalized. The child experiences fear and is trained to respond to similar experiences in similar ways. This training involves a use-mention confusion, but we have tolerated use-mention confusions in the acquisition of language since pp. 165–6. The child soon comes to impute similar states to others by induction on their behaviour, and for practical purposes incipient worries about other minds are eased.

What behaviour does the mother look for to help her determine that her child is afraid of mice, and what behaviour is the child trained to look for in others? We have seen that in a sense this quest is underdetermined, but if ever the notion of family resemblance were appropriate, it is here. Some ascriptions of intensional states are based on plasticity of behaviour that observably converges on some

48 *Analysis of Mind* (Allen & Unwin, London: 1921), chap. III.

object like a mouse. These ascriptions are analogically projected to arrays of behaviour in which the appropriate object is not present (see Armstrong). We noted earlier the difficulties that attach to specifying the behavioural criteria we use to extend the core cases. But to suppose that this shows the present account of how it is done to be wrong confuses explicit criteria with the cues which trigger a natural tendency to spot similarities. You might have trouble explaining why and how people recognize new members of the Jones family. There are doubtless hundreds of cues that trigger such judgements (which are neither right nor wrong, just a feature of human nature) even if no one is aware of them. You might be reduced to explaining the unity of the Jones family in terms of the unhelpful predicate 'looks Jonesy'. You might even conclude that Jonesy-ness was irreducible to extensional evidence. And this is how it is with full-blown ascriptions of intensional states. Beginning with core cases that the child masters as he masters sensation words, he and others have a natural tendency to allow different behaviours to cluster together around a common intensional ascription. When the final picture of reality is drawn, the family resemblance marked by an intensional ascription may not correspond to any natural predicate in the physical vocabulary. But the physical vocabulary will be able to describe the family-resemblance class of behaviours the intensional predicate grouped together.

What behaviour leads to and stems from mouse-fear is an empirical question whose answer will rationally retrace how we all spontaneously extend our first bits of intensional vocabulary. Another question is: what enables a mental state m to cause those behaviours that prompt our ascribing content to m? This too is empirical. Sometimes $C(m)$ = a mouse because m is an image of a mouse; sometimes because m is the thought of the word 'mouse'. There are doubtless other ways. It seems to me likely that what has lately come to be called, tendentiously, the problem of 'mental representation'[49] is the conjunction of these questions. Answering them is all there is to knowing how 'mental representation' is possible.

[49] See e.g. H. Field, 'Mental Representation', *Erkenntnis* xiii (1978): 9-61.

VI

Computers, or, Is there Intelligent Life on Earth?[1]

0. *Introduction*

MATERIALISM implies that an unproblematically physical device could attain every mental state men ever do. Such a device could think, feel, joke, create, love. Indeed, the materialist maintains that we ourselves are machines of that sort. One might be reluctant to call anything sentient a 'machine'. Let us then reserve the word 'c-machine' for anything entirely like a machine except that it might be conscious. The problem is: can a c-machine be conscious? This stipulation entered, let us henceforth use the familiar words 'machine' and 'computer' to mean 'c-machine'. We respect linguistic propriety by not asking whether machines (old style) can be conscious; we are asking whether anything just like a machine (old style) but for its making sense to ask if it is conscious, can actually be conscious.

Defending computer consciousness aids in defending materialism, for objections to the former are often focused objections to the latter. As I cannot survey every argument in this sprawling area, I will discuss those issues which, to judge by their currency, seem to strike philosophers as the most plausible grounds for denying mentality to computers: context sensitivity, pattern recognition, language, creativity, the role of human purpose in the creation of computers, and the uniqueness of the human form of life. *The* most popular argument, that machine behaviour is programmed, intersects several of these. It also intersects the claim that computers are deterministic systems while we are not—the topic of chapter VII. In this chapter I treat the first three issues as specifications of the general claim that a machine could not be sufficiently flexible to respond to an environment and initiate action the way men do. I argue that these claims rest on confusion about what context sensitivity amounts to. The

[1] See also G. Robinson, 'How to tell your Friends from Machines', *Mind*, lxxxi. 324 (Oct. 1972), 504–18.

problems of computer creativity and the derivativeness of their purposes are versions of the man's-higher-nature argument (III.1): I argue that computers can be denied creativity only if creativity is understood so strictly that men as well as machines must fall short.

My overall concern in this chapter is the possibility of machine *sentience*. This must be emphasized, since (see IV.6) intelligence and other psychological states have been construed as whatever causes certain behaviour. Asking whether machines can think in this sense simply avoids the question of the capability of machines for consciousness. The proponent of artificial minds has achieved an empty victory if 'mind' is so construed that a being can have a mind without being conscious: he just shifts the philosophical problem to machine consciousness.

1. Turing Machines

Mentality in computers is an ill-posed question until 'computer' has been specified, and two dangers hedge this specification. On one hand, 'computer' must not be construed so widely as to trivialize the claim that computers could think. Neither God, nor a Cartesian ego, nor a physical object with magic powers should qualify as a computing machine. The complementary danger is that of construing 'computer' (or 'machine') so narrowly that it is trivially impossible for a computer to think. This latter proviso blocks the many arguments against machine consciousness that take 'machine' to denote such paradigms as air-conditioners and automobile engines. Paradigm machines are noisy, inflexible, and leaky, while human beings are usually silent, mercurial, and dry to the touch. It is observed, for example, that I would be dismayed at discovering wiring in my wife's arm.[2] True, but why must a machine have wiring? I'm not dismayed by the thought that my wife's arm contains nerves and blood vessels. A philosophically interesting notion of 'machine' should cover more than automobile engines and air conditioners.

It is natural to regard 'Turing machine' and 'computable by a Turing machine' as suitably abstract and theoretically neutral explications of the intuitive ideas of 'machine' and 'mechanical'. The mark of mechanical behaviour on this explication is not stereotype, but the iteration of a few simple operations according to a finite set

[2] L. J. Cohen, 'Can there be Artificial Minds?', *Analysis*, xvi. 2 (Dec. 1955), 36–41; he contrasts human behaviour with such paradigms of mechanical behaviour as the drill of guards.

of laws, which for the moment we suppose to be deterministic. A physical object whose behaviour is random, describable only in an infinitary language, or unanalysable into simple components, is not a machine. To see in more detail what this conception demands, reflect that the overall condition of a machine m at time t is given by its output at t and its internal state at t. For m to be deterministic, these two parameters must be functions of two others: m's input at t', t' just prior to t, and m's state at t'. The sets of internal states, inputs, and 'atomic' outputs must all be finite. These inputs, outputs, and internal states can be schematized in terms of m scanning an infinite (or *very* long) tape running from left to right. The tape is divided into boxes, and a box is either blank or contains a vertical stroke. As m scans the tape one box at a time, the two unit inputs are 'stroke' and 'blank'. The machine can erase a stroke, enter a stroke in a blank, or do nothing; each of these acts may be paired with a one-box move to the left or right, or no move at all. Which twofold act m performs is determined by the input and m's internal state. Since states are individuated by their differences in result, nothing more need be said about them in the abstract description of a machine. The quadruple $\langle F_1, F_2, F_3, F_4\rangle$ says that if m is in state F_1 and is presented with input F_2, m will print F_3 and shift to F_4 (where the one-box moves are included in the range of the variable F_4). A Turing *program* is any finite set of 4-tuples $\langle F_1, F_2, F_3, F_4\rangle$ such that F_1 ranges over a finite set of states, F_2 ranges over a finite set of inputs, F_3 ranges over a finite set of outputs, and F_4 ranges over the set of ordered pairs of members of F_1 and one-box moves.[3] Any object whose behaviour is described by a Turing program is a *Turing machine*. A Turing machine *realizes* its program.

It is customary to remark that nothing in the notion of a Turing program dictates the kind of realization a Turing program can have. There could be Turing machines made of spiritual stuff. But since the mentality of Turing machines serves as a heuristic guide for evaluating materialism only if Turing machines are unarguably physical, let us add the proviso that a Turing machine must be a physical object. This leaves undiminished the force of the Turing explication of 'mechanical', since most of the objections to computer mentality concern Turing programs, not their embodiments.

[3] For development of complex programs from these elements, see Kleene, *Introduction to Metamathematics*, pp. 356–63, and M. Davis, *Computability and Unsolvability* (McGraw-Hill, N.Y.: 1958), chaps. 1–3.

The deterministic character of Turing programs should be relaxed. There may be physical systems which, from the same state, and given the same input, evolve into different states at different times. This seems true of men, at least up to quite refined descriptions of their states and outputs. This is not to deny that human behaviour is determined, since there may be *some* descriptions of human behaviour under which deterministic laws apply to it. But many areas of psychology (e.g. learning theory) attend to features of human behaviour that are merely probabilistically related. These probabilistic laws are not spurious even if determinism is true.[4] The notions of Turing machine and Turing program apply to indeterministic systems if we add *transition probabilities* to the 4-tuples. Associated with each initial state s and input i is a series of pairs (final state, output); to each such pair p a measure is assigned of the probability that the system will go to p if it is in $\langle s, i \rangle$. Any system satisfying this generalization of Turing computability is an infinite probabilistic automaton; if its tape is finite but *very* long it is a finite probabilistic automaton, or fpa. The transition probabilities must be restricted in various ways for an fpa to be interesting.

A Turing machine can handle any problem representable as a series of yes/no choices. This is the essence of digital programming. To use an example to be followed through section 4, a Turing machine can be programmed to recognize a token of the letter A. Its scanner projects the visual pattern onto a grid of photoelectric cells, each cell marking an associated square with a '1' iff it is in shadow. The resulting linear array of 1s and blanks encodes what the scanner is picking up. The program operates on this input to produce an output which, suitably translated, affirms or denies that it is seeing an A.

Much discussion of machine mentality is independent of the details of Turing programming. Why, then, attend to fpa's in particular? Because Turing theory shows that 'mechanical' can be explicated precisely enough to lend interest to the claim that men are machines. Sometimes an explication aims to show that a concept supposedly hopelessly confused is in fact usefully clear. The confusions surrounding 'machine' noted earlier show that a precise explication like Turing's is needed to pose the issue of machine consciousness properly. But there is a deeper justification for the Turing explication

[4] See I. Hacking, *The Logic of Statistical Inference* (C.U.P., Camgridge: 1965), chap. II.

of 'mechanical'. This justification is its response to the perennial suggestion that explications of intuitive notions cannot be *proven*. The explicandum must be inherently vague, or why would it need making precise? The most one can expect, this suggestion continues, is an independently interesting explicans that agrees in critical cases with the pre-analytic usage of the explicandum. This unavoidable stipulative element in explication means that a thesis using a vague explicans is not the same as the verbally identical thesis using the explicandum. Perplexities about the original cannot be resolved by attending to its more precise counterpart.

This may be true of some explications, but there is evidence that Turing machines are what machines really are, what we were always referring to by the word 'machine'. The evidence, in brief, is the convergence of a number of independently formulated explications of 'mechanical' on the class of Turing procedures. These include Turing's characterization of computers; Herbrand-Gödel-Skolem recursion, which concerns the inductive part of arithmetic and its relation to effective provability; and Post-Markov computability and Church's λ-convertability, both concerned with combinatorial intuitions. All these notions are provably coextensive. The class selected thus appears to be a natural one that underlies a wide variety of intuitions. This reduces the force of any argument resting on the arbitrariness of explications. If it turns out to be reasonable to suppose that men are Turing machines, it will be impossible it explain away the claim that men are machines as an equivocation between ordinary usage and a term of art, or pretend that this result was 'built into' the explication.

Relevant computer research is commonly divided into Artificial Intelligence and Cognitive Simulation.[5] AI attempts to create machines that behave intelligently without presuming that their interior organization resembles that of man, or even that the machine is sentient. CS aims at mimicking the actual operations of the brain. I will ignore this distinction for three reasons. First, the very fact that a machine solves problems men solve is evidence that what is going on inside it is similar to what goes on inside human problem solvers. Workers in AI and CS seem to agree that no watertight barriers separate them. Second, the connection between what a computer does and how it does it will be discussed in section 4 from

[5] See K. Gunderson, *Mentality and Machines* (Anchor, N.Y.: 1971).

a broader perspective than the AI/CS distinction admits. Third, success in CS entails success in AI; therefore, many arguments against the possibility of simulating cognition take the form of arguments against the possibility of artificial intelligence. While CS is for present purposes more pertinent than AI, defending the possibility of computer consciousness comes down in practice to defending AI. Most of the objections to be considered in this chapter are objections to the feasability of AI.

2. Implications of Machine Consciousness

Danto has argued that no development in computer technology could have any philosophical bearing and that, in particular, any theory of mind can accommodate anything computers are capable of.[6] Machine thought or consciousness would at best confirm the empirical hypothesis that there is a correlation between certain mechanisms and sentience: 'But the empirical hypothesis thus confirmed is compatible with all main positions on the mind–body problem'.[7] If you believe the mind is a non-physical substance which pops into existence when a brain does, you can take the consciousness of a sufficiently complex machine to be the same mysterious emergence of a non-physical partner. Nothing prevents a mysterious connection from connecting a Cartesian ego with different kinds of hardware. Parallel arguments apply to property dualism, the double aspect theory, etc.

Danto is right: any theory of mind is logically compatible with anything machines do. What Danto has not shown is that the construction of a conscious machine would give equal evidential support to any theory of mind. In fact, such a construction would appear to tell heavily in favour of materialism. Imagine the construction undertaken in the depths of space: every component is checked for being purely physical, and the area is closely monitored for any alien influences. If we constructed a conscious object under those circumstances, would this not be *evidence* that consciousness was a physical property? (Don't object that all we could know is that the computer behaved like a conscious being; a test case for the claim that a conscious machine would cut no philosophical ice must be a

[6] 'On Consciousness in Machines', in Hook, ed., *Dimension of Mind*, pp. 165–71.

[7] Ibid., p. 165.

conscious machine.) True: the results would not entail the falsity of dualism; and true: the soul is almost defined to be something undetectable by sensors monitoring incoming forces. But that is not the end of the matter. For one thing, Danto's argument sins against the precept of I.1 that an anti-physicalist argument must not prove too much. It shows, by parity of reasoning, that any technological development would leave the nature of heat undecided. Suppose under the most scrupulous conditions we increase the velocity of the molecules of a gas, and observe that the temperature of the gas rises. This is compatible with all the main positions on the heat/molecular motion problem: perhaps heat is an emergent property correlated with molecular motion. Whatever the reason, we do *not* regard this observation as supporting the correlation between heat and molecular motion in the way it does their identity. Because Danto's argument entails that we ought to, it proves too much. (Danto's position is even weaker when applied to the water/H_2O problem.) Danto might reply that what warrants choosing the identity interpretation in the heat/molecular motion case is that among the relevant observations we find: the motion of molecules causes what heat supposedly causes, results from what heat is known to result from and so on. We find it simpler etc. to decide that 'heat' is not the name of a property correlated with molecular motion, but what we have been calling molecular motion all the time. But why couldn't something similar be the result of our deep-space experiment? Danto seems to suppress something quite crucial: the detailed knowledge we would have of the construction and behaviour of the computer. If you just imagine a pile of components at t and a finished computer at t', it is easy to suppose that at some point consciousness just—appeared (see I.6). But with detailed knowledge we would doubtless reject this interpretation. Just *how* we would see that consciousness is not a supervenient property cannot be known now, in advance of the experiment. We can only know that we were K-imagining (see IV.5 appendix) consciousness to have been non-physical after the event. But the same was true for heat before Rumford's time.

3. *Context and Flexibility*

A popular argument against the possibility of computer cognition centres on the context-sensitivity of human cognition. Roughly speaking, a response to phenomenon p is context-sensitive if it depends in part on p's surroundings; and a rule is context-sensitive if what it does with p depends in part on p's surroundings. The use of Chomsky's grammatical insights to drive a wedge between man and computer is an issue about context-sensitivity, discussed in section 4. The problem of simulating pattern recognition brings the issue of context-sensitivity into high relief, and is discussed in section 5. But these topics need leading into.

The purported limitations of machines with respect to context are often thought to be of a piece with the *inflexibility* of machines, or, equivalently, the adaptability of men. A man, it is said, can respond differently to each of an unlimited variety of different situations (input), while a machine can emit only a finite number of stereotyped responses. The behaviour of a Turing machine must be stereotyped because of its finite program. Thus H. Dreyfuss:

> The . . . argument, insofar as it is an impossibility argument, depends on the open texture of pattern recognition, the infinity of facts that may be relevant in problem solving, and the correlative flexibility of bodily skills. If experience really has this open character, then any *specific* human intelligent performance could indeed be simulated on a computer after the fact, but *fully* intelligent behavior would be impossible in principle for a digital machine.[8]

This argument is gravely flawed. Consider an air-conditioner C that pumps cool air into a room when the air temperature exceeds 80°. Presumably, each time C starts it will pump in a *slightly* different amount of cold air per unit time. Why not say that C's reaction to an air temperature of 81° differs from its reaction to an air temperature of 82°? Similarly, a Turing machine with even a simple program can execute infinitely many acts that *can* be classified as distinct: it can, say, add 1 to 1, 2 to 2, and so on. Conversely, why not say that a critic reacts the same way to good and execrable performances: he writes a review. What we say in all these cases depends on the scheme of classification in use: there is a clear sense in which the $n+n$ machine is doing the *same* thing every time because there is a coarse-grained criterion of event similarity that puts all its performances into one class, even though a fine-grained criterion of event similarity calls each act different. Relative to a coarse-grained criterion of event similarity, all the acts the critic performs are

[8] 'Why Computers must have Bodies in Order to be Intelligent', *Review of Metaphysics*, xxi. 1 (Sept. 1967), 31.

describable by a single predicate.[9] For various pragmatic reasons we use the coarse-grained criterion for the machine and the fine-grained criterion for the critic.

It must be remembered that the classification of responses, indeed all classification, is a function of theory. It is the system of properties used in articulating a theory that determines what counts, for that theory, as sameness of type and difference of type: no similarity or difference is significant as such, without appeal to some theory. Two responses (or stimuli) count as different only if the differences between them tie into laws. (One *might* say that two things differ absolutely if they differ with respect to the true theory of the world, but even this involves tacit relativization to theory.) Prediction of the critic's behaviour requires that we take seriously the differences in what he writes after each performance; while calling everything the air-conditioner does 'pumping cold air' suffices for prediction of the machine's behaviour. One might, in light of this, propose a relativized general thesis about human flexibility: under any interesting scheme for classifying stimuli and responses, men can react differentially (or appropriately) to every different kind of stimuli. But this thesis is patently false. A man in the vicinity of an atomic explosion of any megatonnage whatever will always react the same way, and the way a computer would: by distintegrating. It is just false that a man can respond differentially to *any* situation he is faced with. The truth appears to be that there is a set of conditions C and a range of responses R such that, for any c in C, a man faced with c can emit some distinct r in R. But this characterization of human flexibility obviously applies to machines and even rocks. The difference between man and machine lies only in the size or extent of C and R. However considerable this difference is, the relativized thesis abandons an in-principle difference between human adaptability and the response capabilities of other natural systems.

The flexibility intuition is not without force, but it cannot be made both precise and plausible. The differences in flexibility between man and machine are matters of degree and are, to an important extent, relative to our theory-bound classifications of stimuli and response. This puts the full burden on pattern recognition and context sensitivity; instead of illustrating the phenomenon of flexibility, they

[9] Cf. A. Newell and H. Simon, 'The Use of Computers in Psychology', in R. Luce, R. Bush, and E. Galanter, eds., *Handbook of Mathematical Psychology* (Wiley, N.Y.: 1963), ii. 393.

may be what it amounts to. But before turning to these issues, it is well to attend to language, another phenomenon which figures prominently in discussions of these topics.

4. Chomsky and Language

Language is often said to be a prime illustration of the difficulties raised by flexibility and context sensitivity for computer cognition. In particular, N. Chomsky's work on the syntax of natural language has been taken to show that no finite automation could produce anything remotely resembling human speech. Since it would follow that we natural language users could not be computers, this argument merits examination here. I will not be directly concerned with whether Chomsky's work supports the doctrine of innate ideas;[10] my chief concerns will be to document the claim that Chomsky's main argument for denying human language to fpa's comes down to the context sensitivity of transformation rules; and to examine this argument.

Chomsky's rejection of a talking fpa derives from his view that no natural language could be acquired by a purely inductive mechanism, for Chomsky takes an fpa to be precisely what a learner who learns only from experience (an *inductive learner*) could learn to be. Each fpa can produce exactly the productions of some inductive learner. Chomsky's ground this appear to be that an fpa's transition probabilities correspond precisely to the relative frequencies of co-occurrence of words that an inductive learner would notice. More exactly, imagine an inductive learner with a repertory of responses $\{r_1,...,r_n\}$ who encounters stimulus s. His rewards are maximized if p_i per cent of the time he emits r_i, $i = 1,...,n$. Eventually this conditioning takes and—ignoring internal state variables—the learner is describable by the triples $\langle s, r_i, p_i\rangle$. The set of similar n_s-tuples of triples for each distinguishable stimulus s is the machine table for an inductive learner. Thus, to ask what an fpa could do is just to ask what an inductive learner could learn. This argument, at any rate, seems to me the best reconstruction of the published discussions of Chomsky and his followers, who treat the two questions as interchangeable.[11] Chomsky's answer to both is that

[10] See D. Cooper's *Knowledge of Language* (C.U.P., Cambridge: 1974) for the latest of many demolitions of this Chomskian thesis.

[11] Thus see D. Slobin, *Psycholinguistics* (Scott, Foresman and Co.: 1969), chap. 1. The idea that Chomsky has 'proven' that language is not inductively learnable has started to become a commonplace in philosophy; see e.g. W. Matson, *Sentience* (U. of California Press, Berkeley: 1976), p. 106.

certain features of natural languages prevent them from being learned inductively, or, equivalently, from being produced by an fpa.

When it comes to specifying these features, however, Chomsky's writings take a curious turn. His chief empirical contribution to this debate has been the claim that the grammars of natural languages are replete with transformation rules (or *t-rules*). And Chomsky often speaks as if 'recent work' in the empirical study of language has shown that language is not 'programmable', or inductively learnable.[12] But in fact most of his arguments for this conclusion make no use at all of t-rules. They are quite general considerations about language that have nothing to do with the specifics of syntax. Whatever the value of these arguments, pretending their probative force has been enhanced by the advent of transformational grammar is sheer obfuscation. Only the claim that t-rules are not inductively learnable can be regarded as Chomsky's distinctive contribution to the present debate. The rest of the present section attempts to show in detail that Chomsky's general arguments are both unoriginal and unsuccessful, and that the argument from t-rules is no advance beyond the general claim that an fpa cannot be as context sensitive as a man.

Chomsky uses two general arguments to show that language is not inductively learnable. The first is the complexity of human language and the great (even infinite) variety of linguistic responses and initiatives a speaker has available. Now the sheer complexity of language has been recognized for many centuries. If Chomsky is saying that the presence of t-rules is an important and hitherto unrecognized kind of complexity, his argument boils down to t-rules and not complexity *per se*. If he is not saying this, he is merely repeating an observation of Descartes which, unamplified, can hardly show that language could not be learned by an inductive learner equipped with a few all-purpose heuristics. Many intellectual skills unarguably acquired by inductive procedures are very complicated, physics for example. The sophisticated ability to recognize different styles of painting is acquired inductively.[13] It is useless to reply (as Chomsky sometimes does) that physics and art history also require a non-inductive component, for the argument from complexity rests

[12] Thus see *Aspects of the Theory of Syntax* (M.I.T., Cambridge, Mass.: 1965), pp. 57–8.

[13] See Goodman, 'The Emperor's New Ideas', in *Language and Philosophy*, ed. S. Hook (N.Y.U. Press: 1960), p. 139.

on *contrasting* language with other intellectual skills. This point is easily overlooked. The hypothesis that X cannot cause Y is ill-posed unless one specifies the likelihood of the available data under the hypothesis that X does cause Y (the 'null hypothesis'). We must know what language learning would be like using purely inductive techniques for the hypothesis that it is *not* so learned to be well posed, and we naturally look to such activities as learning physics as guides to what purely inductive learning is like. If we are told that even *these* have non-inductive components, we are deprived of the null hypothesis said to make the available data too surprising. Chomsky is like a man who says that zebras must have been stretched because they are longer than they ought to be, and then says he has no idea how long they ought to be.

It is worth looking, in this connection, at the familiar sentences 'John is easy to please' and 'John is eager to please'. Chomsky contends that if we learned language by induction on observable (acoustic) signals we would find these two sentences similar in form, whereas in fact we see 'John' is the subject of the first and the object of the second. Hobbes, I believe, considered the quite similar argument that language can't be a physical phenomenon because a man who receives the message 'Your son is dear' reacts quite differently from one who receives the physically similar message 'Your son is dead'. But in fact small physical differences can make a very great physical difference: a raindrop may push a dam beyond the bursting point.[14] As Cooper points out,[15] an explanation would be needed if *all we had ever heard* were the two sentences and we somehow detected a difference between them. But since we also know what 'easy' and 'eager' mean, it is no surprise that we can draw systematic distinctions between the two sentences. We do not miraculously parlay a simple physical input into elaborate knowledge: we have at our disposal a vast history of connected inputs. Of course, one may *assert* that an fpa could not 'know what "eager" means'; but nothing in Chomsky's first argument shows this.

Chomsky's second argument is the creativity of language and language-users. Our virtually inexhaustible capacity for uttering and comprehending new sentences[16] cannot, allegedly, be acquired by

[14] A physically deep example of this is E. Zeeman's 'catastrophe machine', in 'Catastrophe Theory', *Scientific American*, ccxxxiv. 14 (Apr. 1976), 68–70.

[15] *Knowledge of Language*.

[16] Despite Chomsky's asseverations, the performance/competence distinction is an instance of the occurrence/disposition distinction.

an inductive learner. This argument is also ineffective. A pianist can improvise melodies he has never encountered, but this hardly shows that learning to play the piano involves more than habit formation. Indeed, if a computer must, in order to speak, be able to recognize and generate novelties, any computer that adds 1 to each natural number has the requisite ability. One is tempted to dismiss such 'creativity' as spurious, since $n+1$ differs only trivially from $(n+1)+1$. But, as we saw in section 3, difference is relative to theory. What is novel about the computer's response to 547 may not be needed for a theory of its behaviour, but this is not to say the novelty is absent. It must be remembered, similarly, that stimulus generalization is *generalization* from past samples. An inductive learner with even the most poverty-stricken imagination is extending his skills and judgements to new cases. A hen who perches atop egg #113 has done something novel, for she has never climbed atop her 113th egg before. Our current chicken theory does not recognize this as different from what she did before—but another system of predicates, geared to another theory, does.

So Chomsky must claim that there is a creativity specific to language, and here t-rules enter. The sort of novelty Chomsky evidently has in mind is this: a sequence is novel only if it can be generated out of antecedent sequences by certain structure-dependent rules. By saying this the Chomskian argument abandons its generality and reduces to the observation that language is governed by t-rules. The ability to process novelty has been abandoned as a dispensible intermediary. The whole argument from language is left resting on what, if anything, is special about t-rules.

Chomsky's polemics about the failures of inductive theories of language acquisition have been more persuasive than the two positive arguments just reviewed. Before turning to the t-rule argument, some remarks about them are in order. Their principal flaw is that the explanandum Chomsky holds inductive theories obligated to explain differs from the explanandum he holds his own theory obligated to explain. On one hand he complains that no inductive theory can explain or predict the *actual* utterances of an *actual* speaker.[17] But he takes the explanandum of his own theory to be the 'idealized competence' of actual speakers 'abstracted from hesitation, stuttering', and, one might add, occasional ungram-

[17] See e.g., Chomsky's review of B. F. Skinner's *Verbal Behaviour*, in *Language*. 1 (1959), 26–58.

maticality.[18] This double standard encourages three errors. First, it stacks the deck in what seems to be Chomsky's favour, since it is always easier to explain neat phenomena than messy ones. I say 'seems to', because the inductive view is in any case not committed to categorical predications of utterances. A Turing program specifies the probability of a response *given a specified stimulus*. The inductive view is not obligated to predict what I will say upon entering a museum; it predicts that if I am asked 'Are there Rembrandts here?' I will assent.[19] It is hardly clear that Chomsky's approach is more predictively fruitful with respect to actual speech.

Second, Chomsky's double standard deflects attention away from the highly pertinent question of whether the output of *actual* speakers can be replicated by an fpa. There may be 'grammatical' sentences an fpa could not recognize, but 'grammatical' only to Chomsky's idealized speakers. There are sentences too long for actual speakers to process that count as grammatical because they conform to rules adequate for cataloguing sentences that can be processed. Their grammaticality is an artifact of the grammarian's notation. That a computer could not recognize *those* sentences to be grammatical does not show that any actual speaker is not an fpa.

But most important, Chomsky is blind to the aid and comfort consistently idealizing the explanandum of a theory of language gives the inductivist. A theory of idealized competence is just an account of the basic mechanisms of speech, and a theory of the basic mechanisms is not more obligated to predict the actual behaviour of speakers than is classical mechanics to predict the path of a feather in a windstorm. Actual speech is the 'vector sum' of these basic mechanisms (whatever they are), just as the path of the feather is. The only bar to prediction in either case is the unmanageable complexity of the factors involved. That the laws of operant conditioning do not entail that children will learn the active-passive transformation is compatible with operant conditioning being at the bottom of it. A parallel jibe could be directed at Newton's laws. Citing the predictive limitations of learning theory to support a

[18] See, e.g., Chomsky, 'Formal Properties of Grammars', in Luce *et al.*, *Handbook of Mathematical Psychology*, ii. 327.

[19] See Quine, 'Methodological Reflections on Linguistic Theory', in Harman and Davidson, eds., *Semantics of Natural Language*, pp. 442–54, also *The Roots of Reference* (Open Court, La Salle, Ill.: 1974), p. 15; also Cooper, *Knowledge of Language*, pp. 134–6. The point continues to elude Chomsky.

non-inductive approach is a blatant argument from ignorance.[20]

A final point ignored by Chomsky should be kept in mind. The inductive-behavioural view Chomsky excoriates in Quine and Wittgenstein is primarily directed to issues of semantics: the learning of single words or simple sentences. The point of such theories is to discourage Platonism and mentalism, mischievous doctrines when the topic is meaning or reference, but without clear application to syntax. There is almost nothing Quine or Wittgenstein would have to give up if the mechanisms which account for the inculcation of words do not account for the inculcation of grammar.[21]

So the whole burden of Chomsky's claim that an fpa could not produce human speech again falls on the 'structure-dependence' of the rules of grammar. The argument begins with the claim that the syntax of natural languages requires two kinds of rules. *Phrase-structure* rules are what most people think of as 'grammar', a typical one being: sentences decompose into noun-phrases and verb-phrases. Let us call the result of replacing the words of an English sentence *S* by their respective grammatical categories, and analysing *S* according to phrase-structure rules, the *diagram* of *S*. Conversely, a diagram plus a lexicon yields particular sentences. Transformational grammarians allow that an fpa could produce anything describable by phrase-structure rules. Since a diagram is linear, the probability that a certain category or 'lexical item' will appear depends on what appears earlier in the diagram. Per an earlier argument, these probabilities can be construed as transition-probabilities. However, two phenomena show that an adequate grammar of English must[22] include another sort of rule for which a transition-probabilistic

[20] Socialists like to contrast an ideal socialist order with the messy actualities of free markets. They ought either compare actual free market systems with actual socialist regimes or ideal socialism with ideal free enterprise. Chomsky's long practice in socialist polemicizing may have inured him to special pleading; see his 'Comments on Herrnstein's Response' in N. Block and G. Dworkin, eds., *The IQ Controversy* (Random House, N.Y.: 1976), pp. 310–24.

[21] See M. Apter, *The Computer Simulation of Behavior* (Harper, N.Y.: 1970), pp. 137–8.

[22] Chomsky sometimes allows that a phrase-structure grammar could be descriptively adequate for natural language. He insists, however, that a t-grammar is superior because, for example, it can more perspicuously represent the ambiguity of 'Hunting lions can be dangerous' by assigning it two possible deep structures. But a phrase structure grammar can represent this syntactic ambiguity with equal perspicuity by assigning the sentence two possible diagrams. And even if a t-grammar is always *preferable* to a phrase structure grammar, Chomsky's initial concession quite undercuts his own impossibility argument.

account is impossible. The first is the 'cyclic' sentence, which contains pronouns whose antecedents are arbitrarily far away. The second is that some sentences appear to have components missing from their diagrams. For example, the intuitive connection in meaning between 'The boy hit the ball' and 'Did the boy hit the ball?' shows that the correct analysis of 'The boy hit the ball' contains a 'did'—and no 'did' occurs in its diagram. Chomsky proposes that to each sentence of English there corresponds a series of diagrams; the 'surface structure', which is the phrase structure diagram, and a 'deep structure' which is an underlying diagram. It is the deep structure of 'The boy hit the ball' that contains a 'did'. The rules which map diagrams to diagrams are the *transformation* rules, one example of which is the active/passive transformation. T-rules are contextual, since what a t-rule does to a particular word *w* depends on the diagrammatic context in which *w* is situated.[23]

Chomsky holds that a child could not learn so complex a system of rules by induction from the 'fragmentary' input he actually gets. Even before asking why this is so, note that Chomsky is assuming that learning English requires learning how to parse English sentences. As battalions of philosophers have urged, this confuses a theory of what a speaker can do with the rules he actually follows in doing it. We all learn to speak and, perhaps, to recognize certain utterances as deviant. There are doubtless rules we *conform to* in doing these things. But one need not learn that a rule is true of the behaviour of oneself and others to learn (be trained) to act in accordance with it. We needn't learn *that* there is a hidden 'did' in the analysis of 'The boy hit the ball'; we learn to talk and balk at talk in such ways that the best description of what we do puts a 'did' in the analysis of 'The boy hit the ball'. Suppose that, as a matter of brute fact, when I find sentence S grammatical I also find sentences $S_1,\ldots,S_n$ grammatical, all of which, along with S, arise from diagram D (containing components not found in S) by mathematical application of diagram-transforms $t_1,\ldots,t_m$. This does not require that *I* understand S or any of the S_i by tracing them back through the t_j to D, or even that I know this can be done.

This preliminary point improves the prospects for machine language. Even if t-rules are unprogrammable, it would not follow that an fpa could not speak unless one assumes that the *only* way an fpa could produce utterances describable by t-rules is by using

[23] Chomsky, 'Formal Properties of Grammar'.

t-rules. But this assumption is as gratuitous for fpa's as it is for us. It is equivalent to supposing that the only way a computer can compute π is by using Euclidean geometry. In fact, however, quite simple programmable algorithms can churn out π to arbitrarily many decimal places.

But let us allow that learning a language involves constructing a theory, in fact a transformational grammar (so that an fpa can talk only if t-rules can be programmed). Chomsky now asks what a child must come equipped with if he is to infer such generalizations as 'relative clauses can be nested cyclically' from the few thousand hours of speech he hears. Chomsky invariably calls this input 'fragmentary', but he never gives the standard of completeness against which this fragmentariness is being judged. A child, after all, receives thousands of hours' worth of data in preparation for learning to speak. Why not say the input must be complete, since children learn language on the basis of it? Be that as it may, Chomsky claims that a child who used only the inductive techniques that taught him that fire burns and that playing doctor is naughty would never get the hang of t-rules. The sceptic naturally asks why—what is so special about t-rules? Appeal to such global considerations as creativity and complexity moves in a circle; and since Chomsky allows that a child could learn phrase-structure rules by induction, the only pertinent feature of t-rules is their context-sensitivity.[24] Chomsky's whole argument to the effect that language is the distinctive province of man is thus no more than an appeal to, and stands or falls with, the so-far unsubstantiated claim that fpa's are not context-sensitive.[25] T-grammar has added nothing to the mind–machine problem.

While this conclusions suffices to move the discussion of automata beyond language, the context-sensitivity of t-rules warrants comment in its own right. Calling t-rules context-sensitive trades on an ambiguity in 'context'. The correct grammatical account of a

[24] Cp. his definition of 'context sensitive grammatical rule' (ibid., p. 294), with that of pp. 191–2 above.

[25] Even this is not clear; see ibid., Thms. 6 and 17. Chomsky also shows that 'Given a context-sensitive grammar G . . . we can construct a P[ush] D[own] S[torage] automation that will accept a string x iff there is a left-to-right derivation of x in G'. Extending the range of fpa's in this way partially abandons the claim that an fpa could not 'accept' the productions of a context-sensitive rule. Chomsky leaves himself with the claim that an fpa could not process strings whose derivations involve nesting rules. It is not clear how much significance attaches to such a specific result.

particular word w depends on the sentential context in which w appears; w is thus treated as context-bound by t-rules, while w is not so treated by phrase-structure rules.[26] However, what a t-rule t does to diagram d is entirely clear independent of d's context. The diagram $t(d)$ is always uniquely determined. When applied to their proper arguments, t-rules are no more context-sensitive than are phrase-structure rules when applied to words. Nor need the fact that $t(w)$ is non-functional impress us; for phrase-structure rules leave undetermined what to do with the letters in the words they operate on. If t-rules are context-sensitive, so are phrase-structure rules.

5. *Pattern Recognition and Context-Sensitivity*

The problem of context-sensitivity is frequently introduced as the problem of determining whether a given inscription is a token of the letter A. The issue of pattern recognition is sufficiently general, certainly; all judgement is pattern recognition. Applying a predicate to an object x classifies x as similar to some past objects, and reidentifying x classifies it as similar to its earlier stages. Thought crystallizes around pattern recognition.

Asking how compliance to type is recognized, in just those words, smudges the distinction between what a recognizer *does* in judging compliance and what *happens* when he judges compliance. Ignoring this distinction for a while brings the main issues into higher relief. Consider these two tokens of the inscription /–\: c/–\t and /–\ope. You doubtless took the first to be an A and the second to be an H. Since the two tokens are physically identical, your discrimination must have involved their surroundings as well as their physical characteristics. So a program for recognizing compliance to type must not only attend to the physical properties of inscriptions but must include a way of attending to context as well. Now, one of the distinctive features of human pattern recognition is that we can cast the net of attention ever wider if the *immediate* context does not remove an ambiguity, and in fact there seems no limit to how far out we can go. This is another capacity that a recognition program will have to have.

Dual to the compliance of physically indiscriminable tokens with distinct types is another allegedly distinctive facet of human pattern recognition: the compliance of physically dissimilar tokens with the same type. More specifically, tokens t_1 and t_3 can both comply with

[26] Ibid., p. 294.

type T even if some token t_2 which is physically more similar to t_1 than is t_3 does not comply with T. (Cf. our propensity to classify physically diverse objects as tables.) This 'family resemblance' dimension of pattern recognition is another capacity a pattern-recognizing computer must mimic.[27] I will, however, defer explicit discussion of the family resemblance phenomenon for now.

There is one other noteworthy ambiguity in the notion of recognition. It is not quite accurate to speak of 'recognizing' that /–\ in c/–\t is an A when, as here, there is no objectively correct decision. One's natural reaction is 'A', but there is no antecedent standard that makes this response correct. You are 'right' only in the sense that everyone would make the same decision. A machine can simulate *this* capacity if it is *as sensitive* to context as you are even if it makes different decisions. Now cases of the sort just mentioned are to be opposed to those in which a recognition response is right or wrong according to some independent standard which we must learn to apply. A machine can simulate this kind of 'pattern recognition' only if it, too, can learn to react *as we do*. We may for convenience call both kinds of cases *recognition problems* and speak of responses in both as *solving* recognition problems. And we must always be clear which kind of recognition problem we want a pattern-recognizing machine to solve. It is unfair to ask it to be right where all there is to being right is *consensus gentium*.

The features of context sensitivity discussed so far have been taken to show the impossibility of encoding a general algorithm for attending to context in a finite program. 'How much context is needed?' cannot be answered, since there is no fixed set of parameters $\{x_1,...x_n\}$ such that the reaction r of man M to any situation S is a function $f(x_1,...,x_n)$ of just those parameters:

> Since there is no limit to the amount of data which may be relevant for solving an ill-defined problem, one cannot even in principle try all the permutations of possibly relevant data in seeking a solution.[28]

Imagine a pattern recognizer P checking inscriptions for the values of some parameters $x_1,...,x_n$. These need not be only physical, for Dreyfuss's argument applies even if some x_i are contextual. Its point is that *whatever* finite set of parameters is chosen P will make 'mistakes'—will diverge in point of sensivity or accuracy from

[27] For doubts about the capacity of computers to handle family resemblance, see Matson, *Sentience*, pp. 104–5.

[28] Dreyfuss, 'Why Computers Must Have Bodies', p. 23.

human responses. We can always put something outside *P*'s ken, however wide it is, since *P*'s ken is fixed. Affine transformations turn *m* into *w*. If *P* has not been given affine transformations, it will be unable to group *m* and *w* together. But a man could always learn affine transformations and use them to reclassify *m*'s if the need arose.

This argument profits from loose statement. Does a man really use *indefinitely* many parameters in determining compliance with type? '[A]n anticipation of an object does not arouse a single response or specific set of responses but a flexible skill that can be brought to bear in an indefinite number of ways.'[29] (We are still ignoring the reason/cause distinction.) This makes as little literal sense as saying that there are indefinitely many mountains. Nothing actual is indefinite. If it is in principle impossible to count the number of mountains in the Rockies precisely, it is because our criteria for 'mountain' leave some intermediate cases unadjudicated. Similarly the claim that a man has indefinitely many parameters available can only mean that our criteria for 'parameter' are vague. If this is its basis, the indefiniteness Dreyfuss notes is of little significance. Relative to a strict criterion of 'parameter', a response either depends on the value of x_i in *S*, or it does not.

It is equally unlikely that men use infinitely many parameters in any sense that *P* cannot. It is hard to contrive cases in which determining compliance literally requires review of infinitely many aspects of a token. If tokens were that recondite, recognition would be a super-task equally beyond the powers of men and machines. There is *a* sense in which recognition may involve infinity. A human mathematician may have to determine if a family of sets *f* is countably disjoint. To do this he must determine whether each of countably many distinct pairs of sets is disjoint. But a computer can mimic this sort of infinitary act. The unremarkable reason why man and computer can determine countably many facts about disjointness is that the process by which either makes its determination need not contain an operation for each pair in *f*. They may decide that *f* is countably disjoint by manipulating a finite formula that generates the sets in *f*. More likely there is a lemma available which says $(x)(F(x) \supset x$ is countably disjoint), and what the mathematician *does* is prove $F(f)$ in finitely many steps. Employing a statement that encodes infinite information does not require infinitely many acts.[30]

[29] Ibid., p. 20.

[30] *Analogue* computers can occupy infinitely many informational states: each

A final version of the flexibility argument uses E. Husserl's observations about the indefiniteness of perception.[31] According to Husserl, to perceive something as an apple is to form a set of expectations about possible future perceptions; the 'apple-hood here' feeling is the feeling that certain perceptions will follow the present one. This 'horizon of possibilities' involves preparedness to act, and hence involves having a body.[32] For example, part of recognizing a pattern as an apple-pattern is my feeling that I would see a back-side if I went behind it. Husserl's main point is the *indefiniteness* of horizons. What makes the apple an objective physical thing is the objective indeterminacy of some of the consequents of conditionals of the form 'If *x* happened, I would experience. . . .' (Husserl sows confusion by calling these consequents 'meanings'.) This indeterminacy in our physical object concepts—we can't say now what experience we would expect under sufficiently strange circumstances—corresponds to Austin's point that we would not know what to say, that past usage has given us nothing *to* say, if a familiar physical object were to behave sufficiently strangely.[33] Husserl and Austin are noting, in different idioms, the open texture of material object concepts, what Dreyfuss calls the 'underdetermined expectation of the whole'.

Let us grant that human awareness of a public world is open-textured in the sense explained, and involves ever-receding horizons of expectation. This is irrelevant to the possibility of machine awareness. One might suppose that, being resoluable into yes/no responses, vagueness is beyond the capacity of an fpa program. This is not so; an fpa could use concepts in an open-textured way. We could for example instruct a goldfinch recognizer to emit 'does not compute' if it spots a pattern that passes exactly 60 per cent of its goldfinch tests. Its use of 'goldfinch' would be appropriately

---

voltage in a wire can represent the value of a real-valued variable. An fpa may need some analogue devices to simulate human estimation of, e.g., acceleration. It seems generally agreed that the prospects for CS by analogue computer are dim.

[31] *Cartesian Meditations*, trans. D. Cairns (Martinus Nijhoff, The Hague: 1960), pp. 44–5; *Ideas*, trans. W. Gibson (Collier, N.Y.: 1962), secs. 44 and 47.

[32] Hence Dreyfuss's title. This last inference is actually fallacious; all that follows is that to perceive I must be capable of kinesthetic sensations, which, so far as Husserl's argument shows, I can have without a body.

[33] Austin, *Sense and Sensibilia*, p. 122, fn. 1; see also N. Malcolm, 'The Verification Argument', in M. Black, ed., *Philosophical Analysis* (Prentice-Hall, N.J.: 1963), pp. 228–79.

indeterminate. More cunningly, we could leave its program open for certain realizable combinations of parameters. We could provide it with as much instruction for applying 'goldfinch' as our past usage of 'goldfinch' has provided us. If we 'would not know what to say' in some novel case, neither will the computer. If the machine can devise new parameters (see below) there is bound eventually to be some objective indeterminacy in its matchings.

It must be remembered, finally, that the relevant class of hypothetical conditions we want to be true of the machine, even if not finitely definable, represents a disposition; what we *would* say under conditions most of which will never be realized. If we are trying to replicate a man, all we must replicate is the occurrent basis of this disposition—whatever actual state created by past encounters with goldfinches makes it true that were so-and-so to happen, we would say 'goldfinch', say 'not a goldfinch', or stand nonplussed. We need not replicate separately every such potential response, for in no literal sense are they in us.

The intuitive unlimited flexibility and context sensitivity of human mental activity thus cannot be explicated by appeal to the indefinite or infinite multiplicity of parameters used in solving recognition problems. Let me propose an alternative explication of these elusive notions, one which allows an fpa to exhibit unlimited flexibility and context sensitivity. Intuitively, 'flexibility' is the use of different parameters for different recognition problems. Only finitely many parameters are ever used to solve any one recognition problem, but each recognition problem has its own set of parameters. If S and S' are recognition problems their associated sets may be disjoint, or partially or wholly overlapping. A pattern recognizer first selects the parameters necessary for solving S and then solves S by attending to values of those parameters in S. Flexibility and context sensitivity amount to the existence of a pair of functions $\langle f, g\rangle$ such that, for any S, f maps S to an n_s-tuple of parameters $\langle x_1,\ldots,x_{n_s}\rangle$, some of which are contextual, and P's solution of S is the application of g to $f(S)$), i.e. $g(f(S))$. On this scheme, P recognizes three broken lines to be an A by first selecting from a standing pool of parameters and then classifying the broken lines on the basis of the values it gives these parameters. P is infinitely flexible if the standing pool is infinite. But this infinitariness need not and ought not be taken literally. 'Infinite' flexibility can be mimicked if the cardinality of the range of f is large: the number, say, of nanoseconds it takes an art historian to verify a disputed Titian.

It is natural to ask how *P* knows what parameters to pick. Positing further global context sensitivity to explain the initial selection leads to a vicious regress. But a completely self-contained procedure suggests itself. We may suppose *P* to come to *S* with a ranking of parameters in order of their expected utility for solving recognition problems. Either through programming or experience, *P* has an idea of which parameters *S* is likely to be a function of.[34] One can even reinforce *P* every time it solves a recognition problem.[35] Most empiricists allow that we are born sensitive to some features of situations; otherwise conditioning would be impossible. If these parameters have no weighting for presumed relevance, imagine *P*'s initial selections to be random. If our initial pool is weighted or ordered for relevance, imagine that *P* will try certain parameters first and more persistently. It is rewarded when it is right; and where rightness is not defined, its reward is coming to a halt with a unique solution. Having in this way ordered the pool of parameters, *P* adds values of parameters further down the ordering until, faced with a given problem *S*, it solves *S*. Nowhere in this does *P* have to recognize *S* or *S*'s context. *P* can even add new parameters to its pool. Programs exist which allow a computer to note, by inspection of its scanner, that radii of curvature are pertinent features of shapes.[36] This seems to me an acceptable schematic description of human pattern recognition as well. Surely it is experience that teaches us what facets of a new object are likely to be the ones that identify it; there is no *a priori* method for selecting the traits to look at. If (as happens in science-fiction movies) we found an altogether strange object, we would examine it seriatim for traits that usually help.

This analysis of recognition nicely accommodates the family

[34] See L. J. Cohen's account of how a scientist learns what variables to include in his canonical tests; *The Implications of Induction* (O.U.P.: Oxford: 1970).

[35] Talk of reinforcement here is not metaphorical: a reinforcer is anything that increases the probability of a response, and programs exist in which the probability of a response is a function of the past consequences of its emission.

[36] Cf. the Uhr–Vossler program, in 'A Pattern-Recognition Program that Generates, Evaluates and Adjusts its Own Operators', in J. Feldman and E. Feigenbaum, eds., *Computers and Thought* (McGraw-Hill, N.Y.: 1963). The Selfridge–Dineen program invents new parameters by transforming the coding of the projected grid pattern by four operations. A result of four such operations is a 'characteristic'. If a characteristic turns out to correlate highly with success in solving recognition problems, it is retained; if not, it is dropped. The program will sometimes, randomly, try new quadruples.

resemblance phenomenon, which turns out to be a problem about the variance of parameters used in certain recognition problems. Wittgenstein, Campbell, and Goodman[37] all explain family resemblance as follows. Consider the five properties A, B, C, D, E. G is a family resemblance predicate if a thing counts as a G if it has, say, *some pair* of A, B, ... The family resemblance anomaly is a two-fold consequence of the presence of family resemblance predicates in language. First, two things with no property in common may be classed as G, and hence similar. $XYZDE$ and $MNOBC$ will be deemed similar, because both are G. Moreover, two things may be deemed dissimilar with respect to G even if they have more in common than some pair of G's. Thus $XYZBA$ will be deemed a G and $MNOPA$ a non-G, hence to that extent dissimilar, even though they are more alike than $XYZDE$ and $MNOBC$.

This human capacity to mark, respond to, or classify in line with family resemblances is no more than a disposition to dip into a standing pool of parameters in a somewhat unorthodox way. A pair of functions $\langle f, g\rangle$ as on p. 206 above can easily solve such family resemblance recognition problems as recognizing upper-case and lower-case tokens of the same letter. The Selfridge–Dineen and Uhr–Vossler programs (see p. 207, n. 36) are promising steps in this direction. More formally, $\langle f, g\rangle$ treats G as an *r-wise* family resemblance predicate if (1) $(\exists m \geqslant r)(S)(f(S) = \langle x_1,\ldots,x_m\rangle)$; and (2) there exist neighbourhoods $n(x_1),\ldots,n(x_m)$ around the x_i such that $g(\langle x_1,\ldots,x_m\rangle) = \mathrm{G} \equiv (\exists_{i_1}) \ \ldots \ (\exists_{i_r})(i_k \neq i_l(k, \ l = 1,\ldots,r) \ \& \ x_{i_1} \varepsilon\, n(x_{i_1}) \ \& \ \ldots \ \& \ x_{i_r} \varepsilon\, n(x_{i_r}))$. The case in the previous paragraph arises when $r = 2$.

P (an embodied selector with evaluator) will not solve every recognition problem. But neither can we. The dying words of a riverboat gambler, 'Put your money in the bank', are for ever ambiguous even to us. Consider Dreyfuss again:

If the machine were to examine explicitly each possibly relevant factor as

[37] K. Campbell, 'Family Resemblance Predicates', *American Philosophical Quarterly*, ii. 3 (July 1965), 238–44; N. Goodman, 'Seven Strictures on Similarity', in Foster and Swanson, eds., *Experience and Theory*, pp. 19–29. Wittgenstein does not use the idea of family resemblance to dissolve the problem of universals (as R. Bambrough, and others, maintain: see his 'Universals and Family Resemblance', in G. Pitcher, ed., *Wittgenstein* [Anchor, N.Y.: 1966]). For one thing, it leaves the status of the A, B, . . . (see below) unexplained. Nor did Wittgenstein hold that *all* predicates are family resemblant; he was only cautioning against the search for sharp definitions of such philosophically prominent words as 'know', 'number', 'intend', and 'mean'.

a determinate bit of information, in order to determine whether to consider or ignore it, it could never complete the calculations necessary to predict the outcome of a single [horse] race. If, on the other hand, the machine systematically excluded possibly relevant factors in order to complete its calculations, then it would sometimes be incapable of performing as well as an intelligent human.[38]

Dreyfuss is rating computers against an implausible idealization of our own capacities. True, on the second alternative a handicapper will sometimes beat a computer; but the computer will sometimes beat the handicapper. As for the first alternative, betters, being human, must sometimes just *guess* at post time. If time presses the computer can randomize its bet too.

If relevance tails off after the first billion parameters, a system that uses ten billion will appear to have an unlimited repertory. Dreyfuss speaks of 'the open texture of pattern recognition which would seem to be impossible for a system with a finite set of states',[39] but a system with an astronomically large finite number of states would surely 'recognize complex patterns by projecting a somewhat indeterminate whole which is progressively filled in by anticipated experience'. A large enough pool of parameters will replicate the 'open texture' of experience by using different parameters for different recognition problems and abandoning parameters in the course of solving single recognition problems. It must be recalled that there is intelligent life on Earth; you and I solve recognition problems although it is far from obvious that we are capable of occupying infinitely many states in any non-trivial sense of 'infinite'.

6. How to Solve a Recognition Problem

The foregoing outline of a pattern recognition program is sometimes taken as a reductio of construing mental activities like recognizing as the activities of a programmed machine. You and I, the objection runs, do not recognize patterns by examining parameters; it is something we do *straight off*, as a basic action or response. I recognize an A in my visual field basically, not by saying to myself 'Three broken lines surrounded by a C and a T; it must be an A'. I may muff some recognition problems, but no act of classifying I do venture involves drawing conclusions from a preliminary analysis of components and surroundings. I do nothing, hence nothing analogous

[38] 'Why Computers Must Have Bodies', p. 24.
[39] Ibid., p. 21.

to what *P* does. Nor do I recognize by using auxiliary devices like scanner, in the way I hit a ball with a tennis raquet. The same holds for reasoning generally. Thus Matson: 'this [breaking a pattern down into units] . . . is not the way *we* recognize pigs or letter C's. Nor is it at all plausible to suggest that we really do go through a rapid and unconscious list. We just recognize them.'[40]

Indeed, if I first recognized the presence of three broken lines and then concluded that I was seeing an A, how did I recognize the more elementary patterns as lines? I must recognize something straight off, so why not the A, as intuition dictates? Similarly, postulating rapid unconscious inference from unconscious recognition of the three lines as lines leaves unexplained precisely what appeal to the unconscious was supposed to explain: how I recognize. At some point we recognize basically. (J. Fodor defends a topsy-turvy version of this insight: a computer *does* everything in its program, so if it simulates some behaviour *b*, a man emitting *b* must also *do* everything that happens in his nervous system in accordance with 'tacit knowledge' of the rules for doing them. This leads Fodor to the regress just adumbrated.[41])

The positive points made by this objection are correct. Recognition is a basic response which occurs at the 'personal' level of description. But this does not show that computer recognition differs from human recognition. *How* the computer recognizes may still be how we recognize. To key to this is the fact that recognitions have causes. An act of recognition is the upshot of underlying mental or neural events; and indeed may be identical to a set of subpersonal processes. Either way, the error spotted by the present objection is that of taking these events to be themselves acts of recognition. However, we must not now forget that things *happen* when recognition occurs: retinal irradiation, neural firing, and the like. Reconsider our A-recognizer *P* with this in mind. *P* is built so that incoming light is projected onto a grid, the pattern there is converted into binary code, and the coded pattern fitted against a template.

[40] *Sentience*, p. 104, also pp. 132–3. Geach suggests this objection in 'What do we Think With?' in *God and the Soul* (Routledge & Kegan Paul, London: 1969); and C. Taylor is evidently thinking of it when he deplores 'the renewed primacy of the explicit which has come with the digital computer': 'Review of Fodor's *Psychological Explanation*', *Philosophical Review*, lxxx. 1 (Jan. 1971), 112.

[41] J. Fodor, 'The Appeal to Tacit Knowledge in Psychological Explanation', *Journal of Philosophy*, lxv. 20 (Oct. 1968), 627–40. S. Morgenbesser spots the regress in 'Fodor on Ryle and Rules', *Journal of Philosophy*, lxvi. 14 (July 1969), 458–72; also see T. Nagel, 'The Boundaries of Inner Space', ibid., 452–8.

But why say that what *P does* is scan an internal grid, encode a pattern, and read off from that pattern whether it is facing an A? Why not say instead that *P* recognizes basically, and that the projection and encoding are processes whose upshot is *P*'s recognition? These processes need no more be taken as *how P* decides what it is seeing, as preliminary recognitions, than we need take the processes in my nervous system as *my* reasons for, how I decide, what I am seeing. My eyes project light onto my retina, but I respond to the A, not my retinal state. The transactions in *P* correspond to the events in me. *P* has sensors, but responds to the *A*, not the states of its sensors. The action/event distinction, buried in section 5, has not yet come back to haunt us.

It is quite true that *P*'s internal states evolve in accordance with a program, and mine do not. But this difference does not bear on the role of the internal states themselves. My retinal states are induced in accordance with causal laws. Would *I* see these states instead of the A if they were induced because somebody built me with my conformity to these laws in mind? Remember that the cause of the evolution of *P*'s internal states is not its program. *P*'s program is an abstract system which *P* satisfies because of the causal laws governing *P*.[42] If internal state *s* of *P* realizes the abstract program state *S*, *P* lapses into *S* just when *P* lapses into *s*; and it lapses into *s* in just the way *I* lapse into my internal states. That nobody intended me to respond to stimuli as I do, and somebody so intended *P*, does not warrant assigning our respective responses different logical roles. Suppose my brain lapses into state *s'* when light from an A-token hits my eye, and that my father knew this and indeed conceived me to bring into the world something that went into *s'* when struck by light from an A. It would be absurd to say that, unlike others with my physiology, I recognize *A*'s by noticing *s'*. There is, however, no difference between the offspring of a physiologically astute parent and a computer.

The presence of intentions in the genealogy of computers is a persistent distraction (particularly in connection with creativity; cf. section 7). Thus Geach denies thought to machines because 'Machines manifestly have no life, no sense, no feelings, no purposes except their makers'.[43] Let us waive the question of machine sensibility, and grant that mentality is impossible for a creature lacking purposes.

[42] See pp. 132 above.
[43] 'What do we Think With?' p. 40.

The fact that *P* aims at *T* because an engineer aims at *T* and built *P* to aim at *T* (perhaps to help him gain *T*) does not entail that *P* does not aim at *T*. Indeed, explaining why *P* aims at *T* presupposes that *P* does aim at *T*. Geach's point might be that it is absurd to suppose that *P* could want *T* if somebody wanted *P* to want *T*. This absurdity is hard to see. There is no incoherence in my fathering a child so that *he* will want to gather food (and perhaps accompany me in harvesting). Even if my desire for a child who wants to gather food is in the service of my own purposes, the child may have all manner of aims. *The intention with which a thing comes into being has nothing to do with what that thing is* (barring descriptions which entail facts about origin).

It might be suggested that the child has aims of his own because the father knows few of the details of gestation. But how can the father's epistemic state at the moment of conception determine whether purposes (will) exist in the child? Had the father known every detail of what he was initiating, the *same child* would have resulted. An agent's epistemic state, of course, influences his productions, but this is beside the point. The suggestion here requires that if two creators, the first of whom knows the details of his product and the second of whom does not, produce otherwise indescriminable objects, only the second creation can have purposes of its own. It is irrelevant that the creation of a knowledgeable creator is likely to differ from that of an uninformed one.

7. Programming Creativity

The fact that the origin of a thing is irrelevant to its nature, and the fact that computers can emit basic responses, both bear on computer creativity. Creativity is a central feature of man's higher nature, and the materialist will be discomfited if computers cannot create. And it has seemed evident to many that they cannot, because they are only following programs designed for them by men.[44] Everything a computer does, it seems, is already contained in its program. This argument is reminiscent of the positivist doctrine that mathematics yields no new information, the theorems of a formal system being contained in its axioms and definitions. A theorem may surprise a

[44] '[There is] an opposition between the . . . concept of mentality and the concept of total subservience to known or knowable rules' (Cohen, 'Can There be Artificial Minds?'). Why subservience? Is a computer anything apart from its rules? I have been programmed by my experiences and genetic endowment; is Cohen saying that I don't have a mind?

mathematician, but only because he has not fully grasped what the axioms entail. Similarly, a computer may surprise its programmer, but only because he has not fully grasped what the program entails. The ability of machines to surprise is a reflection on human limitation.

Two difficulties prove fatal to this view. First, the containment metaphor proves empty when unpacked. Second, the argument, when explicitly stated, pitches the standard of creativity so high that men as well as their machines are likely to fail it. To fix our ideas, consider how one might design a machine that composes music, a paradigmatically creative activity.[45] As a preliminary, we have technicians study the scores of Beethoven and compile tables of transition probabilities for him. We find, for example, that he follows a D-sharp by an E 5 per cent of the time and an F 16 per cent of the time. We make parallel observations about his rhythms. We program a computer *B* to produce scores in accordance with these rules. *B* produces Beethovian music.

Beethoven didn't run through an inner program. He simply concocted melodies, where 'concocting a melody' is a basic act. The presence of a program in *B* does not mean that *B* composes any differently; *B* may concoct melodies, too, without consulting an inner program. Beethoven was so constituted that he produced and adopted *n*-tuples of notes with describable harmonic and rhythmic properties. It is by these properties that we recognize, without analysing it down to transition probabilities, a piece to be Beethovian. (But remember: there are 'formula composers' like Korngold.) The phenomenology of writing music (or words) is that one *writes*: it is for critics to discern what is distinctive or valuable in the product. Perhaps *B* is like Beethoven in that the causal processes culminating in a score are not compositional steps. *B* may select an *n*-tuple of notes because it sounds right, where 'sounds right' denotes a program-governed process of comparing the notes to a template or against an external standard—perhaps a program which alters transition probabilities if a human auditor pushes a button marked 'pedestrian'.

But wasn't *B*'s program cribbed from Beethoven himself, the true creator? The immediate difficulty with this complaint is its concession that, had Beethoven never existed, *B* would have been

[45] The illustrative details in what follows are fanciful, but they represent actual work; cf. L. Hiller, 'Computer Music', *Scientific American*, cci. 6 (Dec. 1959), 109–20.

creative, as creative as Beethoven. The mere contingency of Beethoven's existence can affect nothing more than *B*'s claims to priority for his output. Even though the Pythagorean Theorem is hardly news, a child who divines it on his own is mathematically creative. By parity of reasoning a computer that produces the *Eroica* on its own is creative even if the work has already been produced. After all, what made the initial composer creative was his production of the *Eroica!* If there wasn't something *intrinsically* excellent about producing the *Eroica*, producing it first would not deserve any credit.

Problems generated by cribbed programs can in any case be side-stepped by putting a novel set of transition probabilities in a machine *B'* which produces absolutely new works. Surely we would call *B'* creative if its products are *good*; pleasant, elegant and intelligent in the ways critics struggle to articulate. Whether a product is a creation and its producer creative are not questions about the provenance of the product, but its quality (and perhaps priority). Neither the quality nor the novelty of a product are causal issues, for whether something is good or the first of its kind are normally independent of how it came to be. *B'* must meet the further requirement of being able to perform other creative acts; a tape deck which produces the *Eroica* is uncreative. But *B'* has a general program, and will yield further products. The demand that *B'* exhibit creativity over a *broad* range is an echo of the unhelpful demand for flexibility, and anyway even Beethoven couldn't paint.

One might also want a creator to create out of need or desire; whereas 'the keen awareness of a task to be performed, so evident in human creative work, is absent in the computer'.[46] But while this keenness may be a natural accompaniment of creativity, there are examples of effortless human creation. Mozart wrote his last three symphonies in a few weeks, and Bach improvised his *Toccata and Fugue*. But such feats are rare even in the annals of the greatest geniuses, and who can imagine what it was like to be Mozart or Bach? The need for 'keenness', however, might reflect a demand that sentience is required for creativity. This demand ignores such counterexamples as that of a scientist who awakes from a dreamless sleep with the solution to a problem.[47] Perhaps this demand is meant as a conceptual or linguistic truth: no performance is allowed to

[46] D. Fink, *Computers and the Human Mind* (Anchor, N.Y.: 1966), p. 271.

[47] Meehl, 'Psychological Determinism and Human Rationality', *Minnesota Studies in the Philosophy of Science*, iv. 461 ff.

count as creative unless performed by a sentient being. But this stipulation (or report about ordinary usage) is altogether ineffective, for it leaves open the possibility of an insentient being producing exactly what a sentient being did. To allow this is to abandon the argument that a computer couldn't be sentient because it *lacked that ability*.

The consideration with the strongest grip is that B' is working out a program someone put in it. This grip can be loosened by the standard lemma: that somebody intended B' to act the way it does has nothing to do with *what* B' does or how to describe it. If B' had come into existence by blind natural processes, we could not say that B' is uncreative because it was acting in ways it *could have been* instructed in. *That* would deny creativity to Beethoven, who *could* have copied the *Eroica* from a score of Haydn. But the accidental B' is indistinguishable in structure and activity from the programmed B'. Those worried by the presence of a program may retreat to the claim that B' is uncreative just because it behaves in accordance with a program. This idea is suspect if only because we all behave in accordance with programs—genetic endowment and past experience. As always, the haphazardness of our programming is irrelevant. In any case, the thought that a thing cannot be creative if it works in causally necessary conformity to a rule derives from a mistake about causation. This is the assumption that if x causes y, and y exhibits trait z, z is already 'in' x. More generally: if x causes y, y is already in x. This assumption exacerbates the discomfort produced by creative computers. There is a tendency to think that if something caused Beethoven to think of the *Prometheus* theme, the theme must have existed in that cause. Beethoven becomes, on this picture, a medium through which the theme is transmitted. Since Beethoven was obviously more than a passive observer of the *Prometheus* theme's entrance into reality, philosophers have denied that creative acts are caused because they adhere to this view of causation.[48] It is similarly tempting to think of a symphony that B' produces as already in its program, and of B' as just the vehicle for carrying the symphony into the world. The next step is to credit whoever devised the program with the real act of creation, or to say that no creative act took place if nobody thought up the program.

[48] See R. Abel, *Man is the Measure* (Free Press, N.Y.: 1976); for a particularly direct and confused statement, see Popper, 'Of Clouds and Clocks', in *Objective Knowledge* (O.U.P., Oxford: 1972).

This leads to the unsettling corollary that if all acts are causally necessary, no creative acts ever occur.

This view of causality, along with its implications, is patently absurd. If x causes y, to say that y is contained in x is just a misleading way of saying that if x happens, y must happen; i.e. that x causes y. y itself does not happen until it happens. Even if causally necessary, the *Prometheus* melody did not exist until Beethoven played it, or wrote it down, or heard it in his mind. A computer melody does not exist until the computer emits it or, perhaps, hears it in its inner mechanical ear. 'The program contained the melody' is the misleadingly expressed truism that a machine embodying that program produced that melody (or would produce it under appropriate circumstances). We knew *this* just from the fact that the melody came out of the computer! True, if the program is *trivial*—'Print the score of the *Eroica*'—the computer is no more than an inessential transmitter of something that already exists. And it may be difficult to draw a sharp line between trivial and non-trivial programs. The notion of a non-trivial mathematical proof is comparably vague. But the containment views of programmed behaviour, amounts to the claim that *all* programs are trivial, and that is absurd. Unless the full *Prometheus* melody was implanted in Beethoven's brain, saying it was already in its causes just says, confusedly, that there were causes of Beethoven's writing the *Prometheus*.

The positivist account of entailment also collapses when the containment metaphor goes circular. Saying that $A \vdash T$ because A implicitly contains T gets nowhere, because the only criterion for whether T is contained in A is just whether T is deducible from A. It is the proof that proves, not something behind it.

But surely the containment metaphor has this much literal meaning: *if* one knows enough, one can predict exactly what a computer will do. Cohen, for example, makes much of the potential predictability of programmed behaviour and explicitly attributes unpredictability to the programmer's ignorance. Recalling his worries about the human status of his wife, he says that if his wife's behaviour were in principle predictable, we would say she had 'no mind of her own'.[49] But, again, determinism implies this sort of in-principle predictability of Beethoven: if we had studied him closely enough, known the contingencies of his environment and the laws of nature, we could, if determinism is true, have predicted exactly what he

[49] 'Can there be Artificial Minds?'.

would have done. This is not a decisive reductio because nobody knows if determinism is true. But it is nearly a reductio: we do know that Beethoven was creative, and this assessment is not hostage to determinism. It is an irrelevant contingency that we know more about B' than we do about Beethoven, or that we know more because we programmed B'. There is no absurdity in supposing that the modus operandi of a 'natural' creator be programmable. That by feeding his program into a machine we ensure that his potential products are churned out faster than he churns them out only means that *his creations* become available sooner than they would have in the normal course of events. If in-principle predictability (or stochastic predictability) precludes programmed or programmable behaviour from being creative, it precludes Beethoven from creativity.

The source of the intuitive contrast between 'essentially unprogrammable' beings and beings whose behaviour can be programmed may be our inability to predict, categorically, what a man will create. Our inability to do so, and our cognate inability to program a creative machine, is due to our inability to predict (or simulate) all the pertinent environmental factors that will impinge on a man. To be able to do *that* we would have to be nearly omniscient. This is why we are so sure that, categorically speaking, men will continue to take us by surprise. We are more confident of our categorical predictions about what computers will do because we are surer about what their environment is going to be. But this contrast is illusory. We must accord a computer the capacity to surprise us with its responses to unanticipated inputs. As an inhabitant of the real world, its behaviour is no more categorically predictable than that of a man.

All of us were 'manufactured' in placentas, 'programmed' by a generous endowment of instinct, and are periodically 'reprogrammed' by experience. I can initiate learned behaviour after foetal tenure, but so can a machine built with heuristics to modify its initial program. True, it will alter its behaviour only by reference to an external check of 'success'. If no one tells B' how dreary its melodies are, it will go on producing dreary melodies. But this is true of people as well. Pain—including the adverse judgement of critics—is the external check which modifies human behaviour. The lonely spirit who cares only for meeting his own standards is unusual only in that his standards are internal. But standards can be built into a machine. Program it to calculate π, and instruct it to redo its calculations if it finds that $\Sigma(-1)^{n+1} \cdot 4/2n-1 < 3{\cdot}14$ for even n. Here the problem of explicitness threatens to break out again. A man, unlike a computer, will sometimes make a *gestalt* judgement, like 'I just don't like it', without being able to provide a description of what he doesn't like. This should not mislead us. A man who finds something wanting, even by self-created standards, owes us a description of *what* he doesn't like. He makes no sense if he says he doesn't like a novel, but can't say whether he finds fault with the plot, style, or theme. And even where a 'gut reaction' is acceptable, we expect unarticulated but discoverable cues to have prompted the reaction. These cues can be programmed, and—see section 6—can be used to endow a machine with 'gut reactions'.

I must concede that if we disinterred Beethoven's remains and found 'Made in Andromeda' stamped on his skull, our attitude toward him would change. Even if I had been under no illusions about my wife's looks, intelligence, or personality, I would be disturbed if I found that she had been built in a factory. What is not clear is that I would revise any of my *beliefs* about Beethoven or my wife (other than beliefs about where they came from). This conflict between change in attitude and constancy of belief is due, I think, to our willingness to locate intimates within the causal order only on condition that the causes of their behaviour are varied and heterogeneous. This condition is natural, in light of the empirical fact that only such causal histories have so far generated behaviour that surprises and pleases us. Humanity has come to be associated with heterogeneity of contributing causes. This is why, were x to appear to exhibit personality trait P, and we discovered that someone created x to be P, we would be reluctant to ascribe full possession of P to x: we would not trust x to keep up the P-ish behaviour, its cause being too coherent. This intuition may have to be jettisoned as systems appear with coherent causal histories and a wide range of behaviours. Even if we maintain these intuitions, they claim no incompatibility between humanity and certain kinds of genesis. They are epistemic intuitions instructing us never to *believe* that we have our hands on a certain sort of test case.

8. *Other Capacities*

Even if the general objections to machine mentality fail, there is sometimes thought to be a range of specific aptitudes that a computer could never replicate. Reflection on one or two of these shows how wide a range of performance is in principle programmable, and suggests a general moral about programming mind-like behaviour.

A sense of humour is a distinctive human trait. While a computer doesn't have to have one to behave in a mind-like way, asking how one would write a joke-getting program is instructive. While debate about the nature of humour continues,[50] it would seem that a joke is at least an n-tuple of sentences $\langle S_1,\ldots,S_n\rangle$ such that the probability of each S_j is affected by all the S_i, $i < j$; and in particular the probability of S_n given $\langle S_1,\ldots,S_{n-1}\rangle$ is low. This low probability corresponds to the idea that a punch-line must be a surprise. Laughter is a sudden emission of energy caused by processing the n-tuple. This suggests a first step for making a laughing computer: have it discharge energy when an n-tuple of sentences it scans meets the foregoing conditions. It can be programmed to 'get' or 'not get' special kinds of jokes (e.g. Yiddish or dialect). It needs, of course, a probability function.

The stated conditions and their associated program are clearly deficient, but the remedy for their deficiencies contains a lesson. One missing element is what the n-tuple of sentences is *about*. Some theories (Bergson's and aspects of Freud's) hold that a joke must have a certain content, their evidence being the nearly universal presence of references to excrement or sexual intercourse in humour. This may reflect ill on the human race, but it facilitates programming: one can add the requirement that the n-tuple concern sex or elimination (preferably both), which the computer can check by appeal to a table of 500 dirty words. What of double entendres? Well, human audiences sometimes miss the point. There is risible life on Earth, and we shouldn't ask our program to simulate a dream audience. Other theories locate humour in the *how* of jokes. One example is the Hobbesian theory that laughter expresses the sudden enhancement of one's idea of his own power, the occasion being a suitably distanced presentation of another's disaster. If this is right, we must impose appropriate constraints on n-tuples the computer is to laugh at: such n-tuples must be about the humiliation of computers (e.g. downtime), computers who can't compute very rapidly, Polish computers, etc. Similar remarks apply to the Freudian theory that what is funny about jokes is how they slip their forbidden messages past the normally vigilant censor.

[50] See D. Munro, *Argument of Laughter* (U. of Notre Dame Press, Notre Dame, Ind.: 1951).

The point behind these suggestions is that what was needed to supplement the initially inadequate program was an improved *analysis* of humour. The programmer must wait patiently to incorporate the fruits of improved theories into his program. As our understanding of humour improves, so will programs that transcribe it. The skill of the humourist is just his intuitive grasp of the whole a humour program analyses. As I have stressed, this analysis need not describe what the program does, but how it reacts in distinctively human ways. It would seem that the limitations of computers to ape activities that can be precisely described and unambiguously step-wise arranged is not so stringent a limitation. Even the most 'cloud-like' bursts of behaviour may happen in determinate steps in determinate order. The only *clear* limitation on what is programmable is our understanding of ourselves. This moral covers a wide range of human talents; the difficulty one has in imagining a computer doing *X* may always lie, not in any sensed incompatibility between computers and *X*, but in our own confusion about what *X* is. One can envisage a computer being programmed to fall in love, that most distinctive of man's higher capacities. When young it is full of potential that must be discharged into some or other computer of complementary design. When it gets a bit older, it encounters one such computer it prefers to discharge its energy into exclusively. When the other computer is absent, it wheels about aimlessly on its coasters. All we need to finish the program is a clearer idea of what people in love do.

Programming mind-like behaviour will obviously require ingenuity; but a caution was long ago entered against confusing the ingenuity of a mind-like artefact with the ingenuity of its designer.[51]

9. *Forms of Life*

Assimilating the human realm to the mechanical is alarming because of the *inhuman* way machines do things. Part of the idea of a *human* being is a characteristic way of acting, participation in the 'human form of life'. Wittgenstein says that attributing a mind to a man is not a *belief*, hence not something that evidence could prompt us to extend to something else: 'I don't *believe* he has a mind; I *treat* him

[51] See Matson, *Sentience*, pp. 136–8 for a dissenting opinion on the programmability of a sense of humour. He asks 'how in the world is the poor machine to tell' that 'The best laid plans o' mice and men gang aft a-gley' is for real and 'The best planned lays o' mice and men gang aft a-gley' is the take-off—as if human beings were born knowing Burns.

as a soul'.[52] Some philosophers write as if it is not a contingent fact that human consciousness is possessed by beings who participate in the human form of life, the psychological predicates of natural language being conceptually connected with a certain constellation of behaviour and structure. The only thing enough like a man to warrant fruitful comparison with him is another man. 'There is no reason to suppose that a world organized in terms of the [human] body should be accessible by other means.'[53] If we tried to make a artificial mind, we would have to use so much human hardware, arranged as human hardware is, that we will end by constructing a man, artificially: 'I assume there is no reason why, in principle, one could not construct an artificial embodied agent if one used components sufficiently like those which make up a human being.'[54] This argument must be generalized to the mentalities of other life-forms if it is to oppose computer consciousness: it must say that each kind of mentality is conceptually connected with a distinctive form of life that only a 'machine' with an appropriate hardware can participate in. (This generalized thesis is harder to sustain the further one descends the evolutionary ladder: the sentience of creatures is associated with ever more limited behavioural repetories and social lives. Fish don't present the same stumbling blocks to computer simulation that humans do.)

Sometimes the form of life argument seems to be a veiled form of behaviourism. To the extent it is, I will ignore it. But sometimes it seems to be more. 'If a lion could talk, we could not understand him': thus Wittgenstein vivifies the oddity of ascribing human psychological states to non-humans. Did Leo really say, at *t*, that he wanted to read *Word and Object*? Probably not; he produced sounds which, had they been produced by a man, would have counted as an utterance. Given the *lebenswelt* of lions when they are their leonine selves, could what went on in Leo's mind at *t* be what goes on in the mind of a philosopher who says 'I want to read *Word and Object*'? Wittgenstein wants us to conclude that it is not a contingent fact that such psychological states occur in the contexts they do.

Something must be going wrong here. If Leo's brain had miraculously lapsed for a few seconds into the state of the philosopher's

[52] *Investigations*, p. 297.
[53] Dreyfuss, 'Why Computers Must Have Bodies', p. 32.
[54] Ibid., p. 26.

brain, it seems likely that Leo and the philosopher would have had the same experience. The impossibility that Leo wants to read *Word and Object* seems at best contingent; we are unwilling to treat Leo's words as an utterance because it is *extremely unlikely* that he meant them. A Wittgensteinian might reply that one cannot, logically, want to read a book one has never heard of; and where could Leo have heard of *Word and Object*? Well, Leo cannot in logic bear the *dyadic* wants-to-read relation to *Word and Object*, but that is compatible with him satisfying the *monadic* predicate 'is a reading-*Word-and-Object*-wanter' (cf. V.4). Even waiving this distinction, what is now being taken to prevent Leo from wanting to read *Word and Object* is *not* his state of mind at t but his *history*.[55] The argument does not even claim that Leo's *mental state* must be different from the philosopher's; only that certain *descriptions* of his mental state are inappropriate because he has never before heard of *Word and Object*. It is worth while dwelling on this point. The surface logical form of a psychological predicate $P(x,t)$ often suggests that it describes something about x at t. The materialist is committed to holding that a wide variety of objects could be in the state $P(x,t)$ seems to express. The form of life argument is launched against this, to show that only one sort of object can satisfy $P(x,t)$. But how does it do this? By arguing that, surface form notwithstanding, $P(x,t)$ does not ascribe to x a state x is in at t; its satisfaction condition involves times other than t! The form of life argument capitalizes on the fact that, for many psychological predicates $P(x,t)$ (e.g. 'wants at t to go to Medical School') of ordinary language, x cannot be in P at t unless x was in some other state at some earlier time t^- or some later time t^+.[56] But it is surely a confusion to argue that there is an occurrent state P a computer cannot occupy on the grounds that P is not an occurrent state. The materialist can reply more positively: 'Let $P(x,t)$ have its heterotemporal conditions C. A computer can occupy whatever occurrent state S it is which is such that: anything in S at t can be said to be "P" at t if it satisfies C.' He grants the form of life argument its bar against ascribing certain predicates to computers, and asks us not to be so hypnotized by language that we individuate occurrent mental states in terms of

[55] A clear endorsement of the move criticized here is C. Diamond's 'The Interchangeability of Machines', in S. Coval and I. MacIntosh, eds., *The Business of Reason* (Humanities, N.Y.: 1969).

[56] See J. Bennett, *Locke, Berkeley, Hume*, p. 9.

psychological predicates. It is easy, in general, to extrude an occurrent description $P'(x,t)$ of x at t from $P(x,t)$ even if $P(x,t)$ has heterotemporal condition C: $P'(x,t)$ expresses the state such that, if x is in it at t, then $C(x) \supset P(x,t)$.

The style of argument under examination occasions mischief elsewhere. P. Foot has argued that it is *logically* impossible to have certain moral attitudes without the right social setting.[57] Now the thesis that it is logically impossible to disapprove of Jones's marriage unless you know him will puzzle someone who thinks it is merely contingently impossible that my brain be in precisely the state of the brain of one of Jones's intimates. Couldn't I suddenly feel the feeling which, if felt by someone who knows Jones, would be called 'disapproval of Jones's marriage'? But the *nervus probandi* of Foot's argument is precisely that 'x disapproves at t of Jones's marriage' analytically entails that x has had certain dealings with Jones. This point of usage is not worth debating. If Foot's linguistic claim is right, the mooted predicate does not ascribe an occurrent mental state. She will not have shown that a certain *experience* is impossible without the right social setting; only that, if the social setting is wrong, certain *predicates* cannot be applied to that experience. This result will not worry anyone who believes that a Maori *could* be in the same conscious state I am in when I am in that state correctly describable as 'thinking about the continuum problem'.

Still, Wittgenstein seems to have a point, which is best expounded by example. Consider the affection of a dog for his master. When thinking about the mind–body problem uncritically, one may suppose that what Fido experiences when his master returns is what you feel when you see a long-lost friend; Fido only *expresses* it differently. Fido can't talk or embrace his master, so he must be satisfied with jumping around and licking his master's face. But can the feeling be so easily prised off its expression? *You* would feel silly licking your friend's face, although Fido evidently doesn't. Nor does Fido *resign* himself to mute expressions of joy, as you would if your vocal chords were paralysed. If you were confined to putting your hands on your friend's lapel you would feel frustrated. But Fido isn't frustrated—it isn't as if hugging his master is a natural way to express the feeling he has, but which anatomy has denied him. No: it is part of our concept of the human (and canine) feeling of affection

[57] 'Approval and Disapproval', in P. Hacker and J. Raz, eds., *Law, Morality, and Society* (O.U.P., Oxford: 1977), pp. 229–46.

that it is expressed that way. It is not a mere verbal truth that certain behaviours are *appropriate* to certain inner states. A computer couldn't have *this experience* without a body with which to express it appropriately.

This Wittgensteinian *aperçu*—it is less than an argument—undoubtedly suggests something interesting, even profound, about the embodiment of mind. It casts doubt on crude forms of dualism which leave unexplained the appropriateness of bodily states to the mental states they are associated with. It may show that beings with disjoint behavioural repertories could not use their repertories to express precisely the same mental state. But this does not provide sufficient ground for denying even human mentality to beings very different from ourselves in construction and behaviour. It does not show, first, that minds are necessarily embodied. Even if mental state *m* cannot possibly be expressed by behaviour *b*, it does not follow that *m* is expressed by some other behaviour. It might go unexpressed. Even if *m* can only be expressed by *b*′, it is possible that *m* go unexpressed. Moreover, the tight link between feeling and expression cannot show that the only thing similar enough to a man to have his mental states is another man without supplementation by a quite strict standard of similarity. No non-human being can have *precisely* those experiences whose expression requires a human body. A precisely man-like artefact will converge at the limit on man himself, and perhaps the only suitable manufacturing facility will be a placenta. But this is compatible with a computer having experiences somewhat like ours. And it is certainly compatible with computers having experiences of a perhaps unimaginable sort. And if this standard of similarity becomes too strict, you and I will be unable to share mental states. After all, how I register enjoyment or anger doubtless differs a bit from how you do. They are part of my form of life. Is the only thing sufficiently like me to warrant comparsion, me?

The deepest problem in the assessment of Wittgenstein's *aperçu* is that it once again brings us into collision with Hume's law. The materialist is committed to holding that the intuition of a necessary connection between inner states and their expression teased out by such examples as the one on p. 223 is illusory. How would a plausible argument to this effect begin? It is well known that a long habit of association can make a contingent connection appear even deeply necessary. Some cases of perceived appropriateness can be explained this way. Remember how difficult Huck Finn found it to explain to Jim that other languages are possible. A milestone just before my house seems, after years of passing it, the *right* thing to indicate that I am near home. Is *this* why a smile is the *right* expression of pleasure? I find adopting this conclusion uncomfortable, but not as uncomfortable as abandoning Hume's law. Remember, finally, that our standard descriptions for mental states refer to overt behaviour. Our descriptions of the inner causes of bodily events normally refer to the bodily events: the inner causes are called 'the cause of this behaviour'. This adds an extra legitimacy to the illusion that the inner is necessarily connected to the outer.

Appendix: Gödel's Theorems

Much ink has been poured over the implications of Gödel's First Theorem for the mind–machine problem. I want here merely to indicate that much of this literature rests on an almost universal misstatement of the Gödel result.

It is usually said that Gödel showed that, for any fpa F, there is a statement G_F which is both true and unassertable by F. Since *we* know G_F is true, and F was any fpa, we transcend any fpa. One reply is that an infinite hierarchy of fpa's can be constructed, each knowing the Gödel statement of its predecessor. A similar tactic is used in chapter VII against prediction paradoxes. J. Smart suggests supplying F with learning heuristics so that F can induce that G_F is true. But it is much more to the point to remark that this standard characterization of Gödel's First Theorem is simply wrong. Let A_F be the axiom system which F represents. Gödel showed that there is a statement G_F of formal arithmetic such that $-[A_F \vdash G_F]$ and $-[A_F \vdash -G_F]$. *If* one now adopts the hypothesis that formal arithmetic has a standard model N, *and* one interprets G_F under the natural interpretation of formal arithmetic in N—the numeral $k^{(n)}$ denotes the number n, and every predicate denotes the property it numeralwise represents—then G_F is true (in N). But the truth of G_F is no part of the First Gödel Theorem itself. The First Gödel Theorem doesn't say that every formal theory of the relevant sort fails to entail some truth. It says only that every formal theory of the relevant sort is incomplete in a much weaker, syntactic, sense. The claim about truth only follows if one adds (an admittedly natural) semantics.

What of the Second Gödel Theorem? Take the statement 'A_F is consistent'. This statement is representatable in formal arithmetic, indeed in A_F, by a wff C_F. The Second Gödel Theorem is that —$[A_F \vdash C_F]$. But this marks no superiority on our part, since *we* cannot prove the consistency of A_F by elementary means either.[58] To be sure, we can prove the consistency of A_F if we allow ourselves transfinite induction. But if we supply F with transfinite induction, $F' = F+$transfinite induction will also generate C_F.

[58] See Putnam, 'Minds and Machines', p. 142.

VII
Free Will

I TURN now to free will, an issue that the materialist view of man can hardly avoid. I argue here that, because the doctrine of compatibilism is true, materialism presents no threat to human freedom or moral responsibility. Materialism is consistent with our intuitions concerning our special status as moral beings. The right kind of material object can possess intrinsic worth.

It is natural to reason that if mental events are physical events, and all events in the physical order are causally determined, all that happens to anyone is causally determined. One might object to thus burdening materialism with determinism on the grounds that dualism is compatible with determinism. We rejected a version of the argument from man's higher nature in II. 1 just because we could find no obstacle to a physics of spiritual substances. However, since the physical realm is the only one for whose deterministic structure we have positive evidence, it is pointless to speculate about spiritual physics. Materialism is the best candidate for bringing man under the sway of causation. A different reason one might offer for not burdening materialism with determinism is the allegation that there is no clear non-trivial formulation of determinism. It is sometimes said, for example, that determinism is not a thesis about the world, but a guiding principle of science. This allegation ignores recent analytical developments that suggest determinism is capable of clear and non-trivial statement.[1] Quantum phenomena aside, it seems on the evidence true. At any rate, no one disturbed by the deterministic implications of materialism is likely to be mollified by infirmities in actual or possible statements of determinism.[2]

1. Compatibilism: Initial Statement

It is often thought that if determinism is non-trivial and true of the human realm, man does not have free will, and the categories of

[1] Cf. Nagel, *The Structure of Science*, chap. 10; R. Montague, 'Deterministic Theories', in R. Thomason, ed. *Formal Philosophy* (Yale U.P., New Haven, Conn.: 1973).

[2] Matson argues that the (alleged) gap between ourselves and computers is a

moral assessment—praise, blame, responsibility, desert—are inapplicable to him. I will argue that free will is compatible with determinism (hence with materialism and determinism) since, roughly speaking, freedom is doing what you want to do. This being so, one can be free even if one's acts are caused by wants, and one's wants are caused by other factors out of one's control. Compatibilism is not a new thesis. But it is a lesson that merits, and requires, periodic relearning. New objections are always being mounted against it, and there are new things to be said in its defence.

In what follows I treat willing, choosing, opting, deciding, wishing, electing, and desiring as all roughly equivalent. I mark no distinction between formulations of compatibilism that use one or the other of these notions. This policy, which has the obvious advantage of expository convenience, may seem philosophically insensitive. In some situations freedom is more clearly connected with (say) the effectiveness of decisions rather than wants, while in others freedom is closer to the effectiveness of wants. I may want to be in Florida, but what makes me free to go is the fact that I could be in Florida if I decide to go. Here decision is what counts. On the other hand, if I want a hamburger in a vegetarian restaurant, I can't, am not free to, have a hamburger. Here wanting is what counts. A consistent and complete formulation of compatibilism would involve a cumbersome disjunction of all the notions lately cited, and others besides. However, since these notions overlap in complex ways, and are all to some extent vague, neither the clarity nor the plausibility

---

major point favouring free will: it shows that human actions cannot be predicted without reference to deliberation, and for Matson *A* is free if a full explanation of *A*'s actions requires such reference (*Sentience*, p. 166). But since 'sizing up' and deliberating are physical events (178), it shouldn't matter that such things are non-digitalizable. Matson says that what makes for unfreedom is that it be 'possible in principle for an outsider to know what I am going to do before I do it' (172). If determinism is true, my actions and deliberations are causally necessary even if action explanations must refer to deliberations. Yet Matson says (141 n.) that his account of freedom is compatible with determinism—his reason being, apparently, that a Laplacean intelligence could predict my actions only by using premises of the form 'reason *R* will impress Levin'. But (a) as my being impressed by reason R = a brain process, Matson ultimately grounds my freedom in how an external predictor would refer to certain physical events; and anyway (b) if predictability entails unfreedom, why should the sorts of premises used matter? If what disturbs Matson about digital processes is the predictability of their outcomes, he should be equally disturbed by predictable non-digital processes. Matson's mysterious materialism catches up with him when he concludes, in his penultimate sentence, that men deserve praise for their free actions *only* in the way a well-wrought urn does.

of compatibilism is enhanced by registering all the distinctions the list suggests. Sometimes I will use the contextually most natural notion, but usually 'want' and 'decide' will go proxy for the rest. Davidson's portmanteau phrase 'primary reason'[3] might serve, had it not been coined for use in another philosophical debate, that over reasons and causes. I shall sometimes use '(having an) end in view' as a neutral portmanteau phrase for the cause of (what the compatibilist takes to be) free acts, a phrase which is also quite useful when considering whether reasons and decisions are causes. There is the problem that when I scratch my head while thinking about a problem I do not antecedently represent to myself my hand being on my head; and yet the act was mine. True: but the reason my *act* was scratching my head and not, say, killing some microbes, is that 'scratching my head' is how I would describe what happened. The concept of an action, as opposed to bodily movement, seems to involve the idea of a distinguished description its participant is willing to give. We may understand 'end in view' simply as what is expressed by such a description.

An objection to compatibilism collateral to the variety of terms that express dimensions of choice is its *vagueness*. J. Glover calls 'incomplete' the version of compatibilism which takes an act to be free if it is unconstrained, because 'the boundaries of constraint are not easy to draw with any precision; [compatibilism does not provide] a satisfactory account of the distinction between normal and impaired psychological abilities'.[4] But even if this is so—much of this chapter is devoted to sketching just such an account—such vagueness need not impair compatibilism. To explicate a precise explicandum, one must provide a precise explicans. But if the explicandum is vague, all that is required of the explicans is that its vagueness match. Thus, even if 'unconstrained choice' is vague, it can still explicate 'freedom' if its vagueness is congruent with that of 'freedom'. Showing that this is not so would be hard work. Given the wide currency of the notion of freedom, it would be remarkable if 'freedom' did not have numerous borderline cases.[5]

[3] 'Actions, Reasons and Causes', *Journal of Philosophy*, lx. 23 (Nov. 1963), 685–700.

[4] *Responsibility* (Humanities, N.Y.: 1970), pp. 82, 86.

[5] Oddly, Glover also writes: 'openness to persuasion is a matter of degree, and also it will be often difficult to assess the extent to which someone is open to persuasion. . . . But the fact that a question is hard to answer does not show that it is not the relevant one to ask' (ibid., p. 136).

As a first approximation, then, the compatibilist holds that '*A* did *X* freely' means '*A* did *X* because *A* wanted to do *X*'. Correlatively, he holds that '*A* is free to do *X*' and '*A* can do *X*' mean '*A* would do *X* if *A* decided to do *X*'. It might seem more in keeping with ordinary usage to say '*A* is free to do *X*' means '*A could* do *X* if he wanted to', but the latter may simply be elliptical for '*A* could do *X and would* do *X*, if he wanted to'. Similarly, '*A* can do *X* by trying' may be elliptical for '*A* can do *X* because he would succeed in doing *X* if he tried'. A fuller explanation of the naturalness of 'could' instead of 'would' in the compatibilist's explicans is that, the world being as it is, we are reluctant to say that *A* is guaranteed of success if he tries to do *A*, especially if this is meant counterfactually. All we are normally prepared to say is that the probability of *A*'s doing *X* (or *X*'s happening) would increase greatly if *A* set about doing *X*. Reluctance to say that *A* would do *X* if he tried acknowledges the omnipresent possibility of failure; but this acknowledgement is in the spirit of compatibilism. This terminological issue is not unimportant; almost all of Austin's celebrated attack on compatibilism[6] is directed against the obviously circular thesis that '*A* could have done *X*' means '*A* could have done *X* if he had chosen to do *X*'. At only one point, on p. 218, does Austin consider the thesis that '*A* can do *X*' means '*A* shall do *X*, if *A* tries', and he concedes that 'There is some plausibility in this suggestion'. The footnote Austin attaches to this concession does nothing to show there is any implausibility in it.

The philosophical heart of compatibilism is its corollary that even if *A*'s doing *X* was *caused* by *A*'s desire to do *X*, *A* did *X* freely. Compatibilism grants that some causes of *A*'s doing *X*—or, more circumspectly, *X*'s happening—do rule out *A*'s having done *X* freely. It insists only that $(\exists y)(y$ caused A to do $X)$ does not entail $-(A$ did X freely). Compatibilism, moreover, is chiefly a thesis about *action*; it purports to show, by analysis, that a man's actions can be free and caused; free if caused by a want or decision. Compatibilism in this first approximation does not purport to show that the will or the desires can be both free and caused. This first approximation does not purport to show that *A* freely desires to do *X* if *A*'s desire to do *X* is caused; just that *X* itself can be both free and caused and hence that doing *X* itself is sometimes free.

[6] 'Ifs and Cans', in J. L. Austin, *Philosophical Papers*, ed. J. Urmson and G. Warnock (2nd ed., O.U.P., Oxford: 1970).

The appropriate extension of compatibilism is, however, immediate. Freedom of desire is just the application of the initial scheme to desiring itself: *A* desires (to do) *X* freely if *A* desires to do *X* because *A* wants (or wanted) to desire to do *X*. There are clear examples of desires free in this sense.[7] Suppose *A* wants to acquire a taste for scotch and takes steps to acquire that taste. He eventually acquires the taste by making himself drink it. This case contrasts with one in which *B* now has a taste for scotch because his boss insisted that he learn to enjoy scotch at business lunches, even though *B* had no desire to acquire a taste for it. One would say pre-analytically that *A* had freely acquired the desire to drink scotch, while *B* did not freely acquire the desire (but when desire to drink leads either man to drink, the act of drinking is free). This is precisely how matters turn out under the extended version of compatibilism.

It has seemed to many philosophers that one need go no further to see that compatibilism is false. Their point, urged in one form or another by many writers,[8] concerns the meaning of 'choice'. It is said to be analytic that the outcome of a choice is unpredictable. Part of what is meant by saying that a man is *choosing* is that what the choice will be is objectively indeterminate. Since the outcome of choice would be predictable if it were caused,[9] choices cannot be caused. Whether he realizes it or not, the compatibilist is, according to this argument, denying that anyone has ever chosen anything. Since this is implausible, so is compatibilism and indeed determinism itself.

This argument plays upon an ambiguity in the word 'choice'. On one hand, there is a sense of 'choice' in which it is indeed analytic that a choice is unpredictable. Call this the *metaphysical* sense.[10] The other sense of 'choice' is that in which it is used to refer to a certain familiar experience: the one which typically precedes the first move toward one of a group of alternatives that stand before

[7] These seem to be cases of what J. Lamb calls 'categorical freedom' ('On a Proof of Incompatibilism', *Philosophical Review*, lxxvi. 1 (Jan. 1977), 20–35). He argues (p. 34) that compatibilism is false because men at least regard themselves as categorically free. But we see here that compatibilism has little trouble accommodating 'categorical freedom'. Lamb's use of the Austinian formulation of compatibilism contributes to his failure to see this.

[8] See e.g. R. Taylor, 'Deliberation and Foreknowledge', *American Philosophical Quarterly*, i. 1 (Jan. 1964), 73–80; and C. Ginet, 'Can the Will be Caused?' *Philosophical Review*, lxxi (Oct. 1962), 340–51.

[9] But see sec. 6.

[10] Cf. K. Campbell, *Body and Mind*, p. 90.

the mind. (Which is the ordinary sense of 'choice' is not central to the issue.) In this purely referential sense, 'choice' is quite innocent of theoretical implications; calling an event a choice in *this* sense does not commit one about its causal provenance. The argument under discussion appears to involve a shift from the first to the second sense of 'choice'. If one means 'choice' in the second sense, it would indeed be paradoxical to deny that there have been choices. But the compatibilist is only saying that there have been no choices in the first, metaphysical, sense of 'choice'. That claim is not paradoxical, and only seems so if one tacitly shifts to interpreting it according to the second sense of 'choice'. It surely cannot be a fact of common experience that some metaphysical choices have been made. One multiplies senses of words with reluctance, but the onus of proof here is surely on the incompatibilist. It is he who must show that the use of 'choice' to refer to certain familiar occurrences implies subscription to a theory about the causal history of those occurrences. It is quite unlikely that 'choice' in its referential role also has the metaphysical sense; but only if it does is the determinist committed to a paradox.

The argument just discussed is akin to one urged by writers from Aristotle on. They begin by emphasizing that, by definition, I can only decide on or deliberate about what is not already fixed. This is why I cannot decide about the past. Therefore, it is said, if what I am going to do is causally determined, then even if *I* do not or cannot know what I am going to do, I cannot *decide* to do it. But surely the Aristotelian aphorism means that I cannot decide about a matter which is fixed *no matter what I decide, no matter what steps I take to implement an end in view*. The past remains out of my scope; but whether I will go to the movies tonight remains something I can decide to do. The compatibilist's insistence on the distinction between an event whose causal history intersects my decisions and one whose causal history does not recalls a point made in VI. That X causes Y does not mean that Y already exists in X. If Y did pre-exist in X, Y would be superfluous. Simply in virtue of the fact that X obtained, it would follow that Y did—Y would not even have to occur for X to bring Y about! Consider how this applies to a typical case of A's doing Z. This involves a causal chain $X \rightarrow Y \rightarrow Z$, where Y is A's decision to do Z. If Y is truly necessary for Z, it is a mistake to think of Y as merely a channel through which X brings Z about. For this is as much as to say that Y is really *un*necessary.

The compatibilist's point is this: the fact that my decision is causally necessary for a certain event cannot be gainsaid by supposing that this decision already exists virtually in its causes, and is, consequently, superfluous. The difference between events dependent on and independent of my decisions remains. The compatibilist takes the Aristotelian point in stride, and need not concede that it applies to the future as well as the past. I cannot make a decision about the past precisely because the past is fixed independently of my present decisions. This is certainly false of the future. What the future will be depends on what I decide now.

This first skirmish in defence of compatibilism, and in fact compatibilism itself, have treated choices, or the making of choices, as events. Melden and Ryle hold that they are not events.[11] Melden argues that since choices are individuated by reference to their contents (see V.4), they are necessarily connected to their contents. By Hume's law, the decision to do *D* cannot be an occurrence separate from *D*. This cannot be right. It is true that *one* individuating description of the decision to do *D*, namely 'the decision to do *D*', refers to *D*. But if *this* entailed the non-distinctness of doing *D* and the decision to do *D*, no two things would be distinct. For let *x* and *y* be any two things. There is bound to be some relation *R* such that $x = (\iota z)R(z,y)$. As *x* can therefore be individuated by a *y*-referring description—namely '$(\iota z)R(z,y)$'—Melden's argument entails the absurdity that *x* is not distinct from *y*. Davidson spotted Meldin's mistake.[12] Melden confuses the claim that *some* individuating description of *X* refers to *Y* with the claim that *all* individuating descriptions of *X* refer to *Y*. The former is too weak to sustain claims of necessary connection, while the second may be strong enough. But Melden's observation about the individuation of choices establishes only the weak claim that some individuating description of the decision to do *D* refers to *D*. (Even this is wrong if 'refer' is used extensionally (V.4). All Melden has really shown is that some description of the decision to do *D* must use '*D*', a fact

[11] Melden, *Free Action.* Ryle ('The Will', *Concept of Mind*) appears to argue that 'volitions' cannot be occurrences because they cannot be counted. It *is* hard to count them, but only because the identity conditions for *what one chooses* are often vague. If I decide to be a doctor and decide to apply to medical school, it is not clear whether I have made one decision or two; but this is because it is not clear whether being a doctor entails applying to medical school. Some decisions are certainly datable and identifiable.

[12] 'Actions, Reasons, and Causes.'

compatible with the non-occurrence of *D*.) Since there are other descriptions of this decision that do not refer to *D* (e.g. 'what occurred at 3.00'), there is no reason to think that the decision to do *D*, or the onset of the desire to do *D*, is not an event distinct from *D*. Perhaps Melden and those sympathetic to his argument have been misled by the fact that 'the decision to do *D*' is an essential, or distinctively informative, description of its descriptum. One might conclude from this that every description of its descriptum must refer to *D*.[13]

A related objection (less popular now, perhaps, than a decade ago) to the compatibilist's view of choices and the onset of wants as cause-events is that acts are done for *reasons*, and reasons are not causes. (This objection parallels the one to the causal conception of belief; cf. pp. 168–70.) Another form of this objection runs that actions are explained by the reasons for which they were done, and explanation by reasons is not causal explanation. Now the grounds for saying that explanation-by-reason is noncausal are hard to discern. It is sometimes said that '*P* is a reason for *Q*' is normative, and sometimes that it requires a logical relation between *P* and *Q*. But whatever the merits of these suggestions, they quite miss the compatibilist's position. The compatibilist maintains that the cause of act *X* is not reason *R*, but agent *A*'s having *R* as a reason, or perhaps the onset of his having *R* as a reason. Here the end-in-view jargon is handy. The cause of *A*'s doing *X* is not the end-in-view *X*, but *A*'s having *X* as an end-in-view. The endless debate about reasons and causes is sustained by unwillingness to register this distinction. Consider Spassky moving his bishop to King's Rook 4. One normally says that the reason Spassky made this move was to trap Fischer's Queen. But this is elliptical: trapping Fischer's Queen cannot be why Spassky moved the Bishop unless *Spassky wanted* to trap Fischer's Queen. If Spassky moved the Bishop because he thought it looked nice on KR4, it would simply be wrong to say that trapping the Queen was the reason Spassky made the move. It was the fact that this reason (which is, to be sure, logically related to the subsequent isolation of Fischer's Queen) was *Spassky's* reason, that brought about the actual event of the bishop moving to KR4. The fact that the end-in-view of capture was Spassky's end-in-view is what explains the occurrence. An end not held by anyone is never

[13] 'The referential character of such states seems, indeed, essential to any proper description of them' (R. Taylor, *Metaphysics*, 2nd ed., p. 33).

why anything happens, not even in the 'reason' sense of explanation. Spassky, of course, is not thinking about causes. He is thinking strategically, and he guides his action by the maxim 'trap the Queen'. But *this whole process* of adopting a maxim and guiding his action by it is the cause of Spassky's move.

The distinction between Y being a reason for doing X and Y being A's reason for doing X is often obscured by our charity when interpreting actions. If A does X, and Y is the only available good reason for doing X, we generally suppose that Y was A's reason; an assumption which is usually correct but can go wrong. Thus, we often answer 'why did A do X?' with 'for Y' simpliciter.

These skirmishes behind him, the compatibilist may continue to develop his picture of free action. But as soon as he does, he encounters difficulties. Few desires are themselves free in the sense compatibilism accords to freedom of desire, and many people have trouble reconciling the freedom of doing X with the patent fact that the desire to do X is itself not freely acquired, not something the agent in question had a say in. Indeed, while we can perhaps ascend a few free steps up the hierarchy of desires, there is a point above which no desire is freely acquired. It is important to stress immediately that there is no *formal* inconsistency in 'E_0 is both free and caused & $-(E_1$ is both free and caused) & E_1 caused E_0'. Indeed, if E_0 is free iff E_1 caused E_0, the freedom of E_0 is formally compatible with the unfreedom of E_1. The incompatibilist cannot be complaining that compatibilism is logically absurd. His complaint, rather, is that the compatibilist's notion of freedom is empty,[14] or that it cannot do justice to important intuitions about what a free being ought to be.

The first and commonsense response to the independence of my desires from my will is that we do not regard ourselves as constrained by the fact that we have the desires we do. Thus while compatibilism rates such desires unfree, preanalytic intuition agrees with compatibilism in allowing that actions springing from desires in whose acquisition one had no say may none the less be free. You grow hungry. As a causal consequence you eat a steak. Common sense says that even though you didn't decide to be the sort of being who gets hungry periodically, and even though you didn't decide to get hungry this minute, your hunger is not an imposition, nor does common sense classify your eating as unfree. If you were imprisoned and forced to eat at 6.00 p.m. no matter what the state of your

[14] Thus A. Plantinga, *God, Freedom and Evil* (Harper & Row, 1974), p. 32.

appetite, then you would not be eating freely. If a man in some sense *is* his system of desires, they of course cannot impose on him. Whatever the reason, it simply never occurs to anyone to regard his normal standing desires—for food, rest, companionship—as constraints. That I get hungry periodically is an absolute boundary condition within which I plan my life; it is not an inconvenience like a faculty meeting I must make time for. Being hungry, I enjoy eating. Think of love. It is inimical to the nature of love that it be in the control of one's will. Yet a man who loves his wife hardly thinks of his emotion as an imposition.

Beyond ignoring the agreement of compatibilism with intuition about where to allot freedom, the worry that our actions cannot be free if their causes are not free rests on a mistaken general principle about causality. This principle, the transitivity of causal chains (TC), runs: if $...E_2 \rightarrow E_1 \rightarrow E_0$ is a causal chain, any characteristic of E_n is transmitted to all of E_n's causal descendants. One application of TC is that if E_n is not a free act, then neither is E_i, $i < n$. Another application is that $-(E_n$ is both free and caused), then for all $i < n$, $-(E_i$ is both free and caused). TC is the missing premise in the argument that my doing *X* is not free because my desire to do *X* is not free and my desire to do *X* caused my doing *X*. TC also plays a role in the general version of this objection: even if my desire to do *X* appears to be free, since at some point in the causal history of my doing *X* there is an event I did not freely perform, my doing *X* is not free.

Hume's equally familiar application of TC reduces TC to absurdity. Hume says that science never explains anything, but only 'staves off our ignorance a little longer'. We never really know *why* anything happens because at some point ascent up the causal-explanatory chain comes to an end with events or laws we must take as brute. But Hume is surely wrong. Suppose someone professes not to know why a car starts when the ignition key is turned, on the grounds that tracing the explanation through jumping sparks, fuel mixtures, and chemistry eventually leads to brute facts about the behaviour of elementary particles. Our man is being disingenuous. He knows quite well why turning the key starts the car. The only link in the causal-explanatory chain whose explanation is *not* known is the behaviour of the elementary particles in the fuel cloud. To reason that he does not know why the car started because he doesn't know this is just to assume TC. There is no formal contradiction in claiming that why E_0 happened is known (namely E_1) but that why E_1 happened is not known. It follows that why E_0 happened is not known if TC is assumed. Since TC entails a patent falsehood, TC is false.

The incompatibilist is unlikely to be satisfied with this dismissal of TC. He may agree that as a general thesis TC is false, but he will also insist that there is a difference between the explanation and action cases. Take the event of the car starting (E_0) and the event of a neutron emitting an electron (E_n). There is an obvious dis-analogy between these two links in their common causal chain: there are laws which in conjunction with E_1 entail E_0, while there are no such laws and corresponding E_{n+1} for E_n. This is what 'E_0 is explainable and E_n is not explainable' means. Since E_n is not explainable, it is natural that E_n will not transmit all its intelligibility properties to E_0. But consider my drinking scotch (X_0) and the onset of my desire to drink scotch (X_1). True, the cause of X_0 differs in *kind* from the cause of X_1. The first was the onset of a desire, the second was (say) a rearrangement of brain molecules. But this dissimilarity is less important than their similarity: both X_1 and X_2 were caused. In *this* case, whatever is true of X_1 in point of accessibility to human control *is* transmitted to X_1's causal consequences.

We need a better grip on what is at stake here if we are not to beg three of the incompatibilist's questions: (1) What is the use of so-called free acts whose causes are not themselves free? (2) How important is the difference between being desire-caused and being caused but not desire-caused? (3) In particular, is the difference cited in (2) sufficient to disrupt the transitivity of causal chains? To decide these matters, we must first ask what we *want* from free will. More precisely: what are we trying to say when we attribute free will to man? We need adequacy conditions, neutral with respect to all competing analyses, on proposed explications of free will. Free will is whatever, if anything, satisfies these conditions, and the claim that we *are* free is the claim that something about us does satisfy these conditions. I suggest the following two claims as just such a neutral statement of what we are talking about when we say 'man has free will':

(1) Mans' causal influence on the world differs from that of other things.

(2) We are sometimes in control of what happens to us.

A third condition might be that there are things we do that we are not forced to do, but this can be taken as a consequence of (2).

One could view (1) and (2) as a theory about man, a theory known to be true. It is certain, for example, that someone has at some time been in control over something. To say that men are free is to subscribe to this theory. Free will is whatever it is in virtue of which (1) and (2) are true, whatever accounts for the difference cited in (1) and the control cited in (2).

Compatibilism satisfies these conditions handsomely. For, first, a salient difference between ourselves (and the higher animals) and the rest of nature is that we causally influence the world through desire and choice. We differ even from animals in making choices about our desires. Things happen in the world as a result of human desires. This cannot be said of electrons; since electrons make no decisions, nothing ever happens because an electron wants it so or decides to bring it about. If freedom is what sets off human causal transactions from those of the rest of nature, involvement of choices fits the bill.

To see that compatibilism fits the second condition, consider what it is for an agent *A* to *control* a situation. More to the point, what is failure of control? When is an outcome beyond *A*'s control? It is almost analytic that this holds if the upshot of a situation is *causally independent of A's desires or choices*. A man is in control to just the extent that what he wants makes a difference to how things go. This is why we say the moon's orbit or a skidding car are out of human control; they will go the way they are going to go whether we like it or not. Put counterfactually: what does happen is what would have happened even if any enmeshed agent had had entirely different preferences. By contrast, we say that the President controls the membership of the Cabinet because the membership of the Cabinet depends on what the President wants it to be. These facts about the moon and the President are firmly established. Unless we turn out to have some unguessed power over heavenly bodies, or someone other than the President turns out to run the executive secretly, no scientific discovery could require that we change our estimate of control in these matters. Even a discovery about what caused the President to select the Cabinet he did would not show that the Cabinet's make-up is out of the President's control. Here we must be vigilant against a fallacy first deplored in chapter VI; that of thinking that the cause of an event has all the attributes of the event itself. It is tempting to say that if some event *c* causes the President to select *N* for the Cabinet, it was not the President but *c* that appointed *N*. But this supposition is as misguided as it was when it raised spurious problems for computer creativity. Even if an event in the President's brain causes him to select *N*, it is still the President who selects, not his brain. In terms of control, this is the plain fact that even if the President's selection of the Cabinet is caused, it is still in the President's control. That it has a cause does not mean that a given Cabinet selection will occur *whether or not* the President concurs. The President has to co-operate; i.e. he is in charge.

It is been remarked innumerable times that the opposite of control is not causation but coercion and force. Just as control is a kind of causality, so are coercion and force. If I am near an ice-cream parlour, feel the urge to have an ice-cream cone, and get one, I am not being forced to eat ice-cream. I would be *forced* to eat ice-cream if someone threatened to kill me unless I ate some. Try to think of a want as forcing you to eat ice-cream. You get the urge for a snack. You find yourself walking into an ice-cream parlour against your will. You would rather not (don't forget, you are being forced), but the desire has got the upper hand. You grab the doorframe, but your feet drag you in. You eventually get an ice-cream cone and manage to cram the odious confection down your gullet. This is, in reality, a situation in which you *don't* want ice-cream, in which you loathe ice-cream, but a power greater than your mere wants has got you in its grip. Attempting to construe your wants as forcing you to act leads to absurdity; it represents your wants as leading you to do what you don't want to. Keeping this in mind, recall those desires that one does not freely acquire. They surely do not coerce. I enjoy bicycling; my possession of just this degree of relish in bicycling is something that, so far as I am concerned, just happened. But to think of this relish as coercing me is to think of me as a slugabed who doesn't enjoy exercise and isn't even very interested in bicyling. My desires and decisions can be thought of as forces acting on me only if they are thought of as distinct from the self on which they act, as external forces impinging on the self.[15] But the correct elaboration of the metaphor is that I *am* the totality of my desires. As the idiom has it, it is part of me to bicycle daily. I don't resent having this desire, for there is no 'I' apart from it and its like.

[15] See Nagel, *The Structure of Science*, p. 596; also Mill's *An Examination of Sir William Hamilton's Philosophy*, xxvi. '[F]or purposes of blame, a person is his intentions' (Glover, *Responsibility*, p. 66).

This appeal to the distinction between causing and forcing is meant only to be a faint echo of the positivist defence of free will. On the positivist theory, laws and causes do not in any way necessitate. We think they do because we mistakenly assimilate causal laws to legal statutes, which do keep us in line and can correctly be said to coerce.[16] To describe the causes of a man's behaviour is not to say how he *had* to act; it is only to cite a lawlike proposition about the way in which he and others do in fact act. It is surprising that this effort to reconcile free will and determinism has gained wide adherence, since it confers free will on everything. Suppose *A* can be said to do *X* freely while being caused to do *X* by *Y* because '*Y* caused *A* to do *X*' just means 'people regularly do *X* in circumstance *Y*'. By parity of reasoning we should analyse 'The spark caused the gas to ignite' as 'Gas regularly ignites when exposed to sparks' and say on this basis that the gas was not *forced* to ignite, that it ignited freely. To keep his peace with adequacy condition (1), the positivist must somehow distinguish the laws describing human behaviour from the laws describing the behaviour of inanimate nature. The only plausible distinction is that the relevant laws about men refer to motives, desires, and choices. It is *this*, not the contrast between natural and statutory laws, which even on the positivist theory is the guarantor of free action. The positivist's Humean account of causality plays no role in his reconciliation of determinism and freedom. Without the clause about desires, the positivist account violates adequacy condition (1). The popular idea that incompatibilism is a mistake about lawlikeness is unfounded.

By just the same token, compatibilism does its work even under a non-Humean account of causality. Suppose someone came up with a clear notion of causal necessity stronger than constant conjunction, and that causes really *necessitated* in this strong sense. A distinction would remain between necessitating causal nexuses in virtue of which the two adequacy conditions would be met—the distinction between events necessitated by choices and events otherwise necessitated. Compatibilism is invariant under a shift to a non-Humean account of causality.

I end this section with two further points of agreement between compatibilism and intuition. First, both allow and even require *degrees* of freedom. Both allow changes in how free a man is over

[16] M. Schlick, *Problems of Ethics*, trans. D. Rynin (Dover, N.Y.: 1962), pp. 146–9.

time. He is the more free as there are more matters he can affect by his choices and efforts. If at t A lacks the stamina to run two miles, he is not free at t to run two miles since he won't run two miles even if he tries. If A has somehow acquired the stamina by t', he is free at t' to run two miles. For at t', A will succeed if he tries. Both compatibilism and common sense give this account of the situation.

Second, compatibilism forges an analytic link between metaphysical and political freedom. This confirms compatibilism, since any analysis of freedom which offers a unified or univocal treatment of the two excels in point of parsimony. In particular, what does it mean to say that America is a free country and Russia is not? Surely not that events in Russia have causes while those in America don't. On the contrary, we rely on the causal processes that build roads and elect officials. What we do mean is that in America you can, within limits, do what you want; and that the desires of the governed influence the actions of the government. In Russia, if you try to do what you want you are liable to find yourself in Siberia; and the actions of the government are determined solely by the Politburo. This is not political theory; the correctness of a compatibilist account of *political* freedom is self-evident. Everyone agrees that the *political* distinction between freedom and unfreedom is a distinction between two kinds of causes. This supports the presumption that the free/unfree distinction in other areas is also a distinction between two kinds of causes. Certainly anyone denying this must take the fact that we call both individuals and societies 'free' as mere homonymy.

2. A Problem about Changes in States of Knowledge

The acquisition of knowledge presents a problem for compatibilism. Consider a dime in my pocket that I do not know about. Suppose it is true that *if* I decide to spend that dime, I will spend it. By compatibilism's lights I am free to spend the dime, but intuition seems not to agree. Now suppose I come to know about the dime at t, perhaps through my own exploratory efforts. In some intuitive sense I have *first* become free at t to spend the dime; I bring the disposition of the dime within my power at t.[17] But the compatibilist cannot say

[17] S. Hampshire discusses this phenomenon, especially its bearing on self-knowledge; see his *Thought and Action*; his *Freedom of the Individual*, 2nd ed. (Princeton, U.P., N.J.: 1975); and his *Freedom of Mind* (Princeton U.P., N.J.: 1971), pp. 3–20, 183–256.

this. He grants that at *t* it becomes possible for me to decide what to do with the dime (*qua* determinist he thinks that exactly one decision is causally possible at *t*), but he cannot say that I become free at *t* to spend the dime. Similarly: if at *t* I first become aware of a neurotic symptom, I have not, according to the compatibilist, *become* free to alter my behaviour if before *t* I would have altered my behaviour had I wanted to. If the compatibilist allows that my discovery at *t* freed me to spend the dime, he admits that for some *X* and *t* I am *not* free to do *X* at *t* even if I would have done *X* had I decided to: I am not free to do *X* at *t* because it is causally impossible for me to decide to do *X* at *t*.

We can begin to address this objection by distinguishing between those acts *X* that *A* is free to do, and those world-states it is causally possible for *A* to make a decision about. Every act *X* that an agent can perform takes place in some world-state *S*; viewed broadly, *X* is *A*'s answer to the practical question 'What shall I do about *S*?' Let $w(X)$ be the world-state associated with act *X*. If *X* is spending the dime on a candy bar, $w(X)$ is the presence of the dime in *A*'s pocket. It can of course happen that $X \neq Y$ but $w(X) = w(Y)$. The set of acts associated with world-state *S* is $w^{-1}(S)$; when $w^{-1}(S)$ is a unit set or only one member of it is under discussion, we may refer to that single act as $w^{-1}(S)$. Now, let *A*'s *horizon* be the set of $w(X)$ such that it is causally possible for *A* to make some decision about $w(X)$. Intuitively, *A*'s horizon is the set of world-states corresponding to acts that *A* can decide to do. What the example of the dime shows is that the acts *A* is free to do may outrun *A*'s horizon; *A* may be free to do *X* even if $w(X) \notin$ *A*'s horizon. The point of this interpretation of the dime case is sharpened if we suppose that I don't know about the dime because I have temporarily *forgotten* it. It seems intuitively clear in that case that I *am* free to spend it precisely *because* I would succeed in spending it if I tried; the limitation my forgetfulness has imposed on me is the removal, from my horizon, of my ownership of that dime. Thus, it may be true in $S = w(X_i)$, $i \leqslant n$, that

If *A* decides to do X_1, then *A* will do X_1

....

If *A* decides to do X_n, then *A* will do X_n

and *S* be out of *A*'s horizon because all *n* antecedents are impossible.

There is, finally, a notion distinct from both *A*'s horizon and the set of acts A is free to do. This is A's *power to act*: $\{X: A$ is free to do X and $w(X) \in A$'s horizon$\}$.

We can now address the problem of the acquisition of knowledge. The acquisition of knowledge does *not* make A free to do anything A was not previously free to do; it *is* distinctive because it expand's A's horizon. Acquisition of knowledge of $w(X)$ makes it causally possible for A to make a decision about $w(X)$. (If it is causally *necessary* that A decides to do X once A knows about $w(X)$, it is causally *possible* for A then to make a decision about $w(X)$.) Acquisition of knowledge expands A's power to act by expanding A's horizon. This makes it seem that knowledge expands freedom.

To bring this schema down to earth, suppose I am tied to a chair. Consider the difference between acquiring knowledge and being untied. Suppose, first, I come to know about S, that ice-cream is on sale at Baskins and Robbins. Even though I am tied, S may enter my horizon: it is causally possible for me to decide to buy vanilla at Baskins and Robbins if I ever get untied. Getting vanilla at Baskins and Robbins is $w^{-1}(S)$. Let us suppose I make this decision: S is in my horizon, but I am still not free to do $w^{-1}(S)$ because my preference is causally inefficacious. Untying me makes it true that if I want vanilla I will get vanilla: untying me increases the number of acts I am free to perform. Acquiring knowledge and being untied both enlarged my power to act; the crucial point is that they did this in different ways. Being untied contributed a new act that I was free to do, an act whose associated world state was already in my horizon. Acquiring knowledge expanded my horizon; in general, acquiring knowledge may expand my horizon to include world-states associated with acts I may already have been free to perform. In this quite different way it contributes to my power to act. The argument under discussion confuses the fact that acquiring knowledge enlarges one's power to act with the false claim that knowledge enlarges the set of acts one is free to perform.

It is an important fact that at any time a man is free to expand his horizon. Within limits he can add to his knowledge by investigating. It is even fair to say that if a man has an inkling that an S-like situation obtains, he is free to bring S into his horizon. Moreover, since a man is responsible for whatever he is free to do, he is to that extent responsible for the extent of his horizon. There can be wilful ignorance. A yet deeper fact is that, within limits, each man is in his own horizon, and each man can bring himself ever further within his horizon. Thus, a man is, within limits, responsible for actions that proceed from causes he is unaware of. This is the bite of the existentialist indictment of bad faith against those who accept themselves as they are and take refuge in a bad upbringing, a theme I return to in section 7.

3. Counterexamples and Refinements

It is time to sharpen compatibilism through attention to more focussed objections and counterexamples.

The kleptomaniac is the most obvious counterexample. He certainly *wants* to steal the pocketbook, and he may bring it off, yet neither he nor his acts are normally regarded as free. Compatibilism is obligated to distinguish the kleptomaniac from others who act on their wants. It is clear enough that the kleptomaniac is a compulsive. He *must* have that pocketbook. Many compulsions—voyeurism, fetishism—culminate in masturbation, and the insouciant compatibilist might simply observe that standard actions proceeding from wants do not culminate in masturbation. A deeper difference is that kleptomania is compulsive because it arises from an urge that temporarily overtakes the kleptomaniac and plays no role in the rest of his life. A man who regularly steals, who organizes his life around pelf, is simply a thief and most assuredly acts freely when he steals. So compatibilism adds that an act is free when the desire that causes it is long-standing and stable.

To see how natural this amendment is, consider the typically long-standing and stable desire to be a doctor. A young man conceives this goal early in life. He studies for years, attends medical school, and acquires his M.D. His entry into the profession is not compulsive, and is clearly free. Hanging his shingle is not an urge that overtakes him, precisely because his desire to practice medicine is long-standing and stable. In keeping with an earlier suggestion, one might regard the man as *being*, in part, his desire. Certainly he has identified himself with a system of values of which his decision is an integral part. The decision can no more overwhelm him than a gust of wind can overwhelm the storm it is part of.

There is a further point about compulsion. Compulsive behaviour is associated with symptoms that have doubtless played a role in the development of the idea of free action. Muscular tension and inability to maintin eye contact are signs of compulsiveness; i.e.

unfree behaviour resulting from a desire. In practice, these signs have almost the force of criteria. It is hard to say how we would or should respond to a criterion conflict. Imagine a spasmodic desire that leads to pointless, degrading, heavily penalized behaviour, but behaviour unaccompanied by the usual symptoms of compulsion. Is a man who coolly leaves a getaway car while he steals fifty pocketbooks acting freely? The law says he is; he will have difficulty sustaining a plea of diminished capacity.

Hypnosis provides more realistic examples of criteria conflict, and sharpens this type of counterexample to compatibilism. Suppose a man under hypnosis is given the suggestion that he open windows, and is also instructed to forget that he has been hypnotized. When he awakens he will exhibit none of the kleptomaniac's tell-tale signs. Finally, to satisfy the stability criterion, assume the post-hypnotic suggestion is in force for a long stretch of time. Let us call an act resulting from this kind of post-hypnotic suggestion a *hypnotic act*. The incompatibilist does not see any difference between hypnotic suggestion and any other cause of behaviour. If the understandable reluctance of compatibilism and common sense to call hypnotic acts free is without principle, the free/unfree distinction disintegrates. There is, however, an intuitive basis for denying that the hypnotic act is free: the reason the hypnotic subject offers for his act is not really the reason that he is performing the act. He thinks, and would claim, that he is opening windows because the room is stuffy. He is wrong. Spelling this out involves a foray into the topic of reasons for acting, and the reason-sensitivity of desires.

I agreed in V.4 that in one sense saying 'I am acting the way I am because I want to dissipate stuffiness' is infallible; but this was because identifying the object of your want is not a distinguishable epistemic task from identifying the want you have. This in turn was compatible with the self-ascription of a want itself being something that one could be mistaken about. The same applies, *mutatis mutandis*, to the self-ascription of reasons. In fact, when a man says that his reason for opening the window is that he wants to dissipate stuffiness, he is committing himself to two falsifiable claims: (1) Other things being equal, he would not want the window open were the room not stuffy; and (2) If presented with a reason weightier than dissipating stuffiness for leaving the window closed, he would cease wanting to open the window badly enough to act on that consideration. Normally, when a man offers a want, desire, or end-in-view as his reason for acting, these two counterfactuals are true. In fact, his knowledge of his reason for acting, and of (1) and (2), is normally direct and incorrigible. What is distinctive about the reasons which the subject offers to back up his hypnotic act is that these two counterfactuals are false. The very point of hypnotic suggestion is to induce rigidity in behaviour accompanied by a spurious show of reason. If a cool breeze were piped through the room, the subject would still want the window open and offer a new reason why: perhaps incipient claustrophobia. (Here his behaviour is slipping toward the compulsive.) 'I want so-and-so because such-and-such' is a falsifiable statement involving predictions. The mark of hypnotic acts is that such statements made to justify or explain them are normally false.

It is not just the incorrectness of their self-ascriptions of reasons that sets hypnotic agents apart from normal ones. Since the subject has a false belief about his reason for acting, his actions are insensitive to assessments of the soundness of the reason he proffers. Even his coming to think that the reason he offers for his action is not a good reason cannot affect his action, for the reason he thinks is his is not his real reason at all. His real reason is out of his horizon. When, on the other hand, a man has a correct belief about his reasons for acting, it is analytic that his actions be to some extent sensitive to revisions in his estimate of how good those reasons are. Let us say that such normal desires are *reason-sensitive.* Since the hypnotic subject's true reason for acting is beyond his horizon it is impossible for him to scrutinize his reason for acting, or for any such scrutiny to alter his behaviour. Hypnotically induced desires are reason-insensitive. It seems to be this latter feature of hypnotically induced desires, not their epistemic inaccessibility *per se*, that accounts for the intuitive unfreedom of hypnotic acts. Therefore, compatibilism becomes: *A* does *X* freely if the cause of *A*'s doing *X* is a stable and reason-sensitive desire.

There is an ambiguity in calling a man's desire reason-sensitive if he can be dissuaded from acting on it by sound reasons for not acting on it. Must he himself acknowledge that the countervailing reasons are sound? Suppose the hypnosis is so successful that the subject genuinely believes that preventing some original Raphaels from getting rained on is not a good reason for leaving the window closed, although he allows that he would leave it closed if that were a good reason. Some philosophers hold that certain considerations are intrinsically good reasons for acting,[18] and anyone who does not take them into account at least *prima facie* is necessarily insensitive to reason. Compatibilism ought not be hostage to this adventurous view; it needs only the weaker specification that a desire *D* is reason-sensitive for *A* if *A* can be dissuaded from acting on *D* by considerations *A* acknowledges to be good reasons for not acting on *D*.[19] Even this weak reason-sensitivity requirement segregates hypnotic acts from intuitively and compatibilistically free acts. It is an empirical fact that hypnosis cannot induce global reclassification of reasons. The subject, in the case in question, will still acknowledge that the drawings must be saved—but will try to open the windows anyway. A man *freely* opening the window, a man who says truly that he is opening the window because it is stuffy, will desist if he sees something he values getting rained on.

H. Frankfurt[20] has stressed one particular aspect of reason-sensitivity. Frankfurt argues convincingly that to be free our acts must spring from desires we approve of having and acting from. For an act of mine to be free I must have the second-order capacity to change desires, and the act must be caused by a first-order desire that I have decided to allow to be mine, and to be effective. (Sen (op. cit.) suggests that weakness of will may be impotence to implement second-order preferences.) Compatibilism, then, needs this further clause: *A* acts freely if he acts from an *approved* desire. It seems to me best to include this condition under reason sensitivity. So doing is not meant to suggest that the desirability of desires can literally be established by reason. Compatibilism should not be hostage to cognitivism. But we reason about which desire 'to make our will' (in Frankfurt's phrase) in ways not in principle different from those which incline us away from opening a window to the weather. If necessary, we may suppose compatibilism supplemented by the separate clause that *A*'s doing *X* is free if *A* does *X* out of a desire *A* approves of acting on. (A man *might* approve of having a desire and not approve of (his) acting on it. He may think well of

[18] e.g. B. Gert, *The Moral Rules* (Harper & Row, N.Y.: 1966). The *locus classicus* of the opposite view is pt. III of Hume's *Treatise*.

[19] Glover (*Responsibility*, pp. 98–100) lets persuadability by either kind suffice.

[20] 'Freedom of the Will and the Concept of a Person', *Journal of Philosophy*, lxviii. 1 (Jan. 1971), 5–20; also see R. Jeffrey, 'Preference Among Preferences', ibid., lxxi. 13 (July 1974), 377–91, and A. Sen, 'Choice, Orderings and Morality', in S. Körner ed. *Practical Reason* (Yale U.P., New Haven, Conn.: 1974), pp. 54–67.

himself for wanting to help the starving in India, but he does not want to act on this desire lest he impoverish himself.)

Frankfurt points out that this broadened conception of reason-sensitivity distinguishes the actions of persons, rational agents, from those of animals. Animals act on their wants, but they are indifferent to the desirability of those wants themselves. Frankfurt calls such beings 'wantons', and suggests that we say *A* has a *free will*, in addition to the capacity to act freely, if *A*'s second-order desires are causally efficacious. This suggestion not only provides man with a unique faculty of choice, it does so within the compatibilist framework. Classical compatibilists have tended to reject free will as a pseudo-concept,[21] and this has weakened their case. We do seem to have a capacity that underlies our capacity to act freely, a faculty obscurely designated 'free will'. None the less, I will side with Hobbes and eschew any but informal talk of free will, principally because Frankfurt's insight can be expressed in the present framework. I noted in section 1 that compatibilism about action naturally extends to desire: one's desire to do *X* is itself free if one desires to do *X* because one desires to desire to do *X*. A special case of desiring to desire to do *X* is to value being a person who desires to do *X* and acts on that desire. Freedom of desire is the privilege of man only, as is the performance of free acts from free desires, a fit proxy for free will.

The requirement of reason-sensitivity also sheds light on compulsion. Another mark of the compulsive is that he wishes, impotently, to be free of the desires that overtake him. His acts continue to be caused by desires which, either because they are dangerous or shameful, are unacceptable to his reason. It is hard to say whether the instability or the reason-insensitivity of his desires contributes more critically to his unfreedom. Suppose the compulsive approved of his being an occasional kleptomaniac, taking 'variety is the spice of life' as his motto. We might then call his kleptomania free. But if he approved of his kleptomania only when the kleptomaniacal impulses were upon him, we might regard this seeming acceptability to his reason as simply part of the aberration, and rule his action unfree on grounds of instability.

The extended requirement of reason-sensitivity may seem too

[21] Thus Hobbes in *Leviathan*: '[If] a man should talk to me of a *round Quadrangle*; or *Immateriall Substances*; or of *A free Subject*; *A free will*; or any *Free*, but free from being hindred by opposition, I should not say he were in an Errour; but that his words were without meaning; that is to say, Absurd.'

strong, for surely such ordinary free acts as taking a walk do not proceed from desires we have because we approve of having them. But there does indeed seem to be a sense in which they do. What does it mean to say that I *approve* of world-state *S*? Not necessarily that I actively sponsor *S*; it often just means that I *permit S to persist* when it is in my power to take steps to eliminate *S* (*S* persists because I don't take steps to eliminate it). If my wife is cooking roast beef for dinner, I know that she will change the menu if I ask her to, and I say nothing, then I must find roast beef for dinner *at least acceptable*. Even if I have given the roast beef no particular thought, if I later complain about it I leave myself open to the question, 'If you didn't want roast beef, why didn't you say so?' That I said and did nothing warrants the conclusion that I *accepted* what was happening. It is in this weak but non-trivial sense that I find my desire to take a walk acceptable: if I didn't I would take steps to extinguish it or keep it inefficacious. So let 'approve' mean 'tacitly find at least acceptable' and '*A* desires to do *X* because *A* approves of his desire to do *X*' mean 'however *A* came to desire to do *X*, the desire persists because *A* takes no steps to extinguish it'. Under these readings it is plausible to maintain that actions performed by agents capable of awareness of their desires are free only if they are caused by reason-sensitive desires, desires they approve of having.

The normative component of reason-sensitivity gives some substance to the metaphorical identification of a man with his values. A man embodies his conception of what he *ought* to be to the extent than his desires are his because they have passed the test of his reason. He is, to that extent, a self-created self. He is as much his own creation as a watch is a watchmaker's creation. Indeed, in his capacity to create himself, man exercises a prerogative usually reserved for the Deity.

The discussion of hypnotic acts skirted the possibility of global control by capitalizing on the empirical fact that a hypnotist can make his subject open a window no matter what, but not alter all his desires and values to conform to this local urge. What if global control were imposed? R. Taylor takes the conceptual possibility of such an arrangement to refute compatibilism.

> [W]e can suppose that an ingenious physiologist [*P*] can induce [in *A*] any volition he pleases, simply by pushing various buttons on an instrument to which, let us suppose, *A* is attached by numerous wires. All the volitions

> *A* has . . . are . . . precisely the ones *P* gives *A*. . . . We can suppose that *P* puts a rifle in *A*'s hand, aims it at some passer-by, and then, by squeezing the proper button, evokes in *A* the volition to squeeze his finger against the trigger, whereupon the passer-by falls dead. This . . . is the perfect description of a puppet. . . . The example is somewhat unusual, but it is no worse for that. It is perfectly intelligible.[22]

Being a meaning thesis, compatibilism is obligated to account for Taylor's case: it cannot permit even a logically possible case in which freedom and causation by 'volition' diverge. Appeal to criterion conflict is similarly unavailing. 'Free' may have been coined without benefit of Taylor cases, but compatibilism itself leaves no room for indeterminacy. But compatibilism gets a concession in turn: if, under pressure to maintain its intelligibility, the Taylor case becomes merely a case in which *A*'s actions are caused, it begs the question. It purports to be a special case, which all agree involves unfreedom, of the general causal condition compatibilism identifies with freedom. If the Taylor case loses all its specific features (the wires, the murder), it is no longer an unsettling *specification* of the general case. This means, in particular, that there are two kinds of 'manipulation' *P* cannot impose. *P* cannot put *A* on internal power; he cannot let *A* do as *A* pleases, even if that is caused. Taylor is trying to show that *A*'s doing as he pleases, if caused, is not in principle different from *A*'s being manipulated; it begs the question to classify *A*'s doing what he pleases as a kind of manipulation. Nor can *P* make *A* do exactly what *A* would have done anyway. Aside from the possible causal superfluity of *P*'s input, *A* would once again be calling the shots, and doing what he pleases.

The problem for Taylor is that, given these restrictions, *P* cannot allow the decisions he planted in *A* to be sensitive to *A*'s reason. If *P* causes *A* to approve of his desire to do *X* along with causing *A* to desire to do *X*, he must *also* let *A*'s approval be the cause of *A*'s having the desire and of its being strong enough to lead to action. *A* seems to have gone on internal power. But let us suppose *P* somehow gets around this. His main problem is the fact that part of subjecting one's desires to the scrutiny of reason is finding out where they came from. There need be nothing irrational in this, no fallacy of confusing the origin of a desire with its value. Consider *B*, who realizes that he has unwittingly modelled himself completely after his father. He regards his father as a man of outstanding virtue,

[22] *Metaphysics*, 2nd ed., p. 50.

but feels that it is not good for a man to follow his father too closely anyway. *B* finds each particular desire he has adopted acceptable, but he feels that on the whole he has mimicked his father. This qualm is not irrational. More important, people *do* reason this way. They do take the origin of a desire to be pertinent for answering the practical question of whether to acquiesce in the desire, to take steps to diminish its force, or to take steps to extinguish it. It is certainly part of the general concept of evidence that any fact *can* come to be relevant to any conclusion. Thus, if the origin of a desire is shut off from a man, the desire is to that extent insensitive to his reason.

The question, then, is what *P* is to do if *A notices the wires*. *A* will presumably want to be rid of wire-induced desires; and if *A* is rendered unable to find out about the wires, reason-insensitivity has been imposed and Taylor has no more counterexample. Nor can Taylor stipulate that the wires be undetectable, for that differs only in words from saying that there are no wires. Perhaps *P* prevents *A* from registering selected sensory input. But how is *A* supposed to act, then? 'I see the bushes, I see the man behind the bushes working the control panel. But wires? What wires?' There is no way to cordon off the dangerous perceptions, and *P* must eventually make *A* oblivious to his surroundings. If the evidence trying to come to *A*'s attention is inferential, mission control must prevent *A* from following the inference. But again, the systematicity of evidence will eventually require *P* to stupefy *A* across a potentially unlimited spectrum of cognitive activities.

So *P* must let *A* be able to notice the wires, and Taylor's story must include a coherent account of what happens if *A* does notice them. (The possible world in which *A* notices the wires is accessible from Taylor's possible world, since in Taylor's possible world *A can* notice the wires.) If *P* controls *A*'s desires after *A* has noticed the wires, *A*'s tacit acceptance of the desire to do X would not be a necessary condition for his acting on that desire (in the unlikely event *A* finds the desire to do X acceptable even though imposed by a mad scientist). So *P* has no choice but to put *A* on internal power, and the counterexample ends. Let us say that *A comes to* at *t*, if, at *t*, *A* notices the wires and *P* puts him back on internal power. Taylor might argue that before he came to at *t*, *A* was unfree but still free by compatibilist's lights. Even though he must allow that *A* might find out about the wires, or that *A* eventually does find out about the wires, Taylor can still let *P* put *A* through his paces for a while; and during this time, is *A* not a counterexample to compatibilism? No. A crucial difference between *A* and a normal agent *B* is that we cannot describe a situation in which *B* comes to. *A* is intuitively a puppet because we can *contrast* what he does with the very different things he would do and be if he found out where his desires came from. But *B*'s finding out the origins of his desires (most of which he already suspects) will have no such global impact on him. (To say it *should* begs the question against compatibilism.) What is *B* to snap *into* when he finds out how he came to be what he is? What is *B* to snap into if he finds that he wants to walk because walking has pleased him before?

It is not arbitrary for us to find some causes of desire more disturbing than others. It does not disturb me that my wife wants to cook a roast for dinner because I asked her to. It would disturb me if she wanted to cook a roast because of a Taylor arrangement, for then she would be in the control of a sinister force. Taylor cannot complain that such distinctions are arbitrary, for it was the very distinctiveness of some causes of desire that got his argument off the ground.

4. Strong and Weak Freedom

Another problem for compatibilism concerns *A*'s debate with himself about whether to play tennis while standing outside the gate of a tennis court which is, unbeknownst to him, locked. *A* decides not to play and leaves without trying the gate. Compatibilism says he did not freely forbear from playing, since whether he played or not was (contrary to his belief) independent of his decision. Even had he decided to play, he would not have succeeded in playing. But, it is said, common sense finds *A*'s forbearance free. Locke discusses the striking case of a sleeping man transported to a locked dungeon. Upon awakening, and ignorant of his new locale, he debates whether to take a stroll, decides not to, and goes back to sleep. Intuitively, he seems to be staying in the dungeon freely, while compatibilism says that he does not stay freely since it is fixed independently of his will that he stay. Compatibilism fails the test of intuition.

I think the compatibilist account of these Lockean cases is correct, and it can reconcile its apparent collision with intuition as follows. Actions genuinely dependent on wants, the compatibilist's free actions, are normally accompanied by two concomitants: the agent (correctly) *believes* that the outcome of the situation depends on his choices; and the agent experiences a distinctive feeling of spontaneity. When I act freely, it is a counterfactual truth that had I decided differently, I would have done differently. Not only is this so, I believe it to be so. Conversely, my knowledge of causal relations is so reliable—based as it is on experience in various familiar circumstances—that when I believe such counterfactuals, they are usually true.[23] Lockean miscalculations are rare because I have discovered by observation what doors can be opened and what cannot. The second normal concomitant of events caused by choices are special feelings, not unnaturally called feelings of freedom or spontaneity. And, as with belief in certain counterfactuals, when an agent experiences the sense of spontaneity, the act he is performing usually does depend counterfactually on his decisions. Now, what marks the Lockean cases is the presence of these two subjective factors in the absence of the objective condition they usually indicate: the counteractual *A* believes is actually false. *A* believes, at least tacitly, that if he *had* decided to play he would have played. Singularly enough, this is not so. The problem of what to say about these Lockean cases is exacerbated by the presence of inappropriate feelings of spontaneity that accompany *A*'s departure from the court. (*A*'s feeling can be inappropriate because part of its cause is his belief that his will is making a difference. If the belief is false, the feeling is inappropriate.) Our intuition that *A* forbore freely is, I think, completely explained by the presence of these two regular subjective concomitants of free action. We confuse them with the truth of the counterfactual conditional they usually indicate.

But wait: Lockean cases now threaten compatibilism from the opposite flank. Whatever may hold counterfactually of *A* at the tennis gate, the cause of *A*'s actual behaviour, his forbearance, was *A*'s decision to leave. Therefore, the compatibilist is committed after all to saying that *A*'s action is free. Compatibilism can't seem to give a consistent account of *A*'s forbearance: since it was caused by a desire, it was free; since it would have happened even had *A* decided otherwise, it was unfree.

That compatibilism lends itself to both readings only shows that compatibilism has a strong and a weak version. The weak version is that an act is free if a decision was a sufficient condition for it.

[23] There are well-known difficulties in explaining truth for counterfactuals. But abandoning counterfactuals means abandoning the present objection, for it depends on what would have happened had *A* tried to get on to the tennis court.

The strong version is that an act is free if a decision was a necessary and sufficient condition for it. The weak version entails that *A* forbore freely, the strong version that he did not. Let us call an act *strongly free* when a necessary and sufficient condition for its occurrence is a desire, and *weakly free* if a sufficient but not necessary condition for its occurrence is a desire. Which version of compatibilism should we adopt?—i.e. which version of freedom is closest to our intuitive notion of freedom simpliciter?

One argument that favours the strong version is that even had *A* decided to play, the same thing that actually happened would have happened anyway, namely, *A* would have ended up leaving. Therefore, his desire made no difference. If, intuitively, free actions are those in which desire makes a difference, weakly free acts that are not strongly free are not free at all. One might object that the *same* thing would not have happened had *A* decided to stay. Had he done so, he would have tried to open the gate, found it closed, and stormed away muttering. Even though in one sense his not playing was a foregone conclusion, in another sense his deciding not to play made a difference. But this reply obviously depends on a very generous understanding of making a difference. It would allow that my desire for a Nobel Prize makes a difference to their distribution because I will sulk when I don't get one, and this is absurd. This suggests we opt for the following statement of compatibilism: *A* did *X* freely only if there is some desire D that caused *X* and is such that, if no sufficiently *D*-like desire had been present. no sufficiently *X*-like event would have occurred. But this is just to say that *X* is strongly free where '*X*-like' is allowed to count as a kind of event. We have been led back to the strong version of compatibilism.

Another reason for choosing strong freedom as our explicandum is this. It is intuitively absurd that *A* be free to do *X* but not free to do $-X$. If I am free to do *X*, I am free to do *X or not do X*. If I am not free not to do *X*, I am bound to do *X*, and hence cannot be free to do *X*. But it is clear that I can be weakly free to do *X*, but not weakly free to refrain from doing *X*. This was just *A*'s situation at the tennis court; a desire was sufficient for his refraining, but no desire would have been sufficient for his playing, i.e. his not refraining. So freedom cannot be weak freedom.

Lockean cases are confusing because they are weakly free but not free. They pull intuition two ways. A further contributor to this confusion is the fact that weakly free acts are accompanied by the sense of spontaneity that also accompanies strongly free acts. This happens because the sense of spontaneity is caused not only by the *belief* that one's decisions are causally efficacious, but by the *exercise* of one's decisions themselves. This feeling is the affective accompaniment of the translation of decision into action; it is how it *feels* to act on a decision. And weakly free acts *are* caused by decisions. Since *A*'s decision not to play was a sufficient cause of *A*'s behaviour, *A*'s decision produced a misleading sense of spontaneity.

5. *Why Freedom is Valued*

The foregoing remarks help explain why action, and the capacity to act, from stable, reason-sensitive wants, are valued. Since it is axiomatic that freedom is a good, compatibilism must explain why what *it* takes freedom to be is good. In fact, it is sometimes said that compatibilism cannot explain why the distinction between decisions and other causes of action is as important as the distinction between free and unfree acts. Perhaps compatibilism highlights *a* sense of 'freedom', but not a sense strong enough to support the idea of man's transcendental nobility or confer moral responsibility on him.

One compatibilist response is to recycle the adequacy conditions for freedom in section 1 as adequacy conditions for nobility and the ascription of responsibility. A quite different partial answer focuses on the feelings of spontaneity and control that accompany the acts that are free by the compatibilist's lights. It *feels good* and peculiarly *satisfying* to realize your stable, reason-sensitive desires. Whatever its causal explanation, there is no more basic fact about human nature. The complaint that the value of what the compatibilist calls freedom is elusive, or obviously too weak to support the burden freedom supports in ordinary thinking, is altogether absurd. It is true, as Frankfurt notes, that animals are capable of enjoying unconstrained action. But as we alone are capable of knowing our own states and using this knowledge to influence and create our choices, only man is capable of appreciating *that* he is realizing his choices, and the choices he has chosen. Reason-sensitivity assures man knowledge and appreciation of the fact that he is acting from desires which have passed the scrutiny of his reason. The enjoyment of such action is peculiar to man. Reason-sensitivity knows no bounds; any criterion for sustaining and extinguishing desires can become efficacious. A man may elect to act only on those maxims that satisfy some formal criterion; he may act from the concept of lawlikeness. Surely the capacity to act from the concept of lawfulness is sufficient ground for any transcendence man may aspire to.

It might be thought that we take pleasure in free actions because we believe them free in some incompatibilistic sense. If so, compatibilism would be pragmatically inconsistent with the value of freedom: we would stop valuing the acts compatibilism identifies as free if we became compatibilists. In this, compatibilism would be like psychological egoism, according to which we act on desires we call 'selfless' because we believe we are not psychological egoists. If we thought those 'selfless' desires were really selfish, they would lose their appeal and we would stop acting on them. This worry about compatibilism is not supported by the facts of experience. There is no evidence that people who lack the idea of freedom as such enjoy unconstrained action less than the metaphysically more sophisticated. Unless one has been convinced by argument that causality is incompatible with freedom, one's belief that one's intuitive free actions are caused will not by itself interfere with enjoyment of the actions. I know of no philosopher who reports that his pleasure in spontaneous acts decreased when he became a compatibilist.

The relish men take in freedom is often ignored when philosophers concentrate on the medicinal varieties of will: resolve, effort, setting oneself to do something unpleasant. Resisting temptation and aiding a stranger in distress are typical examples of will studied in moral philosophy. While such exertions are important for ethics, they are no fun. But there is another 'realm of will'[24] exemplified by hiking for no special purpose and fidelity from love. This is the exhilarating kind of will.

The analogy with political freedom sustains the view that freedom is prized for just this reason. Some have suggested that political and civil freedom are good because they lead to the self-development of citizens, or because they are necessary for self-respect. These suggestions are right, but they hardly differ in cash value from the present one. The chief virtue of democracy lies in the exhilaration, the intrinsic satisfaction, of knowing that you, not a commissar, determine your personal life, and that you can influence the character of your society. It is a misguided utilitarianism that concentrates on the instrumental value of democracy. As Lipset has put it, democracy

[24] L. Farber, 'Two Realms of Will', *The Ways of the Will* (Basic Books, N.Y.: 1966).

is not the best means to the good life, it is the good life itself.[25]

It is appropriate here to say a word about the relation of compatibilism to desert. It has been argued since antiquity that determinism entails that no one deserves reward, since it was outside the control of the rewardee that he have the capacities he needed for his outstanding performance. Under the rubric 'the arbitrariness of the natural lottery', this argument plays a crucial role in Rawls's derivation of his 'difference principle'.[26] Its popularity notwithstanding, the argument is hopelessly bad. Rewards are not normally given for the possession of an ability, but for performance. A student gets an A not for being intelligent, but for correctly answering the questions on a test. A weightlifter is given a trophy for *using* his strength to lift a given weight on a set occasion, not for his strength itself. Rewards are *not* given for what the rewardee had nothing to do with, for what, like his talents and dispositions, are not in his control. (Beauty contests are an exception; that is why they are regarded as frivolous.) We are rewarded for deeds, which, unlike capacities, are in our control. Our interest in performance over ability is demonstrated by our disdain for appeal to even freakish accidents to excuse failure in athletic contests. If a clearly stronger weightlifter loses an event to a weaker because his shorts fall down at the crucial moment, the weaker man still gets the trophy. Compatibilism and common sense are at one. Compatibilism calls free just what common sense regards as fit for reward, namely performance. What common sense regards as unfit for reward, namely ability, is not what compatibilism calls free. Compatibilism endorses rewarding a man only for what he has control over.

Some will continue to be nagged by the idea that if determinism is true, a man who does the best does not deserve reward because he couldn't help doing the best: he couldn't help making the right choice or exerting the necessary effort. But what can this mean? Surely not that he would have done the best *whether or not he had tried*. Does it mean that he would have tried whether or not he tried? Does it mean that he was coerced to perform well even if he didn't want to, that he was compelled to make the right choice? Surely there is no such experience as finding an alternative undesirable and finding that one is choosing it anyway. One must remember that

[25] S. M. Lipset, *Political Man* (Anchor, N.Y.: 1959).

[26] J. Rawls, *A Theory of Justice* (Harvard, Cambridge, Mass.: 1971): see index entry 'Distribution of natural assets'.

choosing is choosing, that it involves time and reflection. One must remember that effort is *effort*, that I *exert* the effort I exert. The idea that one can't help make choices or exert effort is not an unpalatable consequence of compatibilism: it is simply an idea without sense.[27] Those bent on using determinism to smudge the evident differences between men will continue to be mesmerized by the phrase 'the exertion of effort was caused'. One may speculate on the sources of their susceptibility to this phrase, perhaps in a fear of competition. But like other hypnotic subjects, they are insensitive to reason.

6. *Paradoxes of Prediction*

The final tangle of problems for a deterministic picture of rational agency begins with two initially plausible principles: (a) if an event is governed by causal laws it is in principle predictable; and (b) if an event is in principle predictable, it is in principle possible for a rational being, hence a rational agent, to come to know or believe the prediction, *and* to come to know or believe that the prediction has been made. But then, the argument continues, it is always possible for a man to *falsify* predictions, or the laws supporting them, made about himself: for he can always find out about them and refute them. A can always find out at t what causal law L_0 says A will do at t', $t' > t$, and do the reverse. Hence L_0 cannot categorically predict A's behaviour at t'; hence rational agents cannot be completely described by causal laws.

Let us call this the *prediction paradox*. There are two dimensions to the paradox. The first is the paradox proper. The second is its link with the capacity of self-knowledge to enchance power. At any time t that A discovers what the truth about A has been up to t, the truth changes; not just in the trivial sense that 'A knows A has trait T' was false before t and true after t, but in the non-trivial sense that what was mere behaviour or habit before t becomes action after t. By discovering that he has trait T, A brings his possession of T into the realm of decision. His being T is now in A's horizon, and A now has the power to change his being T. If T persists it is *now* because A has decided to let T persist; A has then committed himself to finding his being T acceptable. This is why man is doomed to transcend

[27] Not quite without sense. If I must choose between a risky investment in a friend's firm and a sound investment to insure my family's future, then, perhaps, I can't help choosing the sounder investment. If only a supreme effort to lift a stone will save my child, I cannot help but exert the effort. But these are not cases the advocates of the present objection have in mind.

himself, condemned to be free. I will defer further discussion of this second dimension to section 7. I turn now to the paradox itself.

Neither (a) nor (b) is self-evident. A deterministic system could, presumably, fend off predictions about itself by incinerating potential predictors. If we defend (a) by saying that the behaviour of such systems it still in principle predictable, we are using predictability interchangeably with causal determination and (a) becomes vacuous. To see why (b) could be rejected, consider its use in an argument close to the prediction paradox. J. Bennett argues[28] that *A* cannot decide to do *X* if *A* knows he is going to do *X* ('believes' would suffice for present purposes). This principle, in conjunction with (b), seems to entail that, if determinism is true, our capacity to make decisions will shrink to nothing, or at least become inauthentic, as our self-knowledge increases. But it need not. We can take Bennett's argument to show that since there always will be authentic decisions, (b) must be false: there must be causal obstacles to certain systems making predictions about themselves. The existence of beings that would undergo certain changes if they became aware of predictions about themselves may show only that the constraints on possible causal chains are tighter than one might have supposed, tight enough to exclude the chains by which these beings would get hold of self-predictions.

These limitations on (a) and (b) suggest a natural resolution of the prediction paradox. Perhaps *A could* falsify L_0 and would if he found out about L_0. But this is consistent with L_0 being true of *A* if *A* never does, and perhaps never could, find out about L_0. What is logically impossible is that L_0 be true of *A* and *A* know about L_0 and *A* want and be able to act in ways that contradict L_0's prediction. That *A* can refute L_0 in this sense does not show that there can be no such L_0 true of *A*. If L_0 is true of *A* and would be true of *A* in all causally possible counterfactual situations, what follows is that *A* never will and never could find out about L_0. Whether we should use modus ponens or modus tolens on Bennett's argument and the prediction paradox is a matter requiring independent empirical investigation of the causal structure of the world.

My point here runs parallel to a point about time travel. Just as there are arguments against the possibility of completely predicting the behaviour of a rational agent, there are similar arguments against the possibility of time travel. Since Booth shot Lincoln, if it

[28] *Kant's Dialectic* (C.U.P., Cambridge: 1974), p. 217.

were possible to go back in time and prevent Booth from shooting Lincoln, it would be possible for an event to have occurred and failed to occur. However, the fact of Lincoln's assassination only shows that nobody ever will return to 1865 and interfere with Booth, not that nobody could have gone back to 1865 and interfered. What is impossible is *both* that Booth shot Lincoln and that Booth was stopped. Had a time-traveller interfered with Booth, Booth would not have shot Lincoln. Closer to the self-predictor (perhaps to the man who falsifies L_0 if he finds out about L_0) is the time-traveller who goes back in time and prevents the invention of time travel (or his own conception). But all that follows is that *if* time travel is possible, all such paradoxical causal chains are impossible, incompatible with the causal structure of the world. They *seem* possible, but this might be a mistaken causal intuition.[29] Nobody today argues that energy isn't conserved because objects might accelerate by themselves; *since* energy is conserved objects *can't* accelerate by themselves. The analogy of the self-annihilating time traveller to the potential self-predictor is this: if *A*'s behaviour *is* predictable and *A* would refute any prediction he could find out about, then, however much it may go against our causal intuitions, it is causally impossible for *A* to find out about those predictions. Intuitions about what a time traveller could do and what a self-predictor could discover may have to be abandoned just as were the mathematical intuitions that led to belief that $(\exists x)(y)(y \varepsilon x \equiv y \notin y)$.[30]

Attractive though this deflection of the prediction paradox is, it will not satisfy anyone disturbed by *A*'s possession of even an unrealizable capacity to refute theories about himself. Electrons can't even be thought of in such terms; whatever the causal structure of the world, it can't be true that predictions about *A*'s behaviour are *as* inaccessible to *A* as predictions about an electron are inaccessible to the electron. Anyway, *is* there any independent evidence that prediction-paradoxical causal chains are impossible? An adequate resolution of the prediction paradox must attack even

[29] Cf. P. Horwich, 'On the Alleged Paradoxes of Time Travel', *Journal of Philosophy*, lxxii. 14 (Aug. 1975), 432–44; and J. Earman, 'Causation: A Matter of Life and Death', ibid., lxxiii. 1 (Jan. 1976), 5–25.

[30] Arguments against backwards causation use a rejectable assumption about causal possibility: see M. Hesse, *Forces and Fields* (Littlefields, Adams, & Co., Totowa, N.J.: 1965), pp. 285 ff; also see J. Wheeler and R. Feynman, 'Interaction with the Absorber as the Mechanism of Radiation', *Reviews of Modern Physics*, xvii. 2 and 3 (April–July 1945), 157–81; and 'Classical Electrodynamics in Terms of Direct Interparticle Action', ibid., xxi. 3 (July 1949), 425–33.

very weak versions of the claim that *A* has an in-principle prediction-confounding capability. Nor is it clear that determinism would be out of the woods even if the causal structure of the world forbids prediction-paradoxical causal chains. Suppose L_0 is the truth about *A*, and it is causally impossible for *A* to discover what L_0 says about him. Now, very often, we expect a theory to support counterfactuals whose antecedents are logically incompatible with its fundamental tenets. 'If the masses of bodies changed spontaneously, momentum would not be conserved' is a clear consequence of classical mechanics, even though the invariance of mass is one of its fundamental tenets. So, if it is logically possible for *A* to become aware of L_0, any adequate *A*-theory—including L_0—must say what would happen if *A* became aware of L_0. And we are back to the prediction paradox.

Conceding this pushes the determinist up a hierarchy of theories. L_0 cannot contain the expression 'is aware of L_0' on pain of impredicativity, so L_0 cannot be the theory which supports the troublesome counterfactual. The counterfactual must belong to a theory $L_1 \neq L_0$.[31] Nothing is accomplished by adding to L_0 the clause C_0: 'If *A* becomes aware of the foregoing he will... .' Since L_0 & C_0 entails different predictions than does L_0 alone, we must now be able to say what *A* would do if he found out about L_0 & C_0, and for that we would need a new clause C_1... .

So: is *A*'s behaviour predictable? The kind of answer to which this question is susceptible emerges only from a closer examination of the paradox and the hierarchy of theories. The first remark to make is that the laws L_0, L_1,... and the dialectic of their refutation must be pursued into the transfinite if the prediction paradox is to be sustained. The 'finitary' formulation of the paradox is: *A* can falsify any law L_i; only $L_{i+1} \neq L_i$ can describe what *A* would do if he found out about L_i. Since i was any number, no law can describe and predict *A*'s behaviour. But if i ranges over the set ω of natural numbers, the argument is a *non sequitur*. Let us say that L' is the *immediate successor* of L if L' is the law describing *A*'s response to learning of L; and that L' is a *successor* of L if some finite chain of immediate successors leads from L to L'. The 'finitary' argument shows at most that no *successor* of L_0 can describe and predict *A*'s behaviour. The determinist need only posit a *limit* law

[31] Kripke, 'Outline of a Theory of Truth', defends impredicativity, but his own apparatus would create another troublesome hierarchy for the determinist.

L_ω which describes A's reaction to *every* member of the ω-sequence $L_0, L_1, \ldots$. L_ω is not a successor of L_0, so L_ω need not be falsifiable by A even if all the $L_i, i \varepsilon \omega$, are.

The intuitive point of introducing L_ω is that even if A can track down and refute laws forever, there may be a point beyond this entire process from which A's behaviour can lawfully be described. The antideterminist cannot plausibly deny this transfinite perspective to the determinist. The antideterminist allows A to track down each law L_i, $i \varepsilon \omega$; would he not be straining at a gnat to say there is no such collection as $\{L_i: i \varepsilon \omega\}$? To meet L_ω, the antideterminist must extend A's capabilities into the transfinite. He must say that, if α is an ordinal and L_α is a law describing A and all A's reactions to the laws L_β, $\beta < \alpha$, A can falsify L_α. The determinist now replies that there is a law $L_{\alpha+1}$ which describes A's reaction to L_α. The two can now jointly trace this dialectic up to the next limit ordinal $\alpha + \omega$; the ground-rules, to the extent that they are still clear, permit a law $L_{\alpha+\omega}$.[32]

Let us take temporary leave of our bickering metaphysicians. It might seem that by now the prediction paradox has ceased to be a real problem because it involves an unreasonable, even absurd, idealization of man. There is no reason to suppose that any actual rational agent would be able to survey more than a small finite initial segment of the $\{L_\alpha\}$. Any actual man would throw in the towel after L_n, where n is small. To say that he could falsify L_n is simply to cling to the infinitary idealization whose appropriateness is the point in question (cf. 197–99). Perhaps the prediction paradox requires empirical resolution, an experimental determination of the point at which human agents become unable to process predictions about their behaviour. The trouble with such a solution is that it would be unprincipled. It would not assign the same n to all agents. It might not even determine a well-motivated maximum n for all agents. Agents could form coalitions to overcome individual limitations. The determinist who has come this far must yield to the idealization and resolve the prediction paradox generally.

[32] The antideterminist loses the argument if he concedes that $S = \{\alpha : \alpha$ is an index of a law A can refute$\}$ is a set, since any set of ordinals is bounded. Suppose S is a set bounded by β. L_β will presumably be the theory which describes the whole process of A's wrestling with $\{L_\alpha : \alpha \varepsilon S\}$. It might be possible, by putting some initial restrictions on L_0, to prove that S is a set. (See Kripke, 'Outline of a Theory of Truth', for a parallel argument about metalanguage hierarchies.)

The one construction that will resolve the prediction paradox in favour of the determinist is a *fixed point*: a law L_α such that the hypothesis that A is aware of L_α makes no difference to an otherwise correction description of A's behaviour, which happens to be L_α itself. Intuitively, L_α is a fixed point if A's behaviour on finding out about L_α is precisely what it would have been had A not found out about L_α. H. Simon has a promising fixed point result.[33] He considers a pollster's published prediction P of voting in an election, and plots P against the actual outcome V given that P was known. It is an elementary theorem of analysis that this curve intersects the graph of correct predictions, predictions which are the same as V (Fig. 2). If V is a function $f(P)$ of P, then for some P_0 and

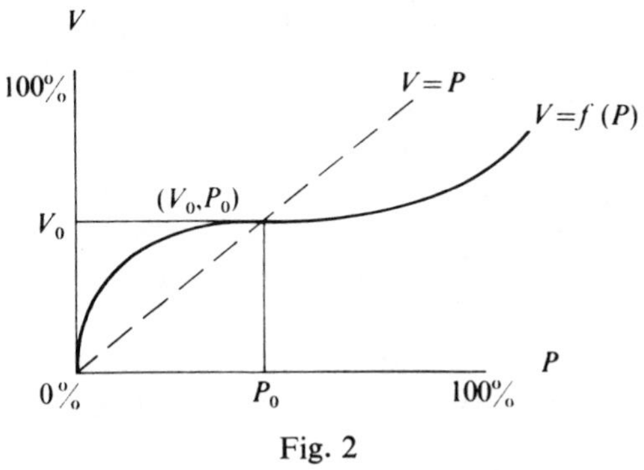

Fig. 2

V_0, $V_0 = P_0 = f(P_0)$. P_0 is a fixed point, and will not falsify itself by being published. (In general, V is a function both of P and what the vote would have been had the prediction not been published; but this refinement is inessential. I will also ignore the fact that we must assume A's response to be real-valued to apply Simon's result.)

The following difficulty, however, presents itself. Simon has shown that there are predictions the net effect of whose publication is null. This does indeed show that, under the right circumstances, a published prediction will be true. But Simon does not show that the theory (if any) on which such a prediction is based would be a correct theory about the population. For let the population number 100, and suppose the underlying theory T entails that voters $v_1,\ldots,v_{51}$ will vote 'yes', and $v_{52},\ldots,v_{100}$ will vote 'no'. T thus predicts a 51 per cent

33 'The Effect of Prediction', in M. Brodbeck, ed., *Readings in the Philosophy of the Social Sciences* (Macmillan, N.Y.: 1968), 447–55.

'yes' vote. Upon hearing the prediction, $v_1,\ldots,v_{20}$ change their vote to 'no' out of contrariness, and $v_{52},\ldots,v_{71}$ switch to 'yes' to back a winner. *T* has misdescribed the internal state of the system but has yielded a fixed point prediction *per accidens*. *T* could be false even if it gave correct 'state descriptions' as well as correct 'structure descriptions': each voter might decide to vote just as he was going to so as not to disappoint the pollster. Surely, in such cases, we would not rate *T* a true fixed point law or theory.

A number of philosophers have thought that considerations like these show that *no* theory *L* about *A* can be wholly correct; even if *L* correctly predicts *A*'s behaviour, *L* cannot take *A*'s awareness of *L* into account. *A*'s knowledge of *L* falsifies *L* even if *L*'s predictive failure has been neutralized. This of course is *not* true about theories concerning non-rational beings, which cannot become aware of theories about them. Ryle presents an argument something like this,[34] but he appears to assume that *L*'s inability to register the change in the knowing subject produced by the subject's becoming aware of *L* means that *L*'s predictions themselves will always be incorrect. Simon has shown that this is not so. The correct version of Ryle's argument is that no theory about *A* can be *correct* because it cannot take into account the effect of its publication on the state of its subject.[35]

The trouble with this plausible objection to Simon's result is that, suitably generalized, it proves that *no theory whatever about anything* can be a true account of its subject. It applies to electrons as well as rational agents after all. Consider any theory *T* about a system *S*. As soon as *T* comes into existence *S* acquires *some* relation *R* to *T*. *R* might be causal: e.g. inscriptions of *T* exert gravitational force on *S*. If *T* is required to account for its own effect or potential effect on *S*, where this includes *R*(*S*,*T*), *T* cannot be the whole truth about *S*. *S*'s relation to *T* can only be described in another theory. *A*'s coming to know about L_α is thus a garden-variety instance of a perfectly general phenomenon sometimes, misleadingly, called the observer effect. The fact that *A*'s internal states are states of *knowledge* does

[34] *Concept of Mind*, chap. VI.

[35] Popper seems to have a similar argument in mind in 'Indeterminism in Classical Physics and Quantum Physics, II', *British Journal for Philosophy of Science*, i. 3 (Nov. 1950), p. 190. He shows that even if *C*'s behaviour can be predicted, the prediction must be based on an incorrect description of *C*'s internal state, but only by placing absurdly restrictive physical limitations on *C* to make determinism 'falsifiable'. Radner replies to Popper in 'Popper and Laplace', in Radner and Winokur, *Minnesota Studies in the Philosophy of Science*, iv.

not distinguish A as especially beyond the reach of deterministic theories. When A comes to know about L_α he enters a relation R, perhaps causally efficacious, with an otherwise true theory. $R(A,L_\alpha)$ makes *some* difference in A that L_α cannot capture. But this was true of *any* subject of *any* theory. One begins to suspect that the prediction paradox rests on a truism, and that the real problem is to circumvent that truism.

These observations suggest an improved form for a fixed point result: a characterization of a fixed point for the $\{L_\alpha\}$ hierarchy, and theories generally, that sidesteps the truism that the one truth about A that L_α cannot capture is A's relation to L_α. This requires a final bit of apparatus. Let V_T be the vocabulary of theory T, and T' be the theory which restates T and records the fact that S bears R to T. T' is the deductive closure of $T \cup \{R(S,T)\}$. Moreover, let us assume that 'R' $\in V_T$. (Obviously, 'R' $\in V_{T'}$). This is reasonable given our ultimate purpose, since, when T is L_α, 'R' is 'x is aware of y', an expression which has long since appeared in the hierarchy. Then evidently $V_{T'} = V_T \cup \{`T'\}$. T' is a *conservative extension* of T: all the theorems of T are theorems of T', and all the theorems of T' not using 'R' are theorems of T. T' differs from T just in containing all the logical consequences of being able to describe the relation of T to S. Suppose, at last, that T would be the truth about S were it not that $R(S,T)$, which, truistically, can only be said in T'. It seems reasonable, in this case, to say that T is a fixed point theory about S. T is a fixed point about S because the truth about S which includes S's relation R to T is the conservative extension of T with respect to 'R'. Similarly, it seems reasonable to say that L_α is a fixed point if $L_{\alpha+1}$—the theory that describes A, including A's reaction to L_α—is that conservative extension of L_α which consists of all the logical consequences of L_α and the result of adding 'L_α' to V_{L_α}.

It is reasonable to suppose that there is such a fixed point in $\{L_\alpha\}$. For V_{L_0} will contain some finite set of variables for describing A. Then let $L_{\alpha*}$ be the theory which attributes to each of the variables of V_{L_0} its fixed point value as in Simon's result. What will $L_{\alpha+*1}$ be like? Since by hypothesis no internal state variable changes through the publication of $L_{\alpha*}$, one would suppose that $L_{\alpha*+1}$ ascribes to A the same behaviours and internal states that $L_{\alpha*}$ does while *correctly* describing what A would do if he became aware of $L_{\alpha*}$. $L_{\alpha*+1}$ is that conservative extension of $L_{\alpha*+1}$ which is such that $V_{L_\alpha*+1} = V_{L_\alpha*} \cup \{`L_{\alpha*}'\}$. $L_{\alpha*}$ is the fixed point in $\{L_\alpha\}$.

Intuitively, A's reactions to published predictions gradually dampen down to nothing, and $L_{\alpha*}$ is the theory that attributes to A all the completely dampened values of his variables. A's awareness of $L_{\alpha*}$ would leave A completely unmoved. We have immunized ourselves against the truism that this cannot be said in $L_{\alpha*}$ by noting that $L_{\alpha*+1}$ is that conservative extension of $L_{\alpha*}$ whose vocabulary exceeds that of $L_{\alpha*}$ in containing '$L_{\alpha*}$'. $L_{\alpha*}$ is a fixed point because of the nature of $L_{\alpha*+1}$.

7. *The Existentialist Interpretation of* $L_{\alpha*}$

There are two interpretations of $L_{\alpha*}$. If certain causal transactions are necessary and sufficient for changes in knowledge states, a knowing subject will be vulnerable to saturation. He will either be unable to register, or integrate, further information. Knowledge acquired but not integrated makes only a *logical* difference in the knowing subject. One can interpret $L_{\alpha*}$ as marking the point at which A has become saturated with information about what he is expected to do. Perhaps A's processing time for $L_{\alpha*}$ lags behind the changes in the variables in A's control.

A quite different interpretation of $L_{\alpha*}$, the existentialist interpretation, is that awareness of $L_{\alpha*}$ does not change A because *A approves of himself being* as $L_{\alpha*}$ describes him. He does not want to refute $L_{\alpha*}$, and he freely chooses to remain an $L_{\alpha*}$-man. Let us bring this interpretation down to earth. Suppose $L_{\alpha*}$ predicts that A will do X, and that X is just what A thinks he should do. His conviction about doing X is so strong that not only can he abide the predictability of his doing X, he is proud that it can be said with confidence that he will do X, and do X because he believes he should. Suppose you are invited to give testimony that will harm you and help a friend. The right path is testimony and, ignoring self-interest, you testify. If you knew beforehand that others were thinking 'He'll testify; his sense of duty is that strong', not only would you not alter your behaviour, you would be proud that this regularity was so conspicuously true of you. You identify yourself, as it were, with that regularity. You resent being predictable only when your actions have causes you do not suspect and your own proffered reasons are dismissed as rationalizations, or when your behaviour is narrow and stereotypic.[36]

[36] Cf. R. Hobart's classic 'Free Will as Involving Determinism and Inconceivable without It', *Mind*, lxiii. 1 (Jan. 1934). 1–27.

It seems counterintuitive that there can be a fixed point—that it makes no difference to *A* at *t* that *L* has been true of him up to *t*—because knowledge of any law *L* brings a stretch of *A*'s biography into his own horizon. When *A* did not know about *L*, the processes *L* describes just worked themselves out as facts of nature. Now that *A* knows about them, their persistence involves a decision on *A*'s part to *let* them continue. Whether he likes it or not, *A* has become responsible for the continued truth of *L*. But letting *L* continue to be true—letting *L* be a fixed point—is just what *A* would do if an *L*-man is just the sort of man *A* wants to be anyway.

Recall how a man becomes responsible for himself. Continuing to satisfy *L* after *L* enters *A*'s horizons is one of *A*'s acts, for an act is an event you are responsible for, of which you approve. You cannot say of an act, as you can say of a natural occurrence, 'Isn't that too bad', for this invites the challenge: 'If it's so bad, why did you do it?' An asymmetry sets in here. *You* cannot reply 'I couldn't help myself'. The fact that you are aware of what you are doing and the causes leading up to it means that you were in a postion to at least take steps to prevent yourself from doing it. Since your dissent would have been sufficient to prevent it, a necessary condition for its happening was your concurrence. Only someone else can say of you that you couldn't help yourself. Existentialists have made this plight familiar.[37] A man who tries to disown responsibility for the way he is by saying 'That's just the way I am' shows by saying this that he is allowing himself to be that way; he knows how he is and he finds it acceptable.

Existentialists speak, inexactly, of a man 'defining' himself through choices. (Words, not men, are defined.) What they mean is that men decide, within limits, what they will be. In fact, since they can know about themselves and influence some of their own states, men are *forced* to decide what they are to be. Sartre expresses this by saying that man's essence is nothingness. This is an exaggeration. What Sartre means to say, quite correctly, is that a man differs from a rock because, relative to the laws of nature but independently of the rock's idea of what it is not but wants to be, the rock's behaviour is fully determinate. But my behaviour requires reference to my idea of what I am not but would like to be. Rocks simply have no ideas

[37] Hampshire, opera citata; J.-P. Sartre, *Being and Nothingness*, trans. H. Barnes, pt. Four and Conclusion (Citadel, N.Y.: 1964); E. Berne, 'Wooden Leg', in *Games People Play* (Grove: N.Y., 1964).

of what they are not. Now men do not differ from rocks in that *all* behaviour presupposes such ideas. If I fall out of an aeroplane, I am as much a 'thing' as any rock would be in that situation. Rather, there are regions of occurrences that depend on my conception of what I would like to be; and among those occurrences are some of the regularities that govern my behaviour. What is up to me is not my logical essence—I cannot choose which essential predicates to satisfy—but my *causal* essence. My connivance is involved in the laws I satisfy. My causal essence is nothing—without my say-so.

These caveats entered, the existentialist account of man's being-in-the-world is correct. Each man is responsible for expanding his horizon with respect of himself; even if he is ignorant that he is an *L*-individual he is responsible for remaining ignorant and hence indirectly responsible for continuing to be an *L*-individual. He is deciding to remain ignorant and must justify so doing.

Nothing in the process by which a man brings himself within his horizon and decides what he is to be need be causally indeterminate. This whole account can be true of rational agents even if determinism is true. Even if determinism is true I am free to choose myself and indeed must choose myself. Even if determinism is true, not choosing myself is to choose to remain ignorant and thereby acquiesce in what I am. Neither determinism nor its recognition relieves the pain or burden of responsibility. There is no subtler insight in all the discussion of free will than Kant's idea that freedom is a necessary postulate of *practical* reason wholly compatible with viewing the world, when divorced from prospects for action, as determined.

So far, then: when I find out what sort of man I am, my continuing to be that sort of man is a choice. Since it is also up to me whether to put myself in a position to make this choice, I am condemned to be free. Only of rational agents is this true, even if the whole process of discovery, deliberation and choice is governed by causal laws. It is time to tie these strands together with our idea of a fixed point. If we choose our natures, there must be principles we employ in making this choice. We must have an answer to the question 'Why are you the way you are?' Leibniz expresses with striking succinctness this condition on all choice: 'It seems that every will presupposes some reason for willing, and that this reason is naturally anterior to the will.'[38] Pressing this challenge will lead to an ultimate goal toward which a man strives, that goal which shapes the shape he

[38] *Discourse on Metaphysics*, II.

gives himself. This is his *ideal*. It may be a conception of what individual persons should be. It may be a picture of what the social world should be, which dictates a picture of what individuals must be. (Such ideals are called ideologies, and eventually suffocate the possibility of individual ideals.) A man may follow an idiosyncratic ideal meant only for himself. As each man ascends through the degrees of freedom, his ideal determines the construction of the thing he is most responsible for: himself.

Imagine, then, a being whose nature is in part determined by the exigencies of the world, and in part determined by an ideal. Imagine, too, that he can discern how closely he meets his ideal, and can bring himself ever closer to it. The closer he gets, the more he is the way he is because he has decided to be that way. What happens if he manages completely to embody his ideal? It seems clear that he would not care that an external observer could predict what he would do. Finding out that he had matched his ideal would have no influence on him. But this is just to say that a description L of a being that completely exemplifies his own ideal is a fixed point for him. It is immaterial whether his information-processing channels are saturated; he would not *want* to be anything other than an L-man. He embraces the description L. *Amor fati*. He is a Kantian holy will for whom 'I will' and 'I ought' coincide. The concept of a holy will is an idealization of man himself, a piece of matter that can alter the laws governing it through self-knowledge and in accordance with an ideal.

A final question presses here. Can the ideal a man chooses be rationally justified, or is the ideal he picks, his picking the ideal he picks, just something that happens to him? Certainly he cannot *believe* that his ideal is just something he has been saddled with, for to so regard it is to say: 'I hold that being a man of such-and-such sort is a goal worth pursuing; but of course whether it *is* worth pursuing is another question.' This is something no one can profess; it is the practical counterpart of Moore's paradoxical '*p*, but I don't believe *p*'. A reason is indeed naturally anterior to every choice, for a choice is something we declare ourselves willing to give reasons for. So it may be impossible for rational agents to *believe* non-cognitivism, as many of its critics have intuited. This would not, of course, show that it is false. At this point the problems of mind and matter become problems of ethics.

Index of Names

Index of Subjects